THE SOUL
AND
BARBED WIRE

THE SOUL AND BARBED WIRE

An Introduction to Solzhenitsyn

Edward E. Ericson, Jr.
Alexis Klimoff

ISI
BOOKS

Wilmington, Delaware

Edward E. Ericson, Jr., and Alexis Klimoff
The soul and barbed wire : an introduction to Solzhenitsyn /
1st ed.—Wilmington, DE : ISI Books, c2008.

       p. ; cm.

       ISBN: 978-1-933859-57-6 (cloth) ; 978-1-933859-58-3 (pbk.)
       Includes bibliographical references and index.

       1. Solzhenitsyn, Aleksandr Isaevich, 1918—Criticism and interpretation. 2. Solzhenitsyn, Aleksandr Isaevich, 1918—Political and social views. 3. Politics and literature—Soviet Union--History—20th century. I. Ericson, Edward E., Jr. II. Klimoff, Alexis. III. Title.

PG3488.O4 Z8883 2008   2007941669
891.78/4409—dc22   0807

ISI Books
Intercollegiate Studies Institute
Post Office Box 4431
Wilmington, DE 19807-0431
www.isibooks.org

Manufactured in the United States of America

Contents

Acknowledgments

This book grew out of a long article that the authors wrote for the *Dictionary of Literary Biography* (vol. 302 [2004]). Our first indebtedness is therefore to Dr. Matthew Bruccoli, president of Bruccoli Clark Layman, Inc., the publisher of DLB, for permission to make use of that article for the present book. Special thanks go to our invaluable friend Daniel J. Mahoney for his encouragement, wisdom, and expertise during many stages of our work. We also gratefully acknowledge the kind treatment and professional support received from the good people at ISI Books, starting with editor in chief Jeremy Beer and including Jennifer Connolly and others. As ever, we thank our wives, Janice Ericson and Louise Klimoff, for their understanding and patience at each step in the process of composing the manuscript.

Edward E. Ericson, Jr.
Alexis Klimoff
December 2007

The line separating good and evil passes not through states, nor between classes, nor between political parties either—but right through every human heart—and through all human hearts. This line shifts. Inside us, it oscillates with the years. And even within hearts overwhelmed by evil, one small bridgehead of good is retained. And even in the best of all hearts, there remains . . . an unuprooted small corner of evil.

Aleksandr Solzhenitsyn, *The Gulag Archipelago*
from chapter 1, "The Ascent,"
of Part IV, "The Soul and Barbed Wire"

Introduction

Rarely does a writer of serious literature become a newsmaker recognized around the globe. This Aleksandr Solzhenitsyn did, and at a single stroke. In 1962 his taboo-shattering *One Day in the Life of Ivan Denisovich* was published in Moscow. This short work of fiction by a previously unknown provincial schoolteacher described life in a Soviet concentration camp, which the author knew from bitter experience. Citizens could glimpse for themselves a secretive and dehumanizing world the existence of which had been officially denied for decades. And, wonder of wonders, the text was allowed into print by no less a figure than the number-one man in the Soviet government, Nikita Khrushchev himself.

The effect was electrifying. The renowned Russian critic and writer Kornei Chukovsky proclaimed *One Day* "a literary miracle." Millions of Soviet readers shared this reaction; for them, the publication signaled a release from a stifling, officially imposed silence. In the West the author was hailed as a truth-telling freedom fighter courageously challenging a repressive system. A man who had lived and labored in utter obscurity for all of forty-three years, more than half a normal life span, became an instant celebrity.

Perceptive critics immediately recognized the outstanding aesthetic qualities of *One Day*, but they did not set the terms for the general public's early reaction. Subsequent events tended to pull popular interest yet further away from the author's literary output and toward his personal story. The escalating conflict between the Soviet state and the defiantly self-directed writer returned Solzhenitsyn's name to the headlines of Western newspapers many times over. His visage graced the covers of *Life* and *Time* magazines. In 1974, after the momentous appearance of *The Gulag Archipelago*, *The Times* of London pronounced him "the most famous person in the western world."[1] Even by the standards of the tumultuous twentieth century, the drama of Solzhenitsyn's improbable life and unprecedented literary career made a sensational story. A literary man, of all people, was shaking up a superpower. By the compelling power of his works, he was discrediting communism. In a face-off with state tyranny, he was triumphantly confirming the old adage that the pen is mightier than the sword.

But the repeated—and repeatedly sensational—presence of Solzhenitsyn in the international news had a downside. For all too many commentators, the writer's name became identified with the purely political issues of the day. This perception was reinforced by the controversies generated by a number of Solzhenitsyn's non-literary pronouncements after his arrival in the West. Of course, the news is not, by its nature, an appropriate instrument for commenting meaningfully on issues of literary quality, although it was precisely the vivid potency of Solzhenitsyn's writing that had led to his prominence in the first place. The unfortunate net result of these factors has been a fading of Solzhenitsyn's name as the Cold War and its associated passions have receded in popular memory. News stories get filed away in a drawer labeled "The Past." Authentic literature does not belong there.

And yet there is a potential benefit in the forgetfulness of an age known for its short attention span. With the eclipse of the polemics of the 1970s and '80s, Solzhenitsyn's total oeuvre can be considered afresh. Seasoned readers of Solzhenitsyn will, we hope, benefit from this book's effort to bring into focus material that has not received critical attention before. They will also, we trust, find in these pages a repository of accurate information on subjects to which many stray bits of misinformation have attached themselves like barnacles. Novice readers are a subset of special interest to us two professors. Today's young could not know the Solzhenitsyn of the headlines. A growing majority of them have not read any Solzhenitsyn nor apparently heard of either his name or *The Gulag Archipelago*, though it was translated into thirty-five languages and sold more than 30 million copies. Some may know the word *gulag* but not how it reached them. With this potential readership in mind, we think of this book as our effort at cultural transmission from one generation to the next. Especially for these readers, the current work functions both as an overview of the huge cultural impact made by Solzhenitsyn and as a nontechnical introduction to the full range of his works.

We begin with an extensive biographical sketch—an appropriate beginning, since so much of Solzhenitsyn's writing is autobiographically based. His personal drama is inextricably intertwined with the main story line not just of the Soviet Union but of the twentieth century, an epoch which Martin Amis has called "our worst century yet," and which Solzhenitsyn has labeled "the cave man's century" and "one of the most shameful centuries of human history."[2] It was of this period that Solzhenitsyn became a—if not *the*—chronicler and analyst, as well as a notable actor in its drama. For it can be argued in retrospect that *One Day in the Life of Ivan Denisovich* inflicted the first crack in the Berlin Wall and that *The Gulag Archipelago* struck a decisive sledgehammer blow against the foundations of the Soviet edifice.

Telling the story of this writer's life necessarily and properly includes conveying considerable information about his writings. Nevertheless, the narrative mode does not lend itself to such an exposition. To accommodate the expository function, after the "Life" chapter comes a section on "Works." Although Solzhenitsyn's most prominent nonliterary proclamations are given their due, the unquestionably literary, or belletristic, works receive greater attention. And while the major emphasis is on works available in English translation, a full awareness of Solzhenitsyn's corpus also requires that attention be paid to important works not yet available in English. Readers will be able to use our focused essays as a reference guide to individual works, each of which has been situated in the context of the author's life and of his writings as a whole. Our approach emphasizes information, and whenever we touch upon issues of interpretation, we attempt to avoid unnecessarily intricate or idiosyncratic readings.

Following the substantial chapters on "Life" and "Works," we have placed a couple of shorter chapters focusing on significant issues. The first of these addresses Solzhenitsyn's basic beliefs. Curiously, until now there has been no single place where readers could find a reasonably comprehensive distillation of the essential convictions that animate his writings. Solzhenitsyn is committed to a vision that is fundamentally moral, and even his political comments, which have drawn disproportionate critical attention, are governed by that commitment. Moreover, this moral vision takes it bearings from a religious view of life and the world. One can certainly see, for example, that his implacable hostility toward Marxism-Leninism is grounded not in some alternative political philosophy but in his Christian perspective. Although his Christian worldview deepened with the years, it never took an idiosyncratic turn, and he is in no sense a speculative theologian.

Ordinarily, an introductory volume on a writer would not devote a separate chapter to his reception, but with Solzhenitsyn we must make an exception. The very fact that he became a highly public figure made him grist for the mills of journalism, and it is journalists in particular who have all too often misunderstood and not infrequently caricatured and maligned him—and then, reverting to a familiar pattern, have relied on these prior journalistic accounts for their basic information. When asked recently how he would like to be remembered to posterity, Solzhenitsyn replied, "I would hope that all that has been said about me, slandered about me, in the course of decades, would, like mud, dry up and fall off."[3] This response, though heated, is not unjust, and the chapter on reception is a modest effort to chip away some of the mud.

The final section consists of a relatively brief selected bibliography. In addition to the journalists featured in the chapter on reception, scholars and critics have written a substantial number of books and articles on Solzhenitsyn. We have attempted to present a list of works that will be helpful to those who wish to pursue more detailed study of the author's life and writings, adding brief remarks on a work's particular focus if it is not clear from its title.

Our book is designed to allow each chapter to stand alone and be read independently. That structure entails some, but only minimal, repetition from one chapter to another.

Our title is drawn from *The Gulag Archipelago*. Although it refers most obviously to Solzhenitsyn's epic writings about prison camps, it also applies, if somewhat obliquely, to his *chef d'oeuvre*, *The Red Wheel*, which limns the episodes leading Russia toward the revolutionary abyss. Solzhenitsyn uses "The Soul and Barbed Wire" as the title for the pivotal middle, or fourth, of *Gulag*'s seven parts, at which point he shifts from the downward movement of lamentation to the upward movement of hope. After an almost unbearable catalogue of the physical torments and cruel limitations to which the unfortunates confined behind barbed-wire enclosures were subjected, the author fixes his gaze upon souls. And readers are invited to see how pitifully unavailing are the devices of detention derived from a materialistic philosophy. As the body is confined, the soul can be refined. Conscience can take root. Faith can take wing. And the prisoner can exult, as Solzhenitsyn does in his own voice, "Bless you prison, for having been in my life!"[4] What does barbed wire have to do with the soul? Irina Ratushinskaya, a poet of the generation after Solzhenitsyn's, had learned from the master how to cope with the gulag when she, too, experienced it: "Yes, we are behind barbed wire, they have stripped us of everything they could, they have torn us away from our friends and families, but unless we acknowledge this as their right, we remain free."[5]

For years, we have immersed ourselves in the details of the events and texts that constitute the story of Solzhenitsyn. Nevertheless, when we step back and survey the record as a whole, we are reminded anew of what we had sensed beforehand: that, in the memorable words of David Remnick, "there is no greater story of human dignity in [the twentieth] century than that of Aleksandr Solzhenitsyn," for with him we have "the rare appearance of the superior and necessary man."[6]

Note on Russian words: All bibliographical citations involving Russian-language titles are given in Library of Congress transliteration. In the body of the text, however, Russian names appear in more relaxed format, typically reflecting the form used in the principal English translations to which we refer.

Life

When Aleksandr Solzhenitsyn was a mere ten years of age, he launched the literary career that he was to pursue for the rest of his life. It was at this time that the precocious lad established a handwritten journal extravagantly titled *The Twentieth Century*, with the equally vaulting phrase "On the Meaning of the Twentieth Century" as the subtitle. The earliest actual products of his juvenile pen, however—illustrations and jokes intermingled with verse, science fiction, and a serialized story about pirates—fell well short of fulfilling the grand design suggested by these titles. More than four decades later, the author himself summed up the beginnings of his career thus: "From childhood on I experienced an entirely unprompted inclination toward writing and produced a great deal of the usual adolescent nonsense."[1] But it was not very long before his choice of subject matter started to catch up with the high ambition that framed his boyish exercises. As his eighteenth birthday approached, Solzhenitsyn, by then an ardent convert to Marxism, set himself the goal of describing afresh the Russian Revolution and its glorious meaning for the world. His innate creative drive had become focused and channeled into a sense of mission. Before another decade had passed, however, Solzhenitsyn came to reject utterly the utopian dreams that had so captivated him in his youth, since the Soviet experiment had by then revealed itself as a murderous sham that was evil in its very design. Yet despite this radical turnaround in his views, he continued to look upon the Russian Revolution as the key turning point in modern history, one that cried out for the intense study conceived in his adolescence. So immense did this project prove to be that it absorbed a large proportion of the writer's time even after he had reached the pinnacle of worldwide fame. When he was finished, in 1991, this epic cycle bore the title *The Red Wheel* and ran to more than six thousand pages.

It was life itself that had led to the sea change in Solzhenitsyn's outlook. His experience of arrest, prison, and labor camp had exposed the harsh truth behind the façade of Soviet life and had driven the aspiring author to turn his new knowledge into literary form. Addressing these contemporary realities distracted him from executing his *chef d'oeuvre,* but he followed the dictates of what he understood to be his duty to his fellow prisoners. The works of fiction that emerged as a result became the most compelling depictions of this information that readers the world over had ever been granted. Nadezhda Mandelstam has written that no work she has read compares to *One Day in the Life of Ivan Denisovich* in its ability to convey the brutal reality of the camps.[2]

Of all the fascinating life stories produced by the turbulent twentieth century, Solzhenitsyn's was surely one of the most sensational. In Soviet terms, such a life should never have happened. By sheer independence of mind, Solzhenitsyn had wandered off the officially sanctioned trail and gone his own way, thinking his own thoughts. What is more, he had turned into a sworn foe of the Soviet state and engaged it in direct conflict in a series of confrontations, each of which has a highly dramatic plot. Indeed, there is a sense in which Solzhenitsyn's life resembles a work of art. Because autobiographical elements provide the foundation of many of his literary products, however, it is better to think of his life and his art as forming a seamless web; neither his life nor his art can be properly understood without reference to the other.

Solzhenitsyn has revealed that in 1985–86 he set down an autobiographical narrative encompassing his life up to the moment of exile;[3] this text remains unpublished, but even without it there is no paucity of autobiographical information. The biographical narrative related in the present chapter comprises three parts: Solzhenitsyn's life in the USSR, his life in exile (both in Switzerland and in the USA), and his life back in post-Soviet Russia. The first part draws as much as possible upon those works which are assumed to be largely autobiographical in character. The overall picture that emerges is one which, in significant ways, happens to parallel the life of the Russian nation. David Remnick has come to the same conclusion, calling Solzhenitsyn "a Russian whose destiny is singular and, at the same time, nearly identical to Russia's."[4]

Russia entered the twentieth century with a thousand-year history rich with religious tradition; it endured a seventy-four-year subordination to an ideologically driven totalitarian regime; and it emerged from that parenthesis of radical dislocation trying to renew its ancient heritage and reinvigorate its society. As a child, Solzhenitsyn was reared in the ways of Russian Orthodoxy; he became a self-professed Communist in his teenage years, but eventually moved on to reclaim his birthright and to search for a better future for himself and for his nation. It is rare for a writer to identify with his nation as closely and as fully as Solzhenitsyn has done. His people's story is what he mainly writes about; it is also his story. His enormous literary corpus could be fairly summarized as an exposition and analysis of the Soviet experiment upon the Russian people. Furthermore, to the extent that totalitarianism, which first waxed and then waned in the twentieth century, gives that century its distinctive character and coloration, the story of Russia during Solzhenitsyn's lifetime is paradigmatic for an entire epoch.

Life in the Soviet Union

Aleksandr Isaevich Solzhenitsyn was born on December 11, 1918, in Kislovodsk, a resort town in the northern foothills of the Caucasus mountain range. This region of southern Russia was ravaged by the civil war that broke out in the wake of the revolution, and

Solzhenitsyn's earliest memory dates from when he was probably three years old and still in Kislovodsk. He remembers being in the church of St. Pantaleimon and seeing the service disrupted by Red Army soldiers who entered the sanctuary in order to seize items of commercial value. (The new regime was aggressively pursuing an anti-religious campaign which then included an ostentatiously brutal confiscation of church property.)[5] The growing boy stored up this and many other vivid impressions of Bolshevik power, but only many years later could he appreciate their significance.

Both parents of the future writer were of peasant stock but had received university educations. Isaakii Semyonovich Solzhenitsyn, Aleksandr's father, enlisted in the army in 1914 during Russia's preparations for war. He served as an artillery officer during World War I and was decorated for heroism. Demobilized and newly married, he died as a result of a hunting mishap, mortally wounded by an accidental discharge of his own shotgun. Aleksandr, his only child, was born six months after Isaakii's death. The mother, née Taissia Zakharovna Shcherbak, was the daughter of a Ukrainian farmer who, though uneducated, became prosperous by dint of his shrewdness and industriousness. This self-made man, much admired by his young grandson, saw his hard-won, extensive holdings expropriated by the new regime. Taissia, barely married and already a widow with a baby on the way, was embarking on a life for which a girlhood in a family of means had not prepared her. She initially took refuge in the home of her older sister, Maria, and Aleksandr spent his first six years living with this aunt in Kislovodsk. The routines of these years were those of a traditional Russian household, including prayers before an icon and attendance of church services, though the boy's mother was not particularly religious. When Taissia went to Rostov-on-Don to look for work as a stenographer, she left her young son in the care of members of her extended family. Her parents took on primary responsibility for little Aleksandr, aided by Taissia's sister Maria and her sister-in-law Irina Shcherbak, wife of Taissia's elder brother, Roman. Aleksandr's summers were spent with his grandparents in 1925 and 1926 and with Aunt Irina in 1927 and 1928. Irina was a spirited young woman with substantial literary interests and deep religious convictions. She made a strong impression on the boy, planting in him the seeds of a love for the Russian classics as well as a sympathetic appreciation for Russian Orthodoxy; in retrospect she appears to have been the strongest childhood influence on the future author.

At the time Aleksandr joined his lonely mother in Rostov, a policy of discrimination against relatives of former officers and landowners was keeping her from finding steady employment. She bounced from one temporary job to another, eking out paltry earnings sufficient only for subsistence living. Virtually destitute, mother and son lived for the next ten years in a ramshackle structure, within which their living space measured twelve by nine feet and lacked plumbing. Solzhenitsyn later summarized his abiding impression of his childhood in one word: "hardships." Until he was forty, he said, he "knew nothing but a kind of dignified destitution."[6] Without a house to call home, he knew only hovels that could not keep out the cold, inadequate fuel to keep warm, and a shortfall of food, despite living in the commercial hub of an agricultural area rich in natural resources. A pair of shoes or an article of clothing had to last for years. Once he sat on a chair with wet ink on it; being unable to wash out the stain, for the next two years he had to wear trousers with an ink spot on their seat.

Solzhenitsyn was an excellent student from the start; among his school subjects were German and English, though more for reading than for speaking. From his Aunt Irina's well-stocked personal library the avid young reader consumed Russian literary classics, as well as works by foreign authors such as Shakespeare, Dickens, and Russians' perennial favorite, Jack London. Irina also presented him with his own copy of Vladimir Dahl's collection of Russian proverbs, a book that he came to treasure greatly.

Solzhenitsyn's youth was passed living among people who were viewed by the Bolsheviks as potential enemies, and whose attitude toward the regime was a mixture of fear and alienation. Solzhenitsyn knew this attitude firsthand. Beyond the deprivations that he and his mother endured together and the dispossession of his maternal grandfather, every day on his way home from school the Rostov boy saw a line of women standing outside the headquarters of the GPU,[7] each one hoping for permission to deliver a parcel to her imprisoned loved one. He also witnessed prisoners being marched through the city's streets by guards who threatened to open fire for a single step out of line. Yet despite such evidence of Bolshevik iniquity he was being ineluctably drawn into Soviet patterns of thinking. At age twelve he joined the Young Pioneers, the Communist Party's organization for children. He had actually hesitated over the decision to enroll because, when he was ten, some Young Pioneers had ripped off the cross he habitually wore around his neck; yet join he did, peer pressure to conform winning out over his precocious sense of independence. (Five years later he took the next step, successfully applying for membership in the Komsomol.) The youth's budding new loyalties troubled his family, especially his maternal grandfather. Subsequent events, however, stoked some misgivings. For example, when, upon the death of her mother, Taissia arranged for memorial services to be sung at Rostov Cathedral and asked Aleksandr to accompany her to church, the boy was unsettled by the public reprimand from his school's headmaster for attending the services.

By Solzhenitsyn's own account, during this time his Christian rearing was severely challenged by the Soviet education he was experiencing every day, with Communist ideological indoctrination emerging as the winner. As he put it, "This force field of Marxism, as developed in the Soviet Union, has such an impact that it gets into the brain of the young man and little by little takes over." By age seventeen or eighteen, he reports, "I did change internally, and from that time, I became a Marxist, a Leninist, and believed in all these things."[8] Conforming to the ideological verities promoted by the regime inevitably entailed rejecting or repressing the religious and patriotic values of his early rearing. The Communists' proclaimed goal of social justice appealed to him, and he also happened to be at an age that was a special target of Soviet propaganda, since the regime was particularly eager to recruit the so-called "October children"—those born during or just after the revolution and who thus were the first wholly Soviet generation. These youths were expected to become the "new Soviet men," to whom would fall the glorious generational mission to move beyond the revolution itself and begin actualizing the radiant future promised by Marxism. As Solzhenitsyn later described this turning point, "The Party had become our father, and we—the children—obeyed. So, when I was leaving school and embarking on my time at university, I made a choice: I banished all my memories, all my childhood misgivings. I was a Communist. The world would be what we made of it."[9] Solzhenitsyn differed from many others among his age cohort in that he did seem to harbor early suspicions about Stalin. And he held back, as if by some inner prompting, when pressure was put on his generation's best and brightest to pursue careers in the security agencies, a surefire ticket to good pay, high status, and accompanying privileges. Yet in all other respects, he became a young Soviet man of his time, a self-labeled Communist.

In 1934, Taissia, who had never remarried, and her son finally found better housing: they moved into a converted stable divided into two rooms, a lodging drier and warmer than their previous quarters. Taissia's work situation also improved somewhat; her excellence as a stenographer earned her evening jobs taking notes at official conferences. At the same time, however, her health took a turn for the worse. She contracted tuberculosis in the early 1930s, her condition deteriorated as the straitened circumstances of years took their toll, and she would die prematurely in 1944. Meanwhile, it fell to her dutiful son to care for his ailing mother, even as he was trying to get out from under her sheltering wing.

Though studious, Aleksandr was far from standoffish, and he formed enduring friendships with other bright young people. His closest friend, from age nine on, was Nikolai Vitkevich, also literarily inclined. With Nikolai and some other good friends, he undertook lengthy bicycle trips during summer vacations, on one occasion going to the republic of Georgia. He kept a journal during these expeditions, writing up his impressions, including nature descriptions.

The Road, an autobiographical poem of some seven thousand lines composed in 1947–52 but not published—except for one chapter—until 1999, contains much information about Solzhenitsyn's early years. In it he recounts a number of memorable episodes from the chaotic postrevolutionary time of civil unrest. Some of these hit close to home, as when the narrator witnesses the authorities harass his mother and visiting grandfather and, later, arrest a friend's father. Yet the omnipresent Soviet propaganda blinds the young observer to the implications of such acts of brutal caprice. The same incomprehension grips the autobiographical protagonist and a similarly indoctrinated friend—based on Nikolai Vitkevich—as they enjoy a leisurely boat ride down the Volga River. They come upon throngs of cowed prisoners. They hear of the terrible human costs of collectivization. But despite abundant evidence of a similarly troubling nature, the Sovietized idealism of the pair keeps them from drawing the appropriate conclusions.

With his heart set on being a writer, Solzhenitsyn wished to pursue literary studies at a Moscow-based university. But because he needed to stay close to his ailing mother, he matriculated in 1936 in a standard five-year curriculum at Rostov University, an institution that then lacked a literary program. He majored, instead, in mathematics and physics. This course of study, though Solzhenitsyn's second choice at the time, would later seem to him providential. For when he was imprisoned, it was his diploma in science that allowed him to transfer out of a labor camp and into a less harsh prison institution devoted to technical work. Solzhenitsyn was a superior university student; his excellent academic record was matched by his energetic involvement in such extracurricular activities as editing the student newspaper. And he found a way to nurture his literary interests while proceeding with his studies of math and science by registering in 1939 for a correspondence course in literature offered by the prestigious Moscow Institute of Philosophy, Literature, and History (MIFLI). Also while at the university, he met and courted Natalia Reshetovskaya, a chemistry major with strong musical interests. They were married in 1940.

Solzhenitsyn graduated with distinction from Rostov University in 1941 and planned to pursue advanced study at MIFLI, but this plan was abruptly cut short by the Nazi onslaught on the Soviet Union on June 22, 1941—the very day that Solzhenitsyn arrived in Moscow to take up his literary studies. He attempted to enlist in the army but was initially rejected on medical grounds. Four months later, however, he was drafted and was assigned to a large horse-drawn transport unit far from the front lines. He describes his experiences at this time in the ironically titled *Love the Revolution,* an unfinished prose work originally intended as a lightly fictionalized account of his wartime career. (Written mostly in 1948, it was published in its unfinished form in 1999.) This was a period of overwhelming frustration for Solzhenitsyn, as he struggled to deal with the entirely unfamiliar ways of horses, and as he tried—fruitlessly at first—to be transferred to a more meaningful army post. Finally, luck smiled on him, and he was accepted in a course for artillery officers.

Solzhenitsyn's university-level training in mathematics led to an assignment to a sound-ranging unit, also known as "instrumental reconnaissance," where dispersed microphones were used to pinpoint the location of enemy artillery. By 1943 he was in charge of a battery on the front lines. Excelling in the army as he had excelled in school, he was decorated for heroism and promoted to captain; his unit also won honors. Wartime did not destroy his Marxist convictions, but it did shake them. He discovered that some Russian military units had joined forces with the Germans against the Soviet army, and he could not help wondering why. By chance, he encountered a Soviet unit composed of political prisoners who had been deliberately assigned to an operation that was likely to get them killed. These and other unsettling experiences he records in *The Road.* One chapter of that long poem, later published separately as *Prussian Nights,* details the Soviet rampage in 1945 through German territory abandoned by the fleeing enemy army; it pays special attention to the profound remorse felt by the protagonist for having joined in the rape and pillage. Another chapter of *The Road* set in 1945 evolved into a play in verse titled *Victory Celebrations.* The play depicts the helplessness of army officers before the unlimited power of a sinister counterintelligence ("SMERSH") operative. It also reveals the playwright's bitter disenchantment with the whole Soviet system. Further insight into Solzhenitsyn's wartime experiences is provided in the texts he composed in the 1990s, the so-called "binary tales."

Solzhenitsyn's military career came to a sudden and disastrous end. He and his old Rostov friend Nikolai Vitkevich, who was also in the army but on another sector of the front, had been exchanging letters that contained some imprudently candid speculations about reforming the Soviet state (they had naïvely assumed that the military censors were on the lookout only for leaks of military secrets). The letters also included poorly camouflaged critical comments about Stalin—for example, the correspondents stated their preference for "Baldie" (Lenin) over "Mustachio" (Stalin).[10] Worse, they contained drafts of a program for a reformist, "purely Leninist" political party. Military censors perused all wartime letters, and the arrest of these letter-writers was only a matter of time. In *The Road* and in volume 1 of *The Gulag Archipelago,* Solzhenitsyn has described the sequence: arrest in February 1945 by SMERSH operatives, transport under guard to Moscow, perfunctory investigation, preordained guilty verdict for "malicious slander" and for founding a "hostile organization." The sentence (considered mild) called for eight years in a forced-labor camp, to be followed by "perpetual exile" in some distant part of the Soviet Union. Thus did Solzhenitsyn enter the world of the *GULag,* the strange-sounding acronym which stands for the state administration of prison camps and which, by virtue of the title of Solzhenitsyn's famous book, was destined to become familiar to the whole world in the form of the common noun *gulag.*

Solzhenitsyn was initially assigned to a labor camp just outside Moscow, then one inside the city. *The Gulag Archipelago* contains an unsparing account of his psychological confusion and of the humiliating moral compromises to which he acquiesced during this time. Prison life also exacted a serious toll on his health, and the combination of these painfully difficult circumstances could not help affecting his view of himself. If wartime experiences had shaken his faith in Marxist dogma, prison experiences now demolished it by providing the kind of insight into Soviet reality that he hitherto could not have imagined. He observed firsthand the systematic brutalization of innocents and, perhaps even more important, saw inspiring models of nobility of spirit among persons officially categorized as "enemies of the people." The views of these individuals clashed with the ideological commitments of his youth, calling them sharply into question. Among many examples, Arnold Susi, a lawyer from Estonia, was steadfast and persuasive in championing democratic values, while Boris Gammerov, a young intellectual from Moscow, radiated conviction in his Christian faith. Solzhenitsyn's intellectual and spiritual turmoil during the first phase of his incarceration provides the context for his early play, *Prisoners*. Written in 1953 and set in a Soviet prison in mid-1945, this play is not as closely autobiographical as *The Road*, but the discordant jumble of clashing opinions expressed by an incredibly diverse cast of characters reflects the maelstrom of perspectives that Solzhenitsyn was trying to sort through at this crucial juncture in his life. Another play, *The Republic of Labor*, written in 1954, conveys yet more of the author's own experiences of bewilderment and humiliation during his early consignment to a hard-labor camp of the "mixed" kind, containing both political prisoners and common criminals.

The tumult of war and initial imprisonment had brought Solzhenitsyn many unsettling experiences to ponder and digest, and it was his next place of confinement that provided him with the opportunity to sort out these impressions. Just as his training in mathematics had made possible his assignment to the artillery corps during the war, so now it became his ticket out of labor camp and into Soviet *sharashkas*, as prison research institutes were unofficially called, where he was destined to stay from 1946 to 1950. After five months at the Rybinsk *sharashka* on the Upper Volga and some months more in Zagorsk, he was consigned for three years to the *sharashka* at Marfino, an outlying district of Moscow, and eventually attached to a group charged with developing a telephone encryption device.

To foster the intellectually demanding scientific projects assigned to the Marfino *zeks* (prisoners), the prison officials provided amenities unheard of in the hard-labor camps. Food was decent and generally adequate in quantity, tobacco was available, and working hours were humane. There was a library, and radios were allowed (some of them often tuned to the BBC). This *sharashka*, originally a seminary complex, had sufficient grounds to accommodate long walks, which the prisoners were free to take several times a day. Most importantly for the writer, Marfino brought together well-educated prisoners with a variety of viewpoints, which they found ways of airing without much difficulty. Solzhenitsyn took advantage of the leisure available there to draft much of the narrative poem *The Road* and the unfinished novel *Love the Revolution,* as well as a number of poems.

The Marfino years provided material for *The First Circle,* a long novel that Solzhenitsyn composed between 1955 and 1968. Many of the novel's characters are literary doubles of fellow *zeks* at Marfino. Two of the most important characters, Lev Rubin and Dmitri Sologdin, are based on Solzhenitsyn's closest companions in the *sharashka,* Lev Kopelev and Dimitri Panin, respectively. Both of these friends have written memoirs of their own that describe life at Marfino, and both vouch for the basic fidelity of Solzhenitsyn's novel. For his part, Solzhenitsyn has noted the accuracy of the way Kopelev has depicted his views at the time.[11] Gleb Nerzhin, the main protagonist in *The First Circle,* is based on the author himself, and Panin considers this fictional character to be "an extraordinarily truthful and accurate picture" of Solzhenitsyn.[12] Kopelev reports many interesting tidbits about Solzhenitsyn. For instance, he was always reading Dahl's famous old dictionary and making notes from it. He taught himself stenography from a home-study book. He read books on history and philosophy, *War and Peace* and stories by Tolstoy, Lao-Tzu and Confucius from a library volume on the ancient East. Finding in Kopelev a friend who was seriously interested in literature and history, Solzhenitsyn sought to expand his understanding of Russia's revolutionary period by drawing out this knowledgeable peer.[13]

Both Panin and Kopelev have expressed great admiration for the Solzhenitsyn of the *sharashka* days. Panin once suggested that a monument should be erected to the writer while he was still alive, even proposing what it should feature.[14] Kopelev praised his friend's "strong, questioning mind," expressed delight in his "unwavering concentration of will, as taut as a violin string," and noted how "unfeignedly sincere and charming" he was in moments of relaxation.[15] The three friends engaged in discussions that typically deepened into heated arguments that turned on the simple fact of incompatible premises: As Kopelev writes, he was then a committed Marxist, Panin was a fervent Christian, and Solzhenitsyn was a skeptic, his main role in their arguments being to challenge the positions of the other two. Kopelev fair-mindedly specifies why he and Solzhenitsyn crossed verbal swords: "He [Solzhenitsyn] said that he used to believe in the basic tenets of Marxism, but then began having more and more doubts. Because he could not believe in the historical analyses of those whose prognoses turned out to be wrong."[16] In sum, the conditions of life in the *sharashka* afforded Solzhenitsyn the relative luxury of time to reassess his ideological convictions and begin constructing an alternative perspective to account for what he had seen and experienced. It is a reorientation that is played out in the mind of the character Gleb Nerzhin. In this time of profound self-examination, Solzhenitsyn moved toward, but not quite to, a reaffirmation of the Christian outlook in which he had been reared. But by the time he departed from Marfino, he had definitively left behind his youthful Marxism.

The relatively mild life of the *sharashka* ended abruptly in May 1950. A conflict with the authorities resulted in Solzhenitsyn's expulsion from Marfino and reimmersion into the world of labor camps. He was shipped off to Ekibastuz, a huge new prison camp in central Kazakhstan. This camp was designed for political prisoners only, in accordance with a decree by Stalin two years earlier that "politicals" be segregated in harsh-regime "Special Camps," because in his view they were far more dangerous than common criminals. Here Solzhenitsyn was involved in physical labor such as laying bricks, working in the foundry, and mining. And here he stayed for the rest of his term of imprisonment, with the years at Ekibastuz providing the raw material for *One Day in the Life of Ivan Denisovich.* Solzhenitsyn also gives an account of his time at Ekibastuz in *The Gulag Archipelago,* starting with his journey there from Marfino. Most importantly, he describes the escalating defiance of the Special Camp prisoners that soon resulted in the systematic assassination of camp informers and culminated in a general strike in early 1952. Solzhenitsyn participated in this strike and later wrote a screenplay, *Tanks Know the Truth,* based in part on this event, as well as upon the much more serious uprising in mid-1954 at the nearby Kengir camp, also recounted in *Gulag.* The authorities at first granted the strikers some concessions but soon crushed the rebellion.

Solzhenitsyn went unpunished for his role in the strike, but only because at the very time the authorities took action he was undergoing an emergency operation for what apparently was abdominal cancer. During his postoperative haze in the recovery room, one of the hospital's doctors, Boris Kornfeld, sat on his bed and recounted enthusiastically his own recent conversion to Christianity. Later that very night, Kornfeld was murdered by persons unknown, probably on suspicion that he had been an informer. His fervent words, perhaps the last of his life, lay upon Solzhenitsyn "as an inheritance."[17] This extraordinary episode, told in one of the most important and moving chapters of *The Gulag Archipelago,* "The Ascent," marks another great turning point in Solzhenitsyn's life. It culminates the process of reevaluation that had begun with his arrest and had proceeded apace throughout his years of imprisonment. His rededication to the religious faith of his early years is commemorated in a poem composed in 1952. The abandonment of Marxism was complete. In a 1989 interview Solzhenitsyn recounted the steps in this process: "In prison, I encountered a broad variety of people. I saw that my convictions did not have a solid basis, could not stand up in dispute, and I had to renounce them. Then the question arose of going back to what I head learned as a child. It took more than a year or so. Other believers influenced me, but basically it was a return to what I had thought before."[18]

Although Solzhenitsyn's term of incarceration officially ended on February 9, 1953, eight years to the day subsequent to his arrest, he was let out of camp on March 5, 1953, the day Stalin's death was announced. But the gulag system was by no means done with the released prisoner. Remaining under control of that system's administration, he was sent into internal exile, which was supposed to be "perpetual." He was assigned to Kok-Terek, a small village in southern Kazakhstan, where he was completely cut off from his earlier human contacts. His wife had earlier filed for divorce to evade the discrimination that befell any citizen who was married to an imprisoned "enemy of the people." (Solzhenitsyn had acquiesced in that decision.) And in 1952 the lonely woman started living with another man. ___

In Kok-Terek Solzhenitsyn made his living by teaching mathematics and physics at a nearby secondary school. In every spare moment he wrote. The first task was to put down on paper the prodigious output that he had composed in his head while in prison and camp. Having given priority to writing poetry, he now feverishly recorded on paper the long narrative poem *The Road*, the two plays *Victory Celebrations* and *Prisoners,* and a number of lyric poems. Without any hope that his works would see print during his lifetime, he was, as the saying has it, "writing for the drawer."

In the fall of 1953 Solzhenitsyn experienced a serious recurrence of the abdominal swelling that had led to his previous emergency surgery. By the end of the year his cancer was diagnosed as terminal. He was given only a few weeks to live. As he recalls, his condition worsened to the point that he was unable to eat or sleep; he seemed "very near death"[19] and was granted permission to take the 300-mile trip to a hospital in Tashkent, Uzbekistan, for treatment. Before departing, he stuffed his manuscripts into a bottle and buried it in his yard. The massive doses of radiation that he received at Tashkent shrank his tumor, and Solzhenitsyn reports that on the day of his release—after the second period of treatment in 1955, when he was declared cured—he decided to turn the raw material of his Tashkent experience into a work of fiction. The resulting text, produced in the early to middle 1960s, is a novel-length "tale" (*povest'*) titled *Cancer Ward*. Its leading character, Oleg Kostoglotov, has, like his creator, known war, prison, and cancer, though in most other regards he is not an authorial alter ego. From Tashkent, Solzhenitsyn returned to Kok-Terek (and his buried bottle) and resumed his routine of teaching and writing.

As if his life had not already been eventful enough, several events of 1956 and 1957 make those years particularly significant for the story of Solzhenitsyn. The first noteworthy event was a speech in February 1956 by Nikita Khrushchev to the Twentieth Congress of the Communist Party of the Soviet Union (CPSU), in which the premier denounced his predecessor, Joseph Stalin, for deviating from Lenin's precepts and, most pointedly, for establishing a "personality cult" that had brought about "a whole series of exceedingly serious and grave perversions of Party principles, of party democracy, of revolutionary legality."[20] This speech, initially secret, was largely intended to strengthen Khrushchev's position in the behind-the-scenes power struggle that had engulfed top Soviet leaders after the death of Stalin. High on the list of charges against the dead dictator was his role in ordering the torture and death of myriads of loyal Communists. In addition, the negative consequences of Stalin's policies were plainly visible to the rulers and the ruled alike; and some of these consequences, such as the gross economic inefficiency of the camp system, had to be undone in order to save the Soviet order itself. Most of the Party members present at the speech presumably knew too much about Stalin to be shocked by any revelations of inhumane actions on his part, but the violence of Khrushchev's attack shattered a hitherto-inviolate taboo and threw them into confusion by the obvious question it raised about the legitimacy of almost four decades of Soviet power. And when the contents of the speech were leaked to the public, the impact was sensational. Communist parties abroad were shaken to their foundations, with many of their members questioning whether their loyalty to the Soviet Union had been misplaced; in fact, numerous Western Communists and fellow travelers date their ideological defection from this occasion. Nations within the Soviet bloc reeled with unrest, and in October of that year Hungary exploded with an ill-fated revolt against Soviet domination.

Soviet citizens, too, felt the aftershocks of the dramatic events in the Kremlin. In cultural matters Khrushchev's speech set in motion the tenuous liberalization known as the "Thaw." This partial relaxation of ideological controls did not last long, and citizens never were sure how far they could go in speaking their minds; but all recognized the break from the strict regimentation of thought that Stalin had imposed. In April 1956 the government canceled all sentences of "perpetual exile," and when his school year ended, Solzhenitsyn returned to Central Russia, moving to a village about a hundred miles east of Moscow named Miltsevo. There he continued to earn his livelihood by teaching school and, as before, devoted every free moment to his writing, just as he would do for the rest of his life. Miltsevo provided the setting for "Matryona's Home," his best-known and arguably greatest short story. Its hero, known only by his patronymic, Ignatich, seeks but fails to find personal peace by burrowing nostalgically into the Russian heartland; this character is thoroughly autobiographical in inspiration. While at Miltsevo, Solzhenitsyn also completed the first draft of *The First Circle*. His situation in life was further improved when in early 1957 he was officially "rehabilitated," with the 1945 charges against him formally erased from his record. Shortly thereafter, he remarried Natalia Reshetovskaya, taking up residence with his wife in Ryazan, a provincial city south of Moscow, where Solzhenitsyn once again

found work as a schoolteacher while continuing his clandestine—
and prolific—writing.

In 1958–60 Solzhenitsyn penned seventeen miniature stories
("Krokhotki," literally "tinies"), which were essentially prose poems. These brief texts, running from a mere dozen lines to a page
and a half, display the sure touch of a poet capable of deft delicacy.
They also reveal a pensive, gentle spirit not readily associated with
an author of long books. Solzhenitsyn would return to the "miniature" genre in later years.

A new injection of high drama into the story of Solzhenitsyn
came in the early 1960s, after Khrushchev gave another speech that
was destined to affect the course of the writer's life. Addressing the
Twenty-Second Congress of the Communist Party of the Soviet
Union in October 1961, Khrushchev pressed the case for liberalizing reform with a vigor that was surprising in light of the shock
waves still reverberating from his "de-Stalinization" speech of 1956.
This congress proved to be the high-water mark in Khrushchev's
campaign to discredit Stalin, and its most visible symbolic result
was the removal of Stalin's embalmed corpse from the Lenin mau-
soleum on Red Square. Another important speaker at the congress
was Aleksandr Tvardovsky, the editor in chief of the USSR's most
prestigious literary monthly, *Novy Mir,* who energetically supported
the premier's reformist position and implied that his journal would
be open to pieces reflecting the new line. The on-again-off-again
"Thaw" was, it seemed, on again. Given this climate, Solzhenitsyn
made the fateful decision to try to get something of his into print. He
set his sights on *Novy Mir* as the outlet most likely to take a risk on
a provocative work of literature. The author's choice of manuscript
for this venture was titled *Shch-854* (for the prison identification
number of its protagonist), a work known later as *One Day in the
Life of Ivan Denisovich;* it had been written in 1959. He handed the
manuscript to Lev Kopelev, his old friend from Marfino days, who
passed it along to a secretary at *Novy Mir;* she, in turn, managed to
present it directly to Tvardovsky. In a well-documented episode,
Tvardovsky took the manuscript home in the evening, changed into

his lounging robe, propped himself up with pillows while sitting on his bed, and started to read. After having read just two or three pages, he got up, put on his office clothes, and resumed his reading. He was, he knew, in the presence of a literary masterpiece, and only dignified attire was fitting for the occasion. Tvardovsky stayed up through the night to read the text twice. In the meantime, Solzhenitsyn was having second thoughts about having revealed himself, even wishing that he could retrieve his manuscript and return to his underground ways.[21] But it was too late: He had set in motion a decade of struggle with the authorities that would lead through hazardous adventure to international fame.

Getting the work published was now Tvardovsky's challenge. The course of action chosen by the highly placed literary man with peasant roots was to hand over the manuscript to the most highly placed political man, also with peasant roots: Nikita Khrushchev himself. Tvardovsky suggested to Khrushchev—a personal acquaintance—that he might find this piece of fiction about prison camp life useful for confirming Stalin's excesses. The book is indeed anti-Stalinist, but almost entirely in the general sense of being opposed to state-sponsored dehumanization in any form. According to Khrushchev's son Sergei, his father listened as the premier's aide, Vladimir Lebedev, read the text aloud.[22] Deciding to have the work published, Khrushchev sought the cover of collective approval by the regime's leadership. He had copies distributed to the members of the Party Presidium, with printed instructions forbidding the duplicating, lending, or keeping of any copy. At the Presidium's next meeting, each member had to speak for or against publishing the book, in this way allowing Khrushchev to determine who was with him in his de-Stalinization drive and who was not.[23] It can be said, therefore, that the very first public use of a Solzhenitsyn work was a politicized *mis*use.

Soon after Khrushchev gave the green light (almost precisely on the eve of the Cuban missile crisis), the work was published by *Novy Mir*, in November 1962, under the title *One Day in the Life of Ivan Denisovich*, Tvardovsky's substitution for *Shch-854*. *Novy Mir* printed many more copies than usual. Within months the mass-circulation magazine *Roman-gazeta* reprinted the work, and it also appeared in book form. The very fact that a depiction of life in a Soviet forced-labor camp was appearing in public guaranteed that the work would create a major sensation. Readers passed along from hand to hand copies numbering in the millions. Translated versions appeared quickly and were similarly numerous. Almost overnight, a hitherto unknown schoolteacher became a household name known around the world. Solzhenitsyn's life had changed course radically and irreversibly. From now on, the writer was to be a highly visible public figure. Khrushchev had let the genie out of the bottle, and there was no stuffing it back in.

Establishment publications dutifully followed the Soviet leader both in embracing *One Day* and in mimicking his instrumental approach of treating this work of literature as a political tool. Early Western responses to the work were profuse and overwhelmingly glowing, though they, too, devoted considerable attention to the work's political significance. The exuberant response to *One Day* at home and abroad went well beyond what Khrushchev and company had expected or desired. It is clear that the Kremlin had hoped for nothing more than servile gratitude that Stalin's terror was over. Instead, the emphasis fell on how much more needed to be told. Other writers, trying to capitalize on Solzhenitsyn's success, bombarded Soviet publishing houses with literary manuscripts challenging Stalinism. And Western commentators welcomed Solzhenitsyn as an anti-totalitarian freedom fighter who had dared to tackle a dangerous subject. Even more significantly, readers in the Soviet Union, the great majority of whom had had friends or family members in the gulag, saw the appearance of Ivan Denisovich's story as an explosive revelation of an officially ignored world, and in this sense as a breathtaking liberation from the chokehold of enforced falsehoods. For many citizens, the publication of *One Day* was an almost mythic moment. The previously unnamable had been named; the link between experience and verbal expression had been reasserted.

The appearance of this story was also a promise of many more stories to be revealed. Readers by the hundreds unloaded upon Solzhenitsyn an avalanche of letters describing their own ordeals or the suffering of others they had witnessed. Solzhenitsyn had once considered writing a history of the whole gulag system, but he had set aside the idea as too vast, given the limited sources available. But now the correspondence precipitated by *One Day* was bringing him exactly the sort of detailed material needed for the gargantuan project he had in mind. The plan was revived, and in 1963–64 the writer met with and interviewed hundreds of the letter-writers. Drawing upon these eyewitness accounts, as well as other sources, he soon set to work in earnest to compose *The Gulag Archipelago*.

At the same time, Solzhenitsyn tried to parlay his success with *One Day* into the publication of other works, but with limited success. Two months after *One Day* appeared, *Novy Mir* carried "Matryona's Home" and another excellent short story, "Incident at Krechetovka Station."[24] Later in 1963 the same journal ran a rather long—and less successful—story titled "For the Good of the Cause." An essay on language (1965) and the story "Zakhar the Pouch" (1966) were the only other works by Solzhenitsyn published in the official Soviet press while he was living in the USSR. In 1963 the literary overlords denied permission to stage his play *The Love-Girl and the Innocent* even in its politically softened version, and in 1965 they effectively closed the door to the publication of any of his longer works (*The First Circle,* then *Cancer Ward*). The author's career as an acceptable Soviet writer was finished, and he would not be published at home again until the Soviet Union was in its death throes.

Meanwhile, *One Day in the Life of Ivan Denisovich* continued to make waves. When Khrushchev was ousted from power in October 1964, one of the points in the Party's indictment against him was his decision to allow the publication of Solzhenitsyn's work.[25] This was preceded, several months before Khrushchev's downfall, by an episode in which Solzhenitsyn was nominated for the Lenin Prize in literature, after which hard-line Party hacks felt sufficiently threatened to launch a shameless last-minute allegation that the writer had collaborated with the Nazis during the war, thus sabotaging his chances. (In retrospect, Solzhenitsyn has suggested that this rebuff was in fact fortunate, sparing him the inevitable extra pressure to conform to the dictates of the state.) The removal of Khrushchev from power left Tvardovsky and *Novy Mir*—and, ineluctably, Solzhenitsyn as well—stripped of their principal protection. The author's position grew increasingly precarious. The short-lived official attitude of favor toward him was now replaced by open hostility, which was soon to deepen into vituperation. The failure of his efforts to get a "lightened" version of his full-length novel, *The First Circle,* into print in the Soviet Union led him to have a copy smuggled West for safekeeping, though not yet for publication. By 1964, however, other works of his had found their own ways westward, and some of them had begun to appear in print—without his permission and against his wishes. The first of these were the miniatures, which turned up in *Grani,* a Russian émigré journal published in Germany.

The KGB was by now tracking Solzhenitsyn's moves, and its more or less discreet surveillance began turning into direct harassment. In 1965 the security agency raided the apartments of two of Solzhenitsyn's friends and made off with a large cache of his notes and unpublished manuscripts. Among the many items snatched was the manuscript of the early play *Victory Celebrations,* which contained passages that were bitterly hostile toward the Soviet regime and thus lent themselves readily to the kind of selective citation soon used to blacken the author's reputation in Soviet eyes. Solzhenitsyn escalated the conflict by circulating statements revealing the KGB's machinations. These increasingly confrontational statements established his reputation as a prominent and eloquent opponent of the regime, and they were typically published in the West and then broadcast back to the USSR over Radio Liberty. Whereas previously Solzhenitsyn had made an effort to stay out of the public eye, by 1965 circumstances had forced him into open defiance. Besides publicizing his fiery denunciations of KGB harassment, he gave public readings from his works and even granted interviews to foreign journalists. His reputation as a shrewd strategist and formidable infighter in his battle with the authorities dates from this time.

The principal means employed by Solzhenitsyn in reaction to the official campaign against him was to circulate his statements, his responses to attacks, and his literary works via the samizdat network, a system of distributing privately printed but officially unacceptable works among other dissenters. In practice this entailed the clandestine reproduction of texts in chain-letter fashion, typically by means of typing while making several carbon copies (access to photocopy machines was heavily controlled). The first work that he allowed to be disseminated via samizdat was *Cancer Ward,* composed during the turbulent, noose-tightening years of 1963–66. He had made every effort to get *Cancer Ward* published in a Soviet-sanctioned outlet, submitting the work to *Novy Mir* and awaiting the censors' clearance after the editorial board gave its approval. A 1966 meeting at which Solzhenitsyn discussed the manuscript with the prose section of the Moscow writers' organization augured well: The fellow writers lavished praise on the work, and in return Solzhenitsyn expressed his thanks and his willingness to consider making recommended revisions. But the manuscript remained hopelessly stalled, and his frustration finally boiled over. In May 1967 this took the form of a blistering open letter to the delegates of the Fourth Congress of the Union of Soviet Writers,[26] even though this statement addresses the specific issue of Solzhenitsyn's languishing manuscript only briefly. For the most part, the letter excoriates the system of censorship that made such problems possible in the first place, and berates the officially approved writers for their shameful docility in the face of a system that routinely disfigures and stunts their own works, as well as for their refusal to protest the active persecution of hundreds of fellow writers. This open letter was Solzhenitsyn's first major act of public defiance, with the text widely distributed in samizdat and receiving considerable publicity in the West. The Fourth Congress, however, refused to take up his proposed agenda items, despite the pleas of a number of delegates. After this occasion Solzhenitsyn began keeping a record of his conflict with the authorities in case they should take action against him. These notes were the genesis of the autobiographical sketches that appeared in 1975 under the title *The Oak and the Calf.*

While all this drama was unfolding on the public stage, Solzhenitsyn was carrying on a second life out of public view. This was his "underground" life as a writer dealing with taboo materials. He was secretly writing what would become *The Gulag Archipelago*, his massive indictment of the Soviet penal system, which he knew could never get past the censors. The riveting story of how he worked under circumstances of nearly unimaginable constraints reached the reading public only in 1991, with the publication of *Invisible Allies*, which he had intended to be part of *The Oak and the Calf.* (Because *Invisible Allies* mentioned the names of the numerous co-conspirators who typed Solzhenitsyn's works and hid copies of them and who would be endangered if their identities were known, he withheld these accounts until after the Soviet Union had collapsed.) The writer labored furtively and feverishly on *Gulag* for some ten years, 1958–68. Much of his work on the book took place in Estonia, where he was provided with shelter by friends of his former *zek* acquaintances. He repaired to what he called his "Hiding Place" four times, with the two most productive periods of creativity taking place in the winters of 1965–66 and 1966–67—a total of 146 days, as he specifies with typical exactness. During this time, Solzhenitsyn recalls, he worked as he never had in his whole life. "It even seemed as if it were no longer I who was writing; rather, I was swept along, my hand being moved by an outside force. . . . Those weeks represent the highest point in my feelings of victory and of isolation from the world."[27] He also reports the astonishing fact that because of security concerns he never once throughout the whole composing process risked having all parts of the work together on his desk at the same time.

With *The Gulag Archipelago* completed in 1968, Solzhenitsyn successfully arranged the nerve-racking operation of getting a microfilm copy to the West for safekeeping. In the same year, both *The First Circle* and *Cancer Ward* were published outside the Soviet Union, both in Russian and in translation. Western reviewers generally welcomed these two long works of fiction with the same warmth they had bestowed earlier on *One Day;* differences among the reviewers focused mainly on which of these new works was the greater. Solzhenitsyn was riding high in world opinion, and his successes in public relations instilled in him a relative sense of immunity despite the sharp hostility of the regime.

In 1969 Solzhenitsyn took up in earnest the vast project that he had set his mind on in his youth—the literary rendering of the historical events that had issued in the Bolshevik Revolution of 1917. He envisaged this as a multivolume cycle of works to be collectively titled *The Red Wheel.* The early version of the first installment ("Knot I"), *August 1914,* was prepared for publication by 1971, appearing in Paris after all attempts to achieve publication in the Soviet Union failed; a highly flawed English translation came out in 1972. The final, considerably expanded, version was published in 1983, though not until 1989 in English (this time in an excellent translation). Despite all the distracting turmoil of his life during the 1960s and early 1970s, Solzhenitsyn's commitment to what he considered his magnum opus never flagged.

The violent displeasure of the regime notwithstanding, Solzhenitsyn formally retained the status of an officially recognized Soviet writer throughout the late 1960s. But from the Soviet point of view this clearly was an unnatural arrangement, and action to terminate it came in late 1969, when the Ryazan chapter of the Writers' Union did the national organization's dirty work by expelling him from the organization for "antisocial behavior." Under Soviet law, a formally unemployed writer could be charged with the crime of "social parasitism," as had happened to Joseph Brodsky in 1964. Solzhenitsyn was probably spared such a fate only because Western writers raised a din of protest on his behalf. On this and other occasions, such outpouring of support in the West unquestionably functioned as a brake on the persecution of the beleaguered writer.

This is of course apart from the courageous support Solzhenitsyn received from numerous prominent Russians such as Mstislav Rostropovich and Kornei Chukovsky.

A tremendous boost to Solzhenitsyn's reputation came in 1970, when he was awarded the Nobel Prize for Literature in recognition—as the citation put it—of "the ethical force with which he has pursued the indispensable traditions of Russian literature."[28] As with prior Western expressions of support for his work, the surge of sympathy on this occasion strengthened his position. Even more than before, the world press accorded him celebrity treatment. The Soviet press, by contrast, overflowed with predictable cries of indignation at this prestigious recognition. Solzhenitsyn did not travel to Stockholm to receive the award, fearing that the Soviet government would strip him of his citizenship while he was abroad and then block his return home. He suggested a ceremony at the Swedish embassy in Moscow instead, but the Swedes, cowed by Soviet threats, chose to forgo that option. Two years later, in 1972, the Nobel Foundation released the text of his lecture, which is normally delivered at some point close to the award ceremony. (And it was not until 1974, when the author was already living abroad, that he received the Nobel insignia in person.)

The intensity of conflict between author and authorities reached its zenith during the years 1970–72. Solzhenitsyn was at that time perceived as one of the two most prominent Soviet dissenters, the other being Andrei Sakharov, a leading physicist known as the father of the Soviet hydrogen bomb who had become sharply critical of the Soviet role in world affairs. Writer and scientist were somewhat uneasy allies because of significant differences between their overall perspectives: Sakharov's secular commitment to Enlightenment principles and Solzhenitsyn's religious convictions were inherently at odds. Nevertheless, the prevailing tone of their relationship was mutual respect, as would soon be demonstrated by Solzhenitsyn's act of nominating Sakharov in 1973 for the Nobel Peace Prize, and then by Sakharov's public protests in defense of Solzhenitsyn both before and after the writer was arrested in 1974. During the tense early 1970s, the crucial cover of Western support extended to both men equally—support for which Solzhenitsyn publicly thanked the press, on behalf of both of them, as soon as he was deported to the West.[29] But both of them also experienced direct physical endangerment. Sakharov was threatened by men posing as Arab terrorists.[30] In Solzhenitsyn's case, KGB agents ransacked his summer cottage and severely beat a friend of his who happened to be there, sent threatening letters to the writer and his wife, and in 1971 even tried to kill him. The attempt on his life was made by poking him with a sharp instrument tipped with poison (ricin, apparently) as he was standing in line at a store in Novocherkassk. Solzhenitsyn was stricken with blisters over much of his body and was bedridden for nearly three months, but at the time did not suspect foul play. This was yet another close call for the survivor of prison camps and cancer.[31] At about the same time, libraries throughout the Soviet Union received orders to destroy their copies of *One Day,* along with issues of *Novy Mir* containing this and other works by Solzhenitsyn.

In 1972 Solzhenitsyn circulated an open letter to Patriarch Pimen criticizing the leadership of the Russian Orthodox Church for its supine inactivity in the face of vigorously promoted atheistic propaganda. It must have been clear to Solzhenitsyn by this time that he could never regain state-approved publication of his works, and it may well be that this realization freed him to reveal sympathies he had not publicized before. In any case, the open letter made clear his allegiance to the church. At about the same time, a prose-poem prayer of his, penned probably in 1962, was printed in *Time* and other Western magazines; it begins, "How easy for me to live with you, Lord! / How easy to believe in you!"[32] (This prayer reached the West at the initiative of Elizaveta Voronyanskaya, one of Solzhenitsyn's "invisible allies." Solzhenitsyn chastised her sternly for this impetuosity, but later he came to view her action as providential, since it was instrumental in leading to his receipt of the Templeton Prize for Progress in Religion in 1983.) Taken together, these two statements brought to the fore the issue of his religious convictions, which previously had drawn little critical attention. Father Alexander Schmemann had written an important essay in 1970 on Christian themes in Solzhenitsyn's writings,[33] but Schmemann's shrewd insights went almost unnoticed.

The publication of *August 1914*—in Russian in 1971 and in English in 1972—changed the landscape of Solzhenitsyn criticism. Some religiously inclined critics observed delightedly that in this work Solzhenitsyn seemed similarly inclined. Moreover, a number of secular critics saw the same signs. The work does not contain explicit assertions of the author's Christian faith. Rather, in this, his most emphatically patriotic literary work to date, the Russia that the author affirms is the historical, religious Russia. The realization thus began to set in across the board that religious convictions lay deep in Solzhenitsyn's outlook. This generated confusion and apprehension among many of Solzhenitsyn's secular admirers in both Russia and the West in the early 1970s and contributed directly to the first significant decline of Solzhenitsyn's standing. In the West, the reviews of *August 1914* were decidedly mixed. While a few were sturdily favorable, most were guarded or ambivalent, and a widespread mood of disappointment was unmistakable. In the words of biographer Michael Scammell, the appearance of this work "disrupted the unanimity of opinion that had enveloped his earlier works."[34] Solzhenitsyn records the same kind of reaction among many of his confederates in Russia, with the book's appearance occasioning a "schism among my readers" and "the steady loss of supporters."[35] The bluntest explanation for the defections came from Mary McCarthy: Solzhenitsyn was "rude and unfair" toward "the 'liberals' and 'advanced circles' of 1914." Assuming a consensual like-mindedness among her readers, she continued, "He has it in for those people, just as he would have it in for you and me, if he could overhear us talking."[36]

Meanwhile, Solzhenitsyn's marriage to Natalia Reshetovskaya was in deep trouble. The strains in their complicated relationship became unbearable. Solzhenitsyn had begun a relationship with Natalia Svetlova, a Moscow mathematician who was one of the "invisible" helpers in his work. Reshetovskaya made a failed attempt at suicide. A divorce petition, initially rejected by the authorities in a mean-spirited attempt to harass the writer, was finally approved in early 1973, clearing the way for Solzhenitsyn and Svetlova to marry. After the divorce Reshetovskaya wrote a memoir about her former husband that blackened his reputation, although she later claimed that Novosti, the official Soviet press agency, which had helped her prepare the book, had edited it in a way that increased its negative slant. The memoir appeared in 1975, with its title rendered in English as *Sanya* (Solzhenitsyn's nickname). Solzhenitsyn has never portrayed himself as blameless in the breakup. Nevertheless, in his second wife he found someone who was his equal in intensity of spirit, fearlessness of character, and enormous capacity for work. She became a full partner in every aspect of his life, including his work as a writer.

The ceaseless hounding of Solzhenitsyn took an alarming turn when in mid-1973 the KGB detained Elizaveta Voronyanskaya. After a microfilm copy of *The Gulag Archipelago* had been transmitted to the safety of the West, the writer had instructed Voronyanskaya to destroy any copies that she still possessed. Voronyanskaya had disobeyed his request, retaining one copy just in case all others were confiscated. The KGB, knowing that Voronyanskaya belonged to Solzhenitsyn's inner circle, brought her in for interrogation (a process vividly described in the third chapter of *Gulag*). After five days and nights of uninterrupted questioning, she cracked and revealed where her copy was located. She died soon thereafter, either by suicide or (as Solzhenitsyn thinks more likely) by murder. Solzhenitsyn was well aware of the KGB's practice of quoting out of context in order to produce an effect opposite of what a writer intended. So, to beat the KGB to the punch, he sent word, through the Swiss lawyer he had engaged, for the presses in the West to roll. The first Russian-language volume of *Gulag* appeared in Paris at the end of 1973, and soon thereafter all eighteen hundred pages were published in the original and in various other languages. Yet another blockbuster episode in the saga of Solzhenitsyn received front-page coverage in newspapers everywhere. (Solzhenitsyn would later view Voronyanskaya's unauthorized hiding of a copy of *Gulag* as providential, much as he came to view as providential her meddlesome role in publicizing his prose-poem prayer.)

Solzhenitsyn had no doubt that *The Gulag Archipelago* was destined to affect the course of history, and many Western critics concurred in their estimates of the work's significance. For that matter, the Soviet authorities themselves seem to have recognized the power of *Gulag* and the perils it posed for them. In a left-handed compliment, the Soviet media ratcheted up to fever pitch the campaign to vilify its author. Even though much of the factual background underlying the *Gulag* narrative was already in the public record, thanks to studies by scholars and memoirs by former prisoners, it remained true that in terms of Western public opinion, the Soviet Union was generally given the benefit of the doubt. It is thus a measure of Solzhenitsyn's literary talent that the force of his voice broke through the wall of Western skepticism and carried the day with general readers and opinion-shapers alike. Two decades later, after the Soviet Union disintegrated, historians would routinely list *Gulag* and *One Day* among the factors contributing to the regime's collapse.

The publication of *The Gulag Archipelago* was also the immediate cause of Solzhenitsyn's expulsion to the West. Although we now know that Yuri Andropov, the head of the KGB in the early 1970s, had been advocating precisely this course of action against the writer for some time, Solzhenitsyn was surprisingly unprepared for this move of Soviet revenge. On February 11, 1974, the Soviet state prosecutor's office issued him a summons. The messenger attempting to deliver the summons was rebuffed at the door by Mrs. Solzhenitsyn, who refused to accept it. Instead, Solzhenitsyn issued a counter-statement of his own, giving copies of it to Western reporters. It read, "I refuse to recognize the legality of your summons and shall not appear at an interrogation in any state institution."[37] Even this episode was not enough to convince Solzhenitsyn that his arrest was imminent. At 5:00 p.m. on the next day (February

12, 1974), eight men—plainclothes KGB agents and uniformed officers—showed up at Solzhenitsyn's door, forced their way into the apartment, and arrested him. Despite his well-honed habit of thinking through the regime's probable moves and trying to stay one step ahead, Solzhenitsyn describes his mental state on this occasion as one of "witless shock."[38] Since several weeks had passed without incident after the initial appearance of *Gulag,* he had let himself slip into a false sense of security and invincibility. Other storms of slander against him had blown over. Why not expect that this latest one, too, despite its intensity, would pass without follow-up action? To the fateful knock on the door, then, he could only react with, "No, I had never thought it would happen. Honestly, I had never expected it."[39] He had time only to put on the old hat and sheepskin jacket from exile days that he had prepared for this eventuality, to kiss his wife and to sign the cross over her head, and to tell her to look after the children.

Solzhenitsyn was about to be stripped of his Soviet citizenship (as his wife would be at a later point), "for systematically performing actions that are incompatible with being a citizen of the U.S.S.R.,"[40] and to be formally accused of treason, a charge that potentially carried the death penalty. He was taken to Lefortovo prison, where he underwent the multiple humiliations described in "Arrest," the opening chapter of *Gulag.* He pondered the possible acts that could be committed against him. The one ultimately chosen was to put him on an airplane and send him away, destination unknown to him until upon landing he saw the airport sign for Frankfurt-am-Main. The world press followed avidly the day-by-day developments in the drama of his exile. Virtually in unison, Western commentators protested the Soviet action against Solzhenitsyn and praised his courage and literary talent. Even Communist parties in the West spoke on his behalf. For Russian public consumption Solzhenitsyn left behind a brief statement titled "Live Not by Lies!"

While Solzhenitsyn's account of his long-running conflict with the Soviet regime is recounted in *The Oak and the Calf* and *Invisible Allies,* the authorities were keeping a record of their own concerning "the issue of Solzhenitsyn." In 1995 the Soviet view of this struggle became public in a substantial volume titled *The Solzhenitsyn Files*.[41] The documents selected for inclusion in this book were drawn from secret, often top-secret, files of the Central Committee of the Communist Party USSR, declassified by President Boris Yeltsin's order after the fall of the Soviet Union. Among the major impressions that can be drawn from these records is how successfully Solzhenitsyn and his helpers outfoxed the KGB and hid their activities from the alleged "Unsleeping Eye."[42] Another major impression is how befuddled and baffled the top officials were in trying to figure out what to do with the recalcitrant author, none more so than the befogged Leonid Brezhnev. Their strategy was ultimately determined by Yuri Andropov. Rather than making a martyr of Solzhenitsyn by killing him or returning him to the gulag, Andropov successfully argued for shipping him West. Allowing him to continue his activities in the Soviet Union was deemed unacceptable, but the sentence of external exile would, Andropov hoped, earn some credit for the Soviet regime in the West by being perceived as a "humane" act. Andropov hoped further that Solzhenitsyn would lose his status and significance once he found himself in the West.[43]

Life in Exile

Solzhenitsyn arrived in the West (in his words) "naked as Adam."[44] After he landed at the Frankfurt airport, his first haven was the home of the German writer and fellow Nobel Prize winner Heinrich Böll, where he was given tea, bread, and bed. The press continued its eager reportage of his every move. Soon he would embark upon a whirlwind of public activity among unfamiliar surroundings for which his prior experiences, despite all their drama, did little to prepare him.

It might seem obvious to Westerners living in comfort and safety that the Soviet authorities could have done much worse by Solzhenitsyn than to send him to live out his days in freedom. But a writer has worries of his own, and Solzhenitsyn had once wondered if "off Russian ground I am doomed to lose my feel for the Russian language."[45] (In fact, he would later acknowledge that he could write another batch of prose poems only after he returned to Russia in 1994; "living abroad—I simply couldn't do it.")[46] So it may be taken as a measure of Solzhenitsyn's inveterate optimism (despite his later reputation as a Jeremiah) that upon his expulsion he remarked, "Even old trees, when they are transplanted, take root in a new place."[47] And, indeed, once in the West he soon settled into a calm routine in which he devoted almost every waking hour to his writing.

It is impossible to overstate the enthusiasm with which the West welcomed Solzhenitsyn. *The Times* of London called him "the man who is for the moment the most famous person in the western world."[48] *Time* magazine declared him "one of the world's great writers, an authentic hero in an age sorely lacking them."[49] Everywhere he went, he received smiles and cheers from well-wishing crowds. Telegrams of support flooded in from all over the world. He was swamped with invitations to speak and requests for interviews. Countries vied with one another in offering him shelter; invitations to settle came from Norway, Denmark, Switzerland, Great Britain, Canada, the United States, Australia, Israel. Less than a month after he was deported, thirty-three US senators cosponsored a resolution to grant him honorary American citizenship.

Because Solzhenitsyn appreciated the Western support he had received prior to his deportation, he felt an obligation to accept at least some of the invitations to make public appearances. After years of living underground, he was being handed the opportunity to speak candidly to audiences clamoring to hear him. And although he would wait until 1975–76 to set out on a major round of speaking engagements, he could meanwhile not avoid dealing with the press in some fashion. He had valued Western journalists as allies when he was battling the Soviet regime, but contending with their hounding ways at close quarters was a different matter, and mere days after reaching the West he was already expressing irritation at the errors (or pure invention) that appeared in their stories. The spirit of conflict between him and the press would only worsen over time. Then there was the matter of interviews, the clamor for which was too great for him to stave them off for long. In 1974 he sat for a formal interview with Walter Cronkite, the prominent American television newsman. In this and other interviews, Solzhenitsyn, relishing his new freedom to speak out, replied unguardedly to questions, sometimes to the interviewer's manifest incomprehension. A number of his remarks here and on other early occasions revealed positions and attitudes of which Westerners were unaware, and his views on nonliterary issues often went against the grain of received opinion. In particular, the cultural elites were often surprised and displeased by his rejection of the West's policy of détente with the Soviet Union, his doubts about Western resolve in standing up for freedom, his apparent coolness toward democracy, and much more. Thus, many of those who had championed the writer for his resistance to Soviet totalitarianism began to have second thoughts. The numerous controversies stirred up as a result may be collectively called "the Solzhenitsyn question."

There was also the problem of finding a place for his family to live. Admirers in Norway, who had proposed as early as 1970 that he might wish to consider moving there, hosted him for an exploratory visit soon after his arrival in the West. He felt drawn to the beauty and the climate of the country, respected the staunch spirit of Norwegians, and enjoyed the company of his hosts. But Norway had its drawbacks, its inconvenient geographical location among them, and Solzhenitsyn decided to make Zurich, Switzerland, his first Western residence. Several weeks later the Soviet authorities allowed his wife and sons to join him there. Their house was right on the street and therefore noisy, and its easy access invited many well-meaning people to approach and thus to distract him from his work. This insufficiently private arrangement could not last, even though the writer spent much time in a considerably more secluded house made available to him by the mayor of the city. Yet living in Zurich had important compensations. For one thing, it was the very city where Lenin had spent a restless year before his fateful return to Russia in 1917, and the writer made a point of familiarizing himself with the Bolshevik leader's way of life during his Swiss sojourn—information that found its way into the Lenin-centered chapters of *The Red Wheel*. Even more useful were meetings with scholars who had investigated Lenin's activities in 1916–17, particularly the much-debated question of his contacts with German agents.

Soon after settling into Switzerland, Solzhenitsyn established the Russian Social Fund, a charitable foundation intended primarily to aid political prisoners and prisoners of conscience, along with their families. The foundation was registered under Swiss law and set up to receive one hundred percent of the royalties from the sale of *The Gulag Archipelago* in all languages. Money was discreetly taken into the Soviet Union and distributed by fearless individuals who braved arrest to carry out this function. (In post-Soviet years the fund has been dispensing modest but regular monetary support to some two thousand indigent former inmates.)

Living in Switzerland was also not devoid of pleasures of a more traditional kind. Solzhenitsyn was eager to meet people for good conversation, and the mayor of Zurich obliged by arranging dinner parties. Other memorable meetings included lengthy discussions with the Orthodox priest and scholar Alexander Schmemann, whose sermons Solzhenitsyn had greatly admired when he heard them on Western radio broadcasts beamed to the USSR.[50] The central location of Switzerland also allowed the writer's first year in the West to be rich in travel experiences. Apart from Norway, Solzhenitsyn traveled to France, Italy, and Germany. He toured Switzerland, too, even arranging a meeting with Vladimir Nabokov in Montreux, to which the elderly writer mysteriously failed to come.[51] In December 1974 he went to Stockholm to collect the Nobel insignia. In his notes on these and other travels,[52] Solzhenitsyn stresses his admiration for the lavish richness of the multilayered cultural heritage visible everywhere in Europe and his equally profound apprehension at signs of modern barbarism—such as the revolutionary graffiti that defaced historical buildings.

Of all the favorable impressions that Switzerland made on Solzhenitsyn, perhaps the most satisfying one involved a visit to the
canton of Appenzell, where he observed direct democracy in action at the canton's annual election of officers. He was much impressed by this session, with its orderly proceedings according to
established rules, and was particularly pleased when citizens talked
back to their elected authorities and even voted down the principal recommendations of the mayor for whom they had just voted.[53]
Solzhenitsyn's admiration for democracy from the bottom up was
later to be reinforced by his experience of the town-hall meetings of
Cavendish, Vermont. These observations accorded with his predilection for the kind of democracy that begins at the local level, then
moves upward from small units to national elections. (Grassroots
electoral arrangements had had an indigenous Russian analogue
in the generally forgotten rural *zemstvos* of the nineteenth century,
which later served Solzhenitsyn as a model for the tiered and gradualist democracy he would recommend for the rebuilding of the
country in its post-Soviet phase.)

While in Zurich, Solzhenitsyn established contact with members of the very large Czech émigré community, who were eager to
help the writer and his family and through whom he hoped—futilely, as it turned out—to have some of his works translated into
Czech. One of these Czechs, a young writer and alleged dissident
named Tomáš Řezáč, turned out to be a Communist agent who
suddenly disappeared from Zurich and resurfaced in Prague with
mendacious radio broadcasts about the community he had just left.
Although he had had no direct contact with Solzhenitsyn, he seems
to have persuaded the Czech security agencies of the opposite, as a
result of which he gained the assistance of the Soviet news agency
Novosti in producing a scurrilous book about the writer in 1978.[54]

During the writer's stay in Switzerland, "the Solzhenitsyn question" began to take on a life of its own. Every new utterance by
the newcomer seemed to reopen the question of what to make of
him. In retrospect, it might be said that his exuberant faith in the
West's vaunted freedom of speech led him beyond the bounds of

prudence that comes from knowing one's audience well, taking their presuppositions into due account, and couching one's formulations accordingly. At any rate, reevaluation became the order of the day. This process of reassessing, it is important to note, was set in motion before Solzhenitsyn's series of major speeches to Western audiences. Those speeches simply became more grist for the mill of ongoing reevaluation.

In fact, an important landmark in the evolution of "the Solzhenitsyn question" can be located in a short piece the author wrote a few months before reaching the West. Titled *Letter to the Soviet Leaders,* it was originally sent privately to its intended addressees on September 5, 1973. In this letter, Solzhenitsyn offered practical advice to the Soviet leaders about how they should chart their course through the period of transition that he believed was in store. Though he granted that they would not willingly give up their power, he urged them to abandon the ideology of Marxism, which he claimed they no longer believed in anyway. When the leaders did not reply, the author released the letter to the public shortly before his arrest, and translations appeared shortly after his expulsion in early 1974. Thus, Westerners had two new pieces to digest at the time the author arrived in their midst, *The Gulag Archipelago* and the *Letter,* and while *Gulag* generally elicited kudos, Solzhenitsyn's *Letter* simultaneously encountered rejection and even rebuke. Incongruously, the little letter had a greater impact on the West's reception of the newly arrived exile than did the massive tome.

Though he was now in the West, Russia clearly remained uppermost in Solzhenitsyn's mind. Shortly before his arrest and exile, he had edited a collection of essays focused on the question of how Russia could shape a postcommunist future for itself. Published in Paris in 1974 and appearing in English in 1975, the collection gave priority to spiritual renewal rather than political reform; it was appropriately titled *From under the Rubble.* The volume comprised eleven essays by seven contributors, three of the essays being by Solzhenitsyn himself, including "Repentance and Self-Limitation in the Life of Nations," according to the writer's own reckoning one of his most important pieces. In short, seventeen years before the Soviet Union collapsed, the authors of this collective manifesto were anticipating the cataclysm and offering advice about how Russia could revive itself on the far side of the Soviet parenthesis.

By the end of 1974 the writer had made up his mind to leave Switzerland and relocate to North America. Canada was his first choice because of its similarity to Russia in terms of climate and geography, and in the spring of 1975 he undertook a fairly extensive search for a suitable property in Ontario. Frustrated by the inability to find anything mutually acceptable to himself and his wife, he broke off the hunt and traveled to Alaska, then to Stanford University's Hoover Institution for a week of fruitful research, followed by a visit to the Old Believer communities in Oregon. It was during this period on the West Coast that an invitation from George Meany reached the writer and led to the major speeches delivered in June and July to the AFL-CIO, America's leading labor organization, in Washington and New York.

It is important to recall the political context of the time. Saigon had fallen to the North Vietnamese in the spring of that year, radical Marxists had seized control of Ethiopia in the preceding year, Angola seemed about to follow suit, and Soviet influence was on the rise in Central America. Yet the official American policy of détente toward the Soviet Union was still in place, and President Ford was preparing to travel to Helsinki in July in order to sign an accord that would in effect legitimize Soviet hegemony over Eastern Europe. In Solzhenitsyn's eyes, the behavior of the West in these circumstances seemed nothing less than a craven retreat before the forces of aggressive communism, and he could not keep his silence. As he explains in his memoirs, it was part of his nature to be forever torn between the need to withdraw from current affairs so as to write and the contrary urge to speak out on the burning issues of the day—"to write or to fight," as he puts it.[55] This time, he fought, with hard-hitting speeches to both the AFL-CIO and a large group of US senators about the growing Soviet threat. (The texts of the speeches were later collected under the title of *Warning to the West*, which also includes two presentations Solzhenitsyn delivered in England the following year.) Although some commentators judged these warnings to be as significant as Churchill's celebrated "Iron Curtain" address of 1946, the major media essentially dismissed them as too militant and strident. The author later became dissatisfied with them as well, albeit for a completely different reason: In retrospect, he deemed it naïve to have viewed the US a staunch ally in the task of Russian liberation. What is more, he felt himself losing faith in the efficacy of his exhortations and practically despaired of the ability—so ringingly affirmed in his Nobel Lecture of 1972—to transmit the experience of one nation to another by verbal means.[56]

Solzhenitsyn returned to Zurich and for a time immersed himself in work on the *Red Wheel* cycle, but by early 1976 he again felt driven to the "fight" mode by what he believed was the further strategic deterioration of the Western world. He appeared first in England, evoking an unprecedented response to his several TV interviews and especially to his speech on BBC radio, all of which concerned Britain's diminished role in world affairs and British cooperation with Soviet demands to forcibly repatriate anticommunist Russians to the Soviet Union after the war. He next went to France and then on to Spain, where he combined extensive touring with another much-noted TV appearance.

Soon thereafter Solzhenitsyn made final preparations for his move to the United States. Several months previously, a friend with whom he had participated in the fruitless search for a property in Ontario chanced upon what he considered a suitable site in southeastern Vermont, and the writer agreed to purchase it on his recommendation. The place was near the village of Cavendish, comprised fifty acres of wooded hillside, and featured a comfortable, unostentatious chalet-like building. The family moved in at the end of June, and Solzhenitsyn had a three-story library built alongside the house; apart from the usual storage space for his books and papers, it featured a spacious study and a small chapel in which church services were occasionally conducted by visiting Russian

Orthodox priests. The advantages of the location included privacy, access to America's rich library holdings via interlibrary loans
(arranged through nearby Dartmouth College), and the chance to
educate his three sons—Yermolai, Ignat, and Stephan—in the English language. (Mrs. Solzhenitsyn's son by a previous marriage and
her mother also were part of the household.) A simple chain-link
fence was put up around the property, which sparked far-fetched
speculation by journalists who wondered whether the ex-prisoner
needed a prison-like enclosure for his work. In reality, the fence's
purpose was merely to keep out hunters and snowmobilers—Mrs.
Solzhenitsyn later semi-playfully added journalists to the list. For
exercise Solzhenitsyn walked in the property's woods, split wood,
and played some tennis on his home court.

Once they were settled in their new surroundings, Aleksandr
and Natalia Solzhenitsyn showed up, in early 1977, at a Cavendish
town meeting, where Solzhenitsyn greeted the family's new neighbors, apologetically explained the need for the fence, and said he
looked forward to the day when the Russian people would be liberated from the Soviet system. "When that day comes, I will thank
you very much for being good friends and neighbors, and I will go
home." A warm ovation ensued. Husband and wife shook hands
with townspeople and then left as the meeting took up its agenda.
Contact with locals was a natural part of the family's routine. The
sons rode yellow school buses to local schools (while receiving an
additional and far more demanding program of studies at home).
The family's Orthodox church (with services in English) was at
Claremont, New Hampshire, some twenty miles away. Cavendish's
protectiveness of the family's privacy was unstudied but firm. A
sign eventually was erected at the town's general store that read:
"No rest rooms. No bare feet. No directions to the Solzhenitsyns."

Even during his stretch of high activity in the public limelight,
Solzhenitsyn sustained his heavy schedule of writing. In 1975 he
released all that was fit to print at the time of *The Oak and Calf,*
which he preferred to call sketches rather than memoirs; its subtitle, *Sketches of Literary Life in the Soviet Union,* strikes a note of

irony in the sense that "literary life" suggests a normalcy absent in the profoundly absurd Soviet circumstances. He had begun writing this extensive account of his unremitting struggles with Soviet officialdom in 1967 and then added supplements to it. This "agglomeration of lean-tos and annexes," as he calls it, opens with his decision in 1961 to risk submitting *One Day* for publication and closes with a rousing rendition of his arrest and exile in 1974. Temporarily left out of the book was "conspiratorial" information, including the names of the author's helpers, which he published as *Invisible Allies* only after the Soviet Union collapsed. (When *The Oak and the Calf* appeared in English in 1980, its reception was somewhat mixed, running along ideological lines that were by then predictable, but its vigorous style impressed many reviewers, some of whom rated it one of the author's most successful books.)

In the same year, 1975, Solzhenitsyn began publishing parts of his works that he had omitted from editions that had appeared earlier—they had been deliberately withheld in the vain hope of making Soviet publication more likely. He recognized, as he stated in a late 1974 interview, that virtually all his writings published hitherto (with the sole exception of *The Gulag Archipelago*) were to some extent distorted by "self-censorship," and that new editions would have to be produced. (The stable environment of Cavendish would soon allow the writer to undertake this task, with his wife doing the typesetting on an IBM compositor and the YMCA Press in Paris producing the actual bound volumes. A *Collected Works* in twenty volumes was produced in this way between 1978 and 1991.)

In 1976, while at work on *The Red Wheel*, Solzhenitsyn pulled out of that work's future volumes eleven chapters focused on Lenin and published them separately as *Lenin in Zurich*, knowing that years of work lay ahead before the whole *Red Wheel* cycle would be ready. A portrait of Stalin was already available in four consecutive chapters of *The First Circle*.[57] For understanding the nature of the Soviet experiment, it was even more urgent to get a fix on Lenin.

In 1977, as part of his endeavor to counter official efforts to distort or erase historical facts about Russia's experience in the twentieth century, Solzhenitsyn initiated a project to gather unpublished materials written by others. He called this archive the Russian Memoir Library. Beyond his solo performance as a restorer of historical truth, he would introduce to the world a chorus of voices. Numerous Russian émigrés submitted memoirs, letters, and photographs. More than a dozen book-length manuscripts eventually appeared in print in a memoir series funded by Solzhenitsyn. As a separate but related venture, he also sponsored a series of scholarly studies on modern Russian history.

A cardinal event in the reception of Solzhenitsyn occurred on June 8, 1978. After avoiding public appearances for some time, the writer broke his silence and delivered the commencement address at Harvard University. With members of the press present in full force, the speech was a media sensation, instantly becoming his best-known public utterance in the West. Given his Western audience, Solzhenitsyn again spoke about Western issues. His list of what he saw as the West's defects included a chiding of the press—in front of the press—for its hasty and superficial judgments. He also scolded the intelligentsia—at this archetypal redoubt of intellectuals—for its loss of will and decline of courage. Before an audience that can be assumed to have been mostly secular in orientation, he offered prescriptive advice cast in openly spiritual, even religious, terms. For a celebratory occasion he did more than a fair share of chastising. This speech had the effect of confirming suspicions that had arisen after the English-language publication of *August 1914* (1972), were intensified by the *Letter to the Soviet Leaders* (1974), and had increased still further with subsequent utterances. The *Harvard Address* can be said to have cemented firmly into place the last brick in the wall of negative consensus among Western elites. But as Solzhenitsyn notes with satisfaction in *Little Grain*, there was a simultaneous—albeit less raucous—chorus of support for his message coming from outside the Washington–New York axis, emanating from that "quintessential, non-elite, and morally sound" America to whom, he claimed, the speech was ultimately addressed.[58] Nevertheless, because of the intense press coverage by the central media, this event marks the time when the insistent criticisms voiced by the elite began seeping into the consciousness of the broad public and solidifying into "common wisdom."

Throughout the 1980s Solzhenitsyn was mostly immersed in work on *The Red Wheel*. He kept to a rigorous daily routine of research and writing, usually composing in longhand at a standup desk. He paused in 1980 to write a long essay titled "Misconceptions about Russia Are a Threat to America" for the journal *Foreign Affairs;* it was published in the same year in book form as *The Mortal Danger*. Appended to the second edition of the book was a lengthy polemical exchange with American Sovietologists who had received this incursion into their specialty with considerable hostility. Another notable polemical piece written in those years was "Our Pluralists," a scathing rebuttal of the accumulated hostile criticism leveled at the writer and his views of Russia by various members of the dissident movement.[59]

In the fall of 1982 Solzhenitsyn traveled to Japan and Taiwan, giving major speeches in Tokyo and Taipei. Conceived originally as no more than a break from the routine of writing, plans for the trip soon evolved to include a serious attempt to gain some understanding of cultures that had long held the writer's interest, as well as an opportunity to again sound the tocsin concerning the dangers of communism, whether of the Soviet or Red Chinese variety. Beyond that, he was eager to make a strong statement in support of diplomatically isolated Taiwan. Apart from his public appearances, Solzhenitsyn did a great deal of touring, especially in Japan, and *Little Grain* contains extensive notes on his impressions.

While the writer's trip to the Far East passed virtually unnoticed by the Western press, his visit to England in the spring of 1983 was fairly well publicized. The occasion was Solzhenitsyn's receipt of the Templeton Prize for Progress in Religion, an award designed to fill a gap in the roster of fields recognized by the Nobel Committee. Solzhenitsyn was the first Orthodox Christian recipient of this honor, the eleventh recipient overall. The ceremony took place in London's Guildhall, and the address he delivered there rivals his

Harvard address in importance. The nature of the Templeton award necessitated an explicit articulation of his religious outlook, a subject that until then he had preferred to leave minimally described. Britain accorded the writer other important occasions. At the invitation of Margaret Thatcher, he met with the prime minister at her official Downing Street residence and had a substantive hour-long conversation with her on current affairs. There was also a cordial meeting over dinner with the archbishop of Canterbury. And after the Templeton ceremony Solzhenitsyn paid a brief visit to Eton College, giving a speech and responding to questions posed by the boys. He then sat for two interviews with sympathetic journalists, Bernard Levin of The [London] Times and Malcolm Muggeridge of BBC-TV. There was, finally, a luncheon hosted by Prince Charles and Princess Diana with only two guests apart from the writer, his wife, and his translator, which made significant conversation possible. The visit and the "Templeton Lecture" generated considerable press coverage in Britain and heated exchanges between Solzhenitsyn's supporters and detractors in the pages of the London Times. Later in 1983, the writer gave an interview to Bernard Pivot, the popular host of the French TV program "Apostrophes," who posed satisfyingly intelligent questions about Solzhenitsyn's work. In all, Pivot interviewed Solzhenitsyn four times; these appearances responded to French interest in the Russian writer and fueled it further. In 1984 Holy Cross College in Massachusetts bestowed upon Solzhenitsyn the honorary degree of Doctor of Humane Letters.

But the 1980s also brought a goodly share of difficulties, anxieties, and disappointments. There were matters of health: The writer dates the first symptoms of heart disease to 1982. In the following year Solzhenitsyn experienced the humiliation of losing in a British court of law to the notorious publisher and purveyor of smut, Alexander Flegon, who sued for libel because the writer had implied that Flegon's piratical publishing ventures had KGB connections. This was followed by profound unhappiness with the 1984 biography by Michael Scammell, who, in the writer's view, misunderstood his works, distorted his motives, and demonstrated a tin ear on all matters having a religious dimension. And in 1985 he was a dismayed observer of the hue and cry raised over the anti-Semitism allegedly present in the new edition of his *August 1914* (which had appeared in Russian in 1983 and a rather far-fetched interpretation of which had been broadcast over US-financed Radio Liberty). The English translation of this version would not become available until 1989, which meant that the vast majority of the furious accusations in 1985 were made by people who had not read the text they were assailing—quite in the Soviet mode of behavior, as Solzhenitsyn noted sardonically. A flood of outraged articles and editorials was followed by a formal hearing scheduled by the Foreign Relations Committee of the US Senate, with the directors of Radio Liberty and the Voice of America giving testimony, but this was over in a single day, as it soon became obvious that the whole thing was a bloated nonissue.

Nevertheless, the readings of *August 1914* that had been scheduled to be broadcast from Radio Liberty were canceled, and Solzhenitsyn's very name was not permitted to be mentioned on the air. And since the writer was at the very same time being attacked in a mendacious Soviet propaganda film as a sellout to the CIA, the "anti-Semitism" episode served to justify the image used by Solzhenitsyn in his title to his sketches of life in Western exile: that of a "little grain" caught between two grinding millstones—one in the East, one in the West.

In 1985, too, Solzhenitsyn made the painful decision not to go through with the process of obtaining US citizenship, which he had initiated more or less unthinkingly. As he explains in *Little Grain*, he could not in good conscience repeat the naturalization oath, which signals agreement "without mental reservation" to take up arms against every external enemy of the United States when so required by law. Essentially, he had no confidence that Americans would or could discriminate between Russia and the Soviet Union if push should come to shove, and his "mental reservation" concerned this very point: He could certainly never take up arms against Russia.[60]

The chapter of *The Little Grain* devoted to the second half of the 1980s is titled "A Warm Wind," and Solzhenitsyn obviously refers to the hopes associated, rightly or wrongly, with the liberalizing reforms launched by Mikhail Gorbachev, notably the much-touted policy of *glasnost,* variously translated as "openness" or "publicity." Solzhenitsyn became one of the beneficiaries of the partial relaxation of cultural controls permitted by the new rules, just as he had earlier benefited from the "Thaw" under Khrushchev. In 1988 one Moscow periodical advocated restoring Solzhenitsyn's Soviet citizenship and dropping the treason charges against him. Such action would have fulfilled two of the author's stated requirements for returning to his homeland. His third requirement—that his works be legally published domestically—also began to be addressed. *Novy Mir* requested and received his permission to publish some parts of *The Gulag Archipelago* in 1989, after which it intended to publish *The First Circle* and *Cancer Ward.* But even as some doors opened, others did not. The Politburo interfered with plans to hold literary gatherings in celebration of Solzhenitsyn's seventieth birthday in 1988; several scheduled events had to be canceled, and those that proceeded were denied media coverage. The regime withdrew approval for the appearance of any selections from *The Gulag Archipelago* and held up the promised publication of his *Nobel Lecture.* In an involuntary compliment to the power of Solzhenitsyn's writings, the Communist Party's chief ideologist of the time asserted that to publish these works in the USSR would be "to undermine the foundations on which our present [Soviet] life rests."[61]

In a matter of mere months, these bans began to be breached. The essay "Live Not by Lies!" appeared in several Soviet periodicals, its first appearance being in an obscure newsletter of the Ukrainian railroad union in October 1988. The classic short story "Matryona's Home" was republished in the mass-circulation journal *Ogonyok* in June 1989 (the journal did not bother to contact the author for permission). Chapters from *Gulag* came out in several issues of *Looming,* an Estonian-language monthly, in the second half of 1989. *Novy Mir* printed the *Nobel Lecture* (July 1989) and reannounced its plans to publish substantial portions of *Gulag* serially. Two large publishing houses openly discussed bringing out editions of selected works. The leadership of the Writers' Union reportedly voted unanimously to support the publication of *Gulag* in full. In sum, at the very time when the chief ideologist was declaring that Solzhenitsyn's works could not be published, Solzhenitsyn's works *were* being published. With what, at least in hindsight, seems like a sense of inexorability, these works were in the process of becoming legally available to the Russian readers who had all along been their primary intended audience. The spate of activity on the publishing front soon became so formidable that *Novy Mir* dubbed 1990 "the year of Solzhenitsyn."

Gorbachev had been elevated to power precisely because the regime sensed that its hold on power was slipping and that it needed the energy of some new approach to keep control of the situation. Gorbachev's challenge was to salvage Soviet communism by reforming it. The foundations of the Soviet edifice were already shakier than the rulers realized, however; and the waves of resistance lapping against the power structure were gathering force and taking on an undermining momentum that was about to prove irresistible. The culmination came at the end of 1989, when, to the surprise of almost everyone, Soviet hegemony over large stretches of Eastern and Central Europe came to a sudden end. The fall of the Berlin Wall was undoubtedly the most visible symptom of this momentous historical earthquake. Together with the hated wall, the Soviet empire disintegrated, followed—after the tumultuous events of August 1991—by the Soviet Union itself, which broke up into its constituent parts, with the red flag over the Kremlin lowered for the last time on December 25, 1991. Soon, pre-Soviet names returned to currency: not the Soviet Union but Russia (or, to be exact, the Russian Federation), Nizhni Novgorod instead of Gorky, St. Petersburg for Leningrad, and so on. The years 1989–91 immediately took their place in history's record as an epoch-defining moment of the magnitude of 1914–17; indeed, together, these two historical moments mark the beginning and the end of the foreshortened century to which the experiment in totalitarianism gave its distinctive character.

Analyzing the causes of the collapse of the Soviet Union will occupy historians long into the future, as will the question of the degree to which Gorbachev's actions led to this outcome. One important factor in the whole process, perhaps the governing one, was that the Soviet Union suffered from a loss of faith in the ideology that had justified its gargantuan social experiment. And here Solzhenitsyn's contribution is undeniable, since no one before him was able to discredit and delegitimize the regime and the Marxist dogma it professed to the extent that he did. In particular, Solzhenitsyn's *The Gulag Archipelago,* without ever having been legally published in the Soviet Union, had struck a mighty blow against the colossus. Back in 1974 American diplomat George Kennan had made a remark about the historical role of this work that in 1991 would sound like prophecy fulfilled: "It is too large for the craw of the Soviet propaganda machine. It will stick there, with increasing discomfort, until it has done its work."[62]

Not only did Solzhenitsyn contribute to the demise of the Soviet Union, but he also saw it coming. Evidence of his prescience in this regard is overwhelming. As *The Solzhenitsyn Files* now reveals, in 1965 a KGB bugging device recorded his remark that "this is a government without prospects," which he followed with the prediction that the inevitable collapse of the whole structure of Soviet communism would entail the need to let every republic go its separate way.[63] And on one of his darkest days, February 12, 1974, when the arrested writer was being prepared for shipment to the West, he ruminated, *"You Bolsheviks are finished—there are no two ways about it."*[64] This conviction that Soviet communism was headed toward extinction he confidently reiterated on various occasions in the following years, as when in a 1983 interview he asserted, "I am absolutely convinced that Communism will go."[65] And more than a year before the Soviet Union expired, he declared, "Time has finally run out for Communism."[66] Hardly anyone else was speaking in that vein at that time, even after the Berlin Wall had come down. After the Soviet Union itself collapsed, Solzhenitsyn could justly observe, "Not only did Gorbachev not want to hear about this, President

Bush and other Western leaders also said the Soviet Union must remain intact. To me [the collapse] had been clear for many years."[67]

In the same vein of prescience, as soon as Solzhenitsyn landed in the West to begin his sentence of exile he confidently declared that he would someday return home in the flesh. In 1974 he told his friend Nikita Struve, "I see the day when I will return to Russia." Pondering this line years later, Struve mused, "It seemed *crazy* at the time to me, but it was a real conviction, a poet's knowledge. He *sees*. The man *sees*."[68] Solzhenitsyn made this prediction publicly as well, telling French TV journalist Bernard Pivot in 1983, "I have the feeling, the deep conviction that I will one day return home alive. And yet, as you may see, I am no longer that young."[69] This confidence about his personal destiny was an unwavering theme, one logically linked to his belief in the impermanence of the USSR.

Some years later, with the Soviet Union's end drawing ever closer, Solzhenitsyn prepared an essay of advice about how to avoid being crushed beneath the rubble of the collapsing structure and how to build a better edifice upon the ruins. This short work, written in July 1990 and known in English as *Rebuilding Russia* (*Kak nam obustroit' Rossiiu?*), appeared in September 1990 in two Moscow-based newspapers that were taking advantage of Gorbachev's policy of *glasnost*. The essay sketches a practical political program for Russia, proposing ways to tackle both short-term and long-term needs; it is best read as a sequel to the 1973 *Letter to the Soviet Leaders,* only addressed this time not to the leaders, who were about to lose power, but to the citizenry at large.

To repair Russia's ruins, Solzhenitsyn saw work to do on every hand. One self-assigned task, which perhaps no one else would have undertaken, was to rescue the Russian language from the ideological depredations inflicted upon it during the Soviet period. To counteract what he considered the radical impoverishment of the Russian vocabulary, he studded many of his works with words of his own devising, put together in accordance with the inherent rules of Russian word-formation. And in a more systematic effort, he diligently collected and published (in 1990) a dictionary of what he called "unjustly forgotten" words culled from various literary works as well as from Vladimir Dahl's much-admired nineteenth-century *Dictionary of the Living Great Russian Language.* His promotion of new elements and old might be likened to a pincer attack on the Soviet linguistic encampment. Solzhenitsyn's *Russian Dictionary of Lexical Augmentation* joins his several earlier statements on language, notably his 1983 essay "Select Observations on Grammar."

With the Soviet leaders' hands no longer on the levers of power, the way was finally clear for Solzhenitsyn to publish those parts of *The Oak and the Calf* which he had been holding back, since the persons named in those parts would no longer be subject to reprisal. This is the material which in English bears the title *Invisible Allies;* the Russian original first appeared in two issues of *Novy Mir* in late 1991, It later took its rightful place as the "fifth supplement" in a new, complete Russian edition of *The Oak and the Calf* (1996).

As the Soviet Union was going through its death throes, the obstacles to Solzhenitsyn's return home—reinstatement of his citizenship, voiding of the treason charge, and publication of all his works—melted away one after the other, thanks in part to pressure from the Russian press. His popularity among Russians soared. A commanding 48 percent of St. Petersburgers polled in the fall of 1993 about who should become the president of the new Russia named Solzhenitsyn, with Boris Yeltsin a distant second at 18 percent.[70] Yet, with the stage seemingly set for his return—almost certainly to a thunderous welcome—he stayed in Vermont, virtually incommunicado. Impatience grew. Why the dawdling? people wondered. Journalists freely declared it a mistake for him to delay. And certainly, if he had sought political power, he was missing his magic moment. Solzhenitsyn has addressed this issue head-on in *The Little Grain.* To have any influence on events in Russia, he writes, one would need to fight one's way to the center of power. But to do so, he continues, would have been

> untrue to my character, unrelated to my desires, and inappropriate for my age.

And so I did not go to Russia at the time when the political expectations associated with my name were exceedingly high. And I am confident that this was no miscalcu-
lation. It was the decision of a writer, not a politician. Not
for a moment have I ever pursued political popularity.

However, if *Rebuilding Russia* had given hope of
changing the country, I would have set off immediately to
take part in that process of reconstruction.

But it was ignored as unacceptable and irrelevant.

And what I could not attain by my pen, I would never
be able to achieve by shouting orders.[71]

Whatever else might have entered into Solzhenitsyn's decision,
it is clear that literary considerations were at the top of the list. And
although the last planned installment ("knot") of *The Red Wheel*
cycle, *April 1917*, was completed in the spring of 1989,[72] there remained many loose ends that the author was most anxious to tie
up. This included Solzhenitsyn's new plan of compiling a detailed
historical outline covering the events from April 1917 to 1922, and
the preparation for print of the journal he had kept during his decades of work on *The Red Wheel*, tentatively titled *The R-17 Diary*.
Only in 1994 could he refer to the completed *Red Wheel* as "this
huge beast now felled."[73]

Preparations for the writer's return to Russia commenced well
before that, of course. Mrs. Solzhenitsyn visited Russia three times
during 1992–93 to lay the groundwork, each time with at least one
son in tow. Her tasks included checking on the construction of
their new home, which was suffering from shoddy workmanship.
Located on a ten-acre plot on the outskirts of Moscow, the brick
structure was V-shaped, with one wing for living quarters and the
other for the library. When Russian president Boris Yeltsin visited
the United States in 1992, he telephoned Solzhenitsyn and, in a
half-hour conversation, personally invited the famous son of Russia to come back home. A Russian documentary filmmaker visited
Solzhenitsyn's Vermont domicile to interview him for a two-part
TV documentary, which aired in September 1992. Solzhenitsyn re-

ported that he was receiving many letters from ordinary Russian citizens, which helped keep him abreast of domestic political developments. When the National Arts Club of New York City bestowed an award upon him in 1993, he wrote an acceptance speech, delivered by one of his sons. Cautioning against the literary penchant for cultural relativism, nihilism, and tastelessness, this address, titled "Playing upon the Strings of Emptiness," is a follow-up of sorts to his *Nobel Lecture.*

To bid farewell to the West, in 1993 Solzhenitsyn set out for Europe, where he felt more appreciated than in the United States. Much of this European tour was devoted to making the rounds to say good-bye to old friends in various countries. He also had a lengthy private audience with Pope John Paul II. Once again, he appeared on Bernard Pivot's TV talk show in France. His largest public speech was also in France, the nation in which his influence upon intellectuals has been the greatest. At the town of Lucs-sur-Boulogne in the Vendée region, thirty thousand people gathered to mark the two hundredth anniversary of the political massacres of those who had opposed the French Revolution. Solzhenitsyn presented "A Reflection on the Vendée Uprising" and helped dedicate a plaque commemorating the ninety thousand who died in the Vendée during the Reign of Terror of 1793–94. The Vendée speech followed by a few days a more important address that Solzhenitsyn delivered to a small audience at the International Academy of Philosophy, a Roman Catholic institution in Liechtenstein. This speech, for which the author's preferred title is "We have ceased to see the Purpose," echoes and updates themes presented at Harvard in 1978, though to some degree the emphasis shifts from the political toward the personal, and the author meditates upon death in a tone mellowed by the passing years. Simultaneously with the Vendée celebration, a crowd of some one hundred thousand people turned out at Moscow's Red Square for an anticipatory celebration of Solzhenitsyn's return home. His close friend, the celebrated cellist and conductor Mstislav Rostropovich, led the National Symphony Orchestra of Washington, D.C., in an outdoor performance.

Ignat Solzhenitsyn, the middle son, was the featured pianist—on his first visit to his homeland since his family left when he was eighteen months of age.

When Solzhenitsyn returned from Europe to the United States, he kept his American leave-taking to a minimum. He submitted to a televised interview by Mike Wallace for the *Sixty Minutes* program. And to David Remnick, editor of the *New Yorker*, he gave a long interview that formed the basis of a substantial article published in that magazine.[74] Solzhenitsyn did take time to bid a warm good-bye to the citizens of Cavendish, Vermont. He thanked the two hundred locals present at the town meeting for accepting his "unusual way of life" and protecting his privacy, telling them that he could not imagine a better place than Cavendish "to live, and wait, and wait for my return home." The assembled neighbors gave him an enthusiastic ovation, as they had at a town meeting seventeen years earlier. For the local public library he left behind copies of his books, each inscribed, "To the People of Cavendish"; he also gave copies to some of the local residents, autographed with personalized notes.[75]

Solzhenitsyn composed the last work of his exile in March 1994, even as he was packing up for his departure from the West. *"The Russian Question" at the End of the Twentieth Century,* published in *Novy Mir,* sweeps through four centuries of Russian history in a little more than a hundred pages, in sharp contrast to *The Red Wheel,* which took almost six thousand pages to address "discrete segments" of the four years 1914–17. The new little book presents a bird's-eye view of Russia's history in order to contextualize properly "the Great Russian Catastrophe of the 1990s," which the author sees as Russia's third "Time of Troubles," similar in magnitude and significance to those of the early seventeenth century and of 1917. That task done, Solzhenitsyn was almost ready to go home. But in April he granted a final interview to Paul Klebnikov of *Forbes* magazine, speaking freely about the political situation in Russia and the West's continuing misapprehensions.[76] Less than a month after this parting shot, he departed from Cavendish.

Life in Russia

Solzhenitsyn arrived in Russia on May 27, 1994. By this time, the dust had already begun to settle upon the rubble of the collapsed Soviet Union. The end of the Cold War had been greeted with euphoria in the West. The free world's number-one foe had vanished. The end of an era had arrived; world history had reached a major watershed moment. Yet it is remarkable how briefly the mood of celebration lasted. Equally remarkable, if not more so, was how slow the West's experts were to move beyond reportage of events to analysis of their significance. One might have expected Western Sovietologists, whose forecasts had proven wildly off target, to be in the vanguard of a process of reconsideration, but their silence was deafening. The time was equally ripe for reassessing Solzhenitsyn, who in the 1970s had been recognized as doing more than his fair share of undermining the legitimacy of the whole Soviet venture but who had since then slipped into eclipse. What he had predicted had, in general terms, now occurred. But no significant reevaluation of the writer emerged as a result. Analysts whom events had proven wrong did not turn their attention to an author whom events had proven right. In the melancholy judgment rendered in 1994 by David Remnick, Solzhenitsyn had been "the dominant writer of this century" in terms of the effect he had had on history, but "when Solzhenitsyn's name comes up now it is more often than not as a freak, a monarchist, an anti-Semite, a crank, a has-been, not as a hero."[77]

Still, when Solzhenitsyn made his trip home, the Western press took notice once again, as it seldom does of the movements of novelists. The headline fonts were not as large nor the tone as adulatory as in the days when he was ejected from his homeland, but the news coverage was extensive and generally respectful. Articles recounted the defiance and courage of his combat against an oppressive state decades earlier. They mentioned that he had been considered Russia's greatest living writer and that many Russians still thought him so, viewing him as a prophet who served as a moral compass in an uncertain world. Some, predictably enough, speculated about which political group, democrats or nationalists, would succeed in their bids for his support. (Neither group did.) Most of all, they were immensely struck by how he chose to arrive back in Russia.

To mark the occasion fulfilling his longstanding prophecy that he would return home in the flesh, Solzhenitsyn showed his flair for the dramatic, as well as his attention to the symbolic. Everyone assumed that he would fly into Moscow's Sheremetevo airport, as most travelers to Russia do. Instead, he reentered Russia through the back door, so to speak, flying from Boston to Anchorage and then across the Pacific Ocean to Russia's easternmost reach. As a Russian critic wrote, "There is hardly a living script writer in the world who could invent such a scenario."[78] But for Solzhenitsyn more than surprise was involved. His goal was not to meet leaders but to talk with ordinary fellow Russians, for it was with these latter that he identified. The drama of his arrival was intensified by his decision to touch down first at Magadan, the capital of the Kolyma region, the region where the harshest Soviet prison camps had been located, making it the symbolic capital of the whole gulag empire. During his years of incarceration, he had identified himself as a member of the "*zek* nation," and it was to this nation-within-a-nation that the former prisoner, now seventy-five years old, symbolically turned. After accepting the proffered bread and salt of the traditional Russian welcome, he kissed the ground, crossed himself repeatedly, and received an emotional embrace from another ex-*zek*. Bowing to the earth of Kolyma, he intoned, "Under ancient Christian tradition, the land where innocent victims are buried becomes holy ground."[79]

The next stop was Vladivostok, Russia's main Pacific port of entry. There he received a hero's welcome from four thousand citizens who had been standing in the rain for hours to greet him. In Vladivostok he also addressed a thousand university students to eruptions of applause. Asked publicly if he still believed in the revival of Russia, he replied, "Yes. It will be difficult, it will not come soon, but it will [come]." He then added, to approving comments from the crowd, that "the turn our life will take depends on us, and not on the decisions bestowed on us from somewhere on high, somewhere in Moscow."[80] At Vladivostok and at all subsequent stops along his way across the country, he reiterated the need for the purification that comes from repentance—repentance for both the individual and national transgressions linked to the Soviet era.[81] He also repeatedly made clear what he considered his new role in life and the spirit with which he approached it. "I'm duty-bound to help Russia with my experience, advice, and influence, but without knowing for certain what result it will have." This was a great applause line. And more applause followed when he explained that he could have stayed in Vermont "peacefully and in great happiness. But it would have been running away from my duty not to have come back. I could not escape our people's pain." He came back, he explained, "not because this country is flourishing and I wanted to join in, or because people were calling me a prophet. I don't need that. I came because of my conscience."[82]

From Vladivostok, Solzhenitsyn embarked on a two-month-long train trip westward to Moscow on the tracks of the fabled Trans-Siberian Railway, spanning 5,778 miles and seven time zones. On board was a crew from the British Broadcasting Corporation, which filmed the cross-country whistle-stop tour. Solzhenitsyn had announced while in Vladivostok, "Everywhere I go, I hope to meet and listen to local residents, to test and revise my own judgments."[83] His efforts to fulfill this intention caused no little consternation among the officials charged with providing pomp and ceremony along the way. "Talk to people, talk to people. That's all he wants," complained one.[84] When it was his turn to speak, he sought to rouse citizens from the torpor to which Soviet rule had reduced them. For instance, at Blagoveshchensk, he declared, "I say this everywhere, and I want to repeat it to you: The future is in our hands."[85] Solzhenitsyn's train kept stopping so that he could address gatherings large and small and could pause for one-on-one conversations with fellow former *zeks*. The format of the public sessions typically featured question-and-answer discussions, rather than formal speeches, and audience participation was lively and intense. (Subsequent to his long train ride, Solzhenitsyn embarked on a month-long odyssey to revisit several locales where he had lived, followed by additional touring in 1995, 1996, and 1997. In all these travels he filled notebooks with statements from the people he met.) The experiences of this trip crystallized for him a sense of obligation to take on the role of spokesman to the new Russia's ruling elites on behalf of the "other" Russia. This was all quite a change from his secluded life in Vermont. His wife observed that, despite the rigors of the trip, he became even healthier. He agreed: Touching his native soil gave him new energy. The train carrying Solzhenitsyn and his entourage finally pulled into Moscow's Yaroslavsky station on the evening of July 21, 1994. A crowd estimated at ten to fifteen thousand turned out to meet it. Yury Luzhkov, mayor of Moscow, was on hand to welcome him. So was a contingent of hard-core Communist opponents, their hostile placards jostling with placards in greater number signaling respect and admiration. Over the next several days, Solzhenitsyn was interviewed on television and in the print media. When the excitement of the journey subsided, the Solzhenitsyns settled into quietness on the outskirts of Moscow.

Western journalists covering Solzhenitsyn's return to Russia typically began in skepticism, but were unprepared for the degree of emotion displayed, and took refuge in nervous bet-hedging, wondering if they had underestimated the writer. In many cases, Solzhenitsyn was pronounced "the most admired living Russian" by a Western press that could not fathom why that should be. Russian reactions were more mixed and more interesting. As predictably as in the West, many big-city intellectuals received him with coolness and even condescension. The general tenor of responses from the populace, however, was more favorable. Russia's mixed reaction to her famous returning son is encapsulated in an episode at one of the train stops, when he encountered this rebuke: "It is you and your writing that started it all and brought our country to the verge of collapse and devastation. Russia doesn't need you. So .

. . go back to your blessed America."[86] Solzhenitsyn's instantaneous riposte was that to his dying day he would keep fighting against the evil ideology that was capable of slaying a third of his country's population. The applause was thunderous.

One sad surprise awaiting the exile upon his return was how little his fellow Russians had read him, even though his works had now been legally available for several years. Solzhenitsyn acknowledged plaintively, "I thought I would come to a Russia that had read me, that knew me as a writer. But, in fact, only the older generation knows me. They remember something about an *Ivan Denisovich*. The rest have never read me."[87] This lack of readership was not limited to Solzhenitsyn. The journal *Znamya* used to sell more than a million copies per month, but by 1994 its sales had plummeted to seventy thousand. *Novy Mir* nose-dived from more than two million per month to fifty-five thousand. The severe dislocations and general chaos of the immediate post-Soviet years disrupted the longstanding Russian habit of reading serious literature, and trashy newsstand magazines flooding in from the West severely eroded old reading patterns. But the author whose main work ran to nearly six thousand pages was prepared to take the long view concerning the possibility of his influencing the future course of his people. Any significant improvement in Russia's health, he acknowledged, would "not be very soon and might not be in my lifetime." But he needed to get a toehold at the starting line, and the social climate into which he came was not conducive to cultivating sustained moral reflection. In fact, he perceived, "The atmosphere remains heavy and stained with communism."[88] He could be, and was, generally honored as a literary giant, as a moral authority, as a man who more than any other had emerged from the Soviet era with his reputation intact. But his message required revisiting past iniquities so that repentance could follow, and not many showed any taste for looking those horrors in the eye, preferring the escape of forgetfulness. "Why should anyone now care about the Gulag Archipelago?" asked one young critic.[89] In this sense—and only in this sense—the many who consigned Solzhenitsyn to the past had

a point, though that consignment carried the high price of forgo-
ing the liberating process of decontamination that could come only
by acknowledging past evils and—Solzhenitsyn insists—genuinely
repenting for them. As he declared, "Cleansing only comes about
through repentance. . . . We need to repent. But no one wants to."[90]
Actually, some did "want to." Some Russians looked to Solzhenitsyn as a sage whose advice was to be heard and heeded.[91] Their
numbers, however, have so far not been enough to form a critical
mass among the citizenry at large and have not included many contemporary opinion-shapers.

Solzhenitsyn kept a relatively high profile during his first year
back in Russia. In fact, he made nearly a hundred public appearances. In a speech given in his very first month back home, he injected into public discourse the word *oligarchy* to describe the real
power structure in the new Russia, and the word stuck, though
credit to the source did not. In his first official speech in Russia, he
addressed the Duma, Russia's legislature, in October 1994, the first
nonmember to be invited to do so. Wearing the same suit he wore at
Harvard in 1978, he declared that he had accepted the Duma's offer
because the people he had met during his travels around the country "have begged me to come to Moscow and tell the Duma and
the president what has been piling up and is boiling in the soul of
an ordinary man." He charged that Russia "is emerging from communism on the most twisted, painful and awkward path" and continues to be run by Soviet-era "nomenklatura turncoats disguised
as democrats."[92] As a result, the current form of government "is
not a democracy, but an oligarchy—rule by the few."[93] The initially
hearty applause turned tepid, then dwindled to silence. The lawmakers grew restless, some of them ostentatiously signaling their
disagreement by sarcastic comments or departure from the hall.
The speech's closing call for faster movement toward democracy
drew only a smattering of applause. Solzhenitsyn then met privately
with President Boris Yeltsin for two hours of intense conversation,
though with no discernible results. When other politicians asked to
speak with him, he obliged them as well.

In addition, Solzhenitsyn was granted a biweekly program ón national television, starting in February 1995, on which he addressed various public issues of his choosing. For a while, the format included a guest in conversation with the host. Among the public positions Solzhenitsyn took was his condemnation of the privatization scheme devised by Deputy Prime Minister Anatoly Chubais, according to which only three percent of the country's property was distributed equitably among the populace, while insiders were allowed to snap up huge industrial enterprises at fire-sale prices. Another of his positions was his strong support for the principle of local governance. As a participant in a Kremlin conference on local government, attended by federal and provincial leaders, he pressed for shifting a degree of power and resources from the federal to the local level. Participants from the provinces enthusiastically cheered him and swarmed around him when the session concluded, seeking his ear and his counsel. This occasion, coupled with a similar conference on the same general topic held soon thereafter in the city of Samara, was to be the high-water mark in Solzhenitsyn's direct influence on politics in the new Russia. On political issues just as on broader cultural issues, Moscow was the locus of greatest resistance to Solzhenitsyn's thinking.

Despite the flurry of activity that followed his return home, Solzhenitsyn faded from the limelight of public attention in less than a year's time. His television program was canceled in October 1995, allegedly for low ratings but undoubtedly also for the writer's disapproval of some state policies. The texts of these talks have been collected in *A Minute a Day* (*Po minute v den,'* 1995). Years earlier, at Harvard, Solzhenitsyn had faulted both the intellectual and the ruling elites of the West, and both had given his chastisements the cold shoulder; now the same pattern of avoidance was playing itself out in the new Russia.

Declining health, including hospitalization in 1997 for heart trouble, also played a part in his gradually diminishing public visibility. Still, in May 1997 he was elected to Russia's prestigious Academy of Sciences, to which he gave a speech in September of that year. In October 1997 he established an annual prize bearing his name to recognize writers who were preserving and advancing the Russian literary tradition. According to Mrs. Solzhenitsyn, the prize is intended to reward not old-fashioned works but simply works that "make people think."[94] Funds underwriting this award of $25,000 per year come from a portion of the royalties generated by *The Gulag Archipelago.*

In 1998, as Solzhenitsyn approached his eightieth birthday, he agreed to be the speaker at the unveiling of a monument honoring Anton Chekhov at a Moscow theater named for the playwright. When his eightieth birthday arrived in December, public celebrations included a theatrical adaptation of *The First Circle* by director Yury Lyubimov and a concert presented by cellist Mstislav Rostropovich, his longtime friend. In addition, several television stations broadcast documentaries on him, and Moscow newspapers published front-page tributes. When, however, President Yeltsin sought to heighten the festive spirit by signing a decree to grant Solzhenitsyn Russia's highest civilian honor, the Order of St. Andrew, Solzhenitsyn turned the offer down, declaring in a sharply worded rebuke of the then-government that he could not accept an award from the state authority that had "brought Russia to its present state of ruin."[95] But in 2001 he welcomed Russian President Vladimir Putin into his home for a private conversation, clearly signaling a degree of hope for a turn in the fortunes of Russia.

One of Solzhenitsyn's latest public appearances occurred on September 2, 2005, when he presented a message at the opening of the Center for Russian Culture Abroad. This center was designed to gather and make publicly available all sorts of materials preserved and produced by the Russian emigration. Solzhenitsyn had begun the collection in Vermont in 1977, as well as historical investigations gathered under the title *Studies in Modern Russian History.* Establishing this archive culminated three decades of his labors to preserve the historical memory of Russia, which her revolutionary upheavals had threatened to destroy.

Despite his public activities and the inevitable encroachments of old age, including serious back trouble, Solzhenitsyn has been able to sustain his lifelong pattern of putting in long days at the writing desk. The result is a body of late-in-life works of impressive size and variety, including prose poems, short fiction, critical essays, and major scholarly texts. In fiction he returned to short stories, a genre he had pursued in earlier years. Now, however, he experimented with a format he has called a "binary tale," in which the narrative structure is divided into two distinct parts that are only loosely linked in terms of plot while conveying meaningful thematic echoes. Eight such short stories appeared in Russian periodicals in 1993–98, notably including two based on material left over from *The Red Wheel*.

Another genre to which Solzhenitsyn returned in his later years is the prose miniature. Having written seventeen miniatures between 1958 and 1960, he had found himself unable to write in this genre while absent from Russian soil. In the 1990s, after returning to his homeland, he wrote thirteen more of them, publishing them in *Novy Mir* in 1997–99. These reflections—mostly on journeys, landscapes, and natural phenomena—are, like the earlier miniatures, imbued with a contemplative tone, now tinged in some cases with an elegiac air. (Solzhenitsyn has since added one prayer apiece to these two sets of miniatures, bringing their totals to eighteen and fourteen, respectively.)

In the category of long works of nonfiction, Solzhenitsyn communicated his view of Russia's vexed post-Soviet condition in *Russia in Collapse* (1998). This essay of grim and almost despairing observations is best approached as a sequel to *Rebuilding Russia*, the 1990 work in which the writer had offered numerous proposals for policies Russia should follow in the wake of the Soviet demise, advice that was not heeded. Now he expresses the fear that post-Soviet Russia might also, in its turn, collapse if it stays on the course of its frightening decline in those spheres of life, such as education and medical care, without which civilized existence becomes impossible. In a very different mode, he published numerous essays of literary commentary on modern Russian authors ranging from Anton Chekhov to Joseph Brodsky, all bearing the series title *Literary Collection*.

Two substantial volumes of a massively researched historical study of the troubled relationship between Russians and Jews, entitled *Two Hundred Years Together,* appeared in 2001–2. Having come upon this theme frequently in his research for *The Red Wheel,* Solzhenitsyn traces the story from the mid-nineteenth century to the Russian Revolution and then on through the Soviet period. With his customary boldness he confronts the multitude of bitter charges and countercharges that had accumulated in the collective memory of both groups. His hope is to clear the air and point out common ground so that Russians and Jews can move toward reconciliation. In this sense, the scholarly work can be viewed as part of Solzhenitsyn's effort to help his homeland find a better future. It also holds interest as the product of an author who has been accused of anti-Semitic tendencies—a manifestly unfair charge in a debate that nonetheless shows no sign of ending.

In another major effort of the author's late years, he prepared for publication a set of memoir-like sketches, *The Little Grain Managed to Land between Two Millstones,* serial installments of which appeared in *Novy Mir* between 1998 and 2003. This work consists of Solzhenitsyn's reminiscences of persons and experiences encountered during his twenty years in the West. It does for those two decades of exile what the final, augmented version of *The Oak and the Calf* has done for the two preceding decades, and it does so with similar verve and immediacy. Humor and startling candor mark many of his comments on his own work and on a variety of current affairs.

Standing apart from the many publications of Solzhenitsyn's own texts that have appeared since his return to Russia, but of great relevance to the story of his life, is a volume the title of which could be freely rendered as *Kangaroo Court in the Kremlin.* Published in Moscow in 1994 and appearing the next year in English in somewhat abridged form under the title *The Solzhenitsyn Files,* it is a collection of initially top-secret Soviet documents detailing the Soviet leaders' anxious and often perplexed reactions to Solzhenitsyn's statements and activities. It describes the confrontation between author and regime during the 1960s and early 1970s from the regime's point of view. Thus, it, too, in its own way, is to be paired with *The Oak and the Calf,* which describes the confrontation from the author's point of view. In terms of the "oak and calf" imagery, the viewpoint of each is represented, a book for one and a book for the other. Taken together, the two books reinforce the author's understanding that the oak was rotten to the core and that the calf's energetic buttings left their mark, unquestionably contributing to the oak's ultimate downfall.

Just when it seemed that attention to Solzhenitsyn, if it were ever to stage a comeback, would probably not be revived until well into the future, that facile expectation was jolted by a surprising development. In early 2006 a Russian television network serialized *The First Circle* in ten installments. Advertising billboards featured the author's smiling visage. The credits listed Solzhenitsyn as the screenwriter, and his consultation on the production ensured its fidelity to the novel, with the author himself providing the voiceover for long passages from the text. The first segment rang up the largest TV audience of the week, and subsequent episodes drew in some fifteen million viewers apiece. Dostoevsky's *The Idiot* and Bulgakov's *The Master and Margarita* had preceded *The First Circle* in the series of televised adaptations of literary classics, with *War and Peace, The Brothers Karamazov,* and *Doctor Zhivago* slated for future release.

Actually, some groundwork had been laid for the strong response to the presentation of *The First Circle* on television. Out of the public eye, Solzhenitsyn's social and political ideas have been slowly but steadily gaining respectful appreciation among citizens and government figures. For instance, in the years immediately following the collapse of the Soviet Union, Solzhenitsyn had been almost alone in pointing out Russia's demographic crisis and the unjustifiable neglect of the twenty-five million Russians stranded in those former Soviet republics which now constituted the "near abroad." President Putin himself has now called public attention to this unacceptable state of affairs. Solzhenitsyn's conception of a strong and traditional Russia that is no longer tempted by Communist ideology or imperial designs was derided during the 1990s, but it now seems to be a factor in shaping a new national consensus. The under-the-radar quietness with which his thinking has gained entry into Russia's civic imagination augurs well for an enduring influence of his articulation of the Russian national tradition.

Scholarly interest in Solzhenitsyn's writing has also been growing in Russia since the late 1990s and has resulted in the appearance of numerous significant articles and monographs.[96] A large international conference on the writer took place in Moscow in late 2003 (marking Solzhenitsyn's eighty-fifth birthday) and the papers presented, together with a large quantity of other valuable material, appeared in a capital volume published in 2005.[97] At the end of 2006, the publishing house "Vremia" announced that it had reached agreement with the author to launch a thirty-volume *Collected Works* encompassing everything that had appeared in print up to that time, as well as several significant items that had not been previously published. By the end of 2007 (when the present book goes to press), the entire corpus of Solzhenitsyn's short prose and most of *The Red Wheel* cycle had appeared in the new series.[98]

How, finally, are we to sum up the meaning of Solzhenitsyn's improbable, even sensational life? Solzhenitsyn has frequently been described as a grim, Jeremiah-like figure; yet he has always considered himself "an unshakable optimist" with "a sort of stupid faith in victory."[99] Beyond the personality trait of optimism lies hope as a habit of his being; his writings, both literary and nonliterary, almost always conclude on the note of hope. Along with faith and love, hope is one of the classic Christian virtues, and Solzhenitsyn's hope is an integral aspect of his religious worldview, in which humanity stands poised on the intersection between time and eternity. In 1994 an interviewer asked Solzhenitsyn if he feared death. "Absolutely not," answered the seventy-five-year-old writer. "As a Christian, I believe that there is a life after death, and so I understand that this is not the end of life. The soul . . . lives on. Death is only a stage, some would say even a liberation. In any case, I have no fear of death."[100]

Throughout a long life packed with high drama, Solzhenitsyn remained vitally engaged with the central issues of his era. Focused predominantly on Russia, just like Tolstoy and Dostoevsky, his great nineteenth-century predecessors, he—also like them—addressed concerns and raised questions that resonated far beyond any national boundary. Fiercely independent, driven by a sense of mission, and possessed of legendary determination and perseverance, he was virtually always in conflict either with the powers-that-be or with conventional wisdom, frequently with both at once. The political dimension of his worldview, while not to be neglected, has unduly preoccupied the majority of commentators, who as a result have conveyed a skewed portrait of the man. The political controversies will fade with the passage of time. What will abide is Solzhenitsyn's sheer literary power. This quality is what gained the attention of the world in the first place, and it will ultimately determine the degree to which he attains the status of an enduring classic author.

Works

This section provides separate entries, most of them brief, on a very large portion of Solzhenitsyn's writings. That it does not provide comprehensive coverage is testimony to the vast body of work that the author has produced. Decisions to include or omit titles necessarily entailed judgments based on this book's intended purpose of offering guidance to a wide range of nonspecialist readers. Works that receive critical commentary in the present book include Solzhenitsyn's best-known literary productions, such as *One Day in the Life of Ivan Denisovich* and *The Gulag Archipelago*, as well as a number of writings that are focused on historical, literary, and philosophical subjects. We also provide commentaries on works dealing with topical issues in Soviet and post-Soviet Russia and on Solzhenitsyn's autobiographical accounts of his struggle with the Soviet regime and of his subsequent life abroad.

There is no perfect pattern for ordering the works of Solzhenitsyn. The two most viable options are by chronology and by genre. Organizing by genre has the greater problems for the simple reason that some of the writer's most celebrated works defy traditional genre categories. Thus, *The Gulag Archipelago* combines historical analysis and personal memoir with an impassioned accusatory brief, while *The Red Wheel* cycle represents a synthesis of the historical-novel mode with a purely historical account.

The sequence we have followed is roughly chronological. While many of Solzhenitsyn's brief works, especially his essays, can be dated exactly, writings of more substantial length were typically produced over a period of many years and in some cases were revised and reissued in substantially new editions. Other works represent installments in an ongoing series that continues as the present book goes to print.

Most of the works discussed here are available in English, but our list of entries includes several important items that have not yet been translated. We give bibliographic data on each work discussed and typically add some comments on the quality of the available English translation(s). The following abbreviations and conventions are used in citing Solzhenitsyn's texts:

Sobranie sochinenii (Moscow)—The Russian-language *Collected Works* launched in Moscow by the "Vremia" publishing house in 2006 and projected to contain thirty volumes: *Sobranie sochinenii v tridtsati* t*omakh*, edited by Natalia Solzhenitsyn;

Sobranie sochinenii (Vermont)—Solzhenitsyn's twenty-volume Russian-language *Collected Works*, compiled in Vermont under the author's direct supervision and published in Paris by YMCA Press in 1978–91;

Publitsistika—A three-volume collection of Solzhenitsyn's essays, speeches, and interviews, published in Yaroslavl by the "Verkhniaia Volga" publishing house in 1995–97;

The Solzhenitsyn Reader—A wide-ranging English-language compilation of works and excerpts from works by Solzhenitsyn: *The Solzhenitsyn Reader: New and Essential Writings, 1947–2005*, ed. by Edward E. Ericson, Jr., and Daniel J. Mahoney (Wilmington, DE: ISI Books, 2006).

Other texts will be cited in full.

Early Works

———————

T he works completed by Solzhenitsyn before *One Day in the Life of Ivan Denisovich* (written in 1959, published in 1962) are here classified as "early," even though their appearance in print occurred much later. The following works are included under this rubric:

> • The narrative poem *The Road* (1947–52; pub. 1999);
> • The unfinished novel *Love the Revolution* (mostly 1948; pub. 1999);
> • Twenty-eight poems composed in prison, forced-labor camp, and exile (1946–53; pub. 1999);
> • Three plays that together constitute a dramatic trilogy titled *1945*, first published in 1981, consisting of *Victory Celebrations* (1951), *Prisoners* (1952–53), and *Republic of Labor* (1954).

Every one of these works was composed in strictest secrecy, and only *Love the Revolution* and the play *Republic of Labor* were not memorized according to the astonishing method Solzhenitsyn has described in *The Gulag Archipelago.*[1]

The Road

This narrative poem of some seven thousand lines, sometimes referred to as *The Way* or *The Trail,* is a poetic autobiography that traces the evolution of a first-person protagonist named Sergei Nerzhin. In terms of biographical accuracy, the account is in accord with the major events of Solzhenitsyn's life known from other sources, the only significant departure being the fictional names given to the major characters.

The Russian title *Dorozhenka,* a diminutive form of *doroga* (road, journey, way), confers a subtle emotional coloration on the familiar metaphor of a spiritual odyssey, and suggests an attitude toward the road traveled that includes equal measures of irony, regret, and affection. In contrast to this note of understanding sounded in the title, the text of the poem is filled with harsh criticism of Nerzhin's prearrest life. In the opening chapter, for example, the twenty-year-old Nerzhin is shown as so blinded by Marxist ideology that he is genuinely baffled by the account of a peasant who suffered dispossession, exile to the tundra, and the death of his children from the privations encountered there, all on account of having been classified a "kulak"—the incriminating evidence having been nothing more than his ownership of six horses. Nerzhin seems little moved by the human tragedy of collectivization revealed by this tale of woe, pausing only to recall the Stalinist edict of the time according to which "kulaks must be liquidated as a class" for the sake of the future social utopia.

In the same opening chapter Nerzhin witnesses other scenes that gain meaning only in the retrospective survey of his life. He observes—with some disdain for the brutal physicality of the work—a multitude of ragged men laboring on a gigantic canal project (they are prisoners); he has a similarly distant reaction during a brush with soldiers pursuing escapees from a prison camp. But when he happens to get a close-up view of a river steamer filled with prisoners under guard, the eye contact that occurs because of the proximity of the ship serves to shake him loose briefly from the ideological distancing that had effectively blinded him to the significance of the other scenes. As a boy who had grown up without a father—just like the real Solzhenitsyn—Nerzhin fancies that the convicts staring at him are reminded of their own sons. Ordinary human instincts here trump ideology for the first time.

Eye contact plays a more critical role in the following chapter, where the newlywed Nerzhin is depicted as virtually obsessed with the Marxist view of the world. As he says of himself:

> I believe to the point of convulsions! Life is clear to me,
> Doubts and uncertainties are not in my nature.

Nerzhin even writes a hymn to the October Revolution and, as his new wife complains, gets out of bed early in the morning in order to read Marx. But he is deeply shocked when the train carrying him and his wife pulls alongside an enormously long assemblage of railroad cars equipped with small barred openings, each revealing shaved heads and eyes staring out with hostility at the happy couple, subjecting him to a seemingly endless succession of hate-filled looks as well as to an ugly curse flung at him through one of the barred windows. This jarring episode clears his ideology-befogged mind long enough to bring into focus suppressed memories sharply at variance with his Communist beliefs.

Three specific events from Nerzhin's earlier years stand out; they are, as he realizes in retrospect, significant practical manifestations of the ideology he has adopted. As a nine-year-old boy he witnessed two OGPU men with "cast-iron chins" terrorize his mother and grandfather; some years later he inadvertently came upon the scene of the arrest of a close family friend who was the father of one of Nerzhin's playmates; and later still he was bewildered to discover that the most brilliant and popular boy in his school was being hunted down for his opposition to Stalin's system.

Several chapters of the poem relate to Nerzhin's army service, and these texts trace his growing recognition that important aspects of reality cannot be accounted for by his view of the world. Thus, he is confronted with what is for him the mind-boggling fact of the existence of Russian units fighting against the Soviets on the German side of the front. And he learns with dismay that it is Soviet military practice to send battalions of men deemed unreliable on missions virtually guaranteed to result in their death.

Nerzhin's new self-awareness is a natural correlative of his greater understanding of the world. He feels guilt over the ways he had unthinkingly taken advantage of his rank to lord over the soldiers in his unit, and the retroactive moral condemnation of his wartime behavior reaches a crescendo in the chapter titled "Prussian Nights." During the Red Army's rampaging advance into Eastern Prussia as the war winds down, Nerzhin at first assumes a stoically passive stance "like Pilate." But the gleeful and totally unchecked savagery of soldiers looting, raping, and setting fires to towns unprotected by the disintegrating German army ineluctably seduces him to join in. He first rummages for stationery supplies in an abandoned post office, then fails to prevent a wanton murder of a German girl whose defiant expression irritated his men. Finally, he forces a terrified German woman to have sex with him. This last act triggers an explosive revolt of his conscience, a reaction of a kind Solzhenitsyn has elsewhere linked to a bolt of lightning passing through one's "inmost being."[2] And Solzhenitsyn ends "Prussian Nights" with an extraordinary statement in which the act of confessing his transgression in a text acquires the force of public penance:

> Where are you, pure light of childhood?
> The flicker of the icon-lamp? The silvery gleam of the
> Christmas tree?
> Is it not a murderer and a rapist
> Who is now reaching for a pen?
> ....
> I step forth to repent publicly
> In the numbing cold of popular contempt.[3]

In this sense, *The Road* is both an effort by the author to expiate his sin and an attempt to cast out the demons of ideology that had long possessed him. Yet it is almost certainly even more, since the immediately following text deals with the dramatic account of Nerzhin's arrest, which coincides in all details, except the names used, with what Solzhenitsyn has related in *The Gulag Archipelago*.[4] For although there is no explicit mention of anything like moral retribution, the structural juxtaposition tends to suggest that Nerzhin looks upon the arrest as in some sense merited by his transgressions. In more general terms, this theme is sounded in the poem's last chapter, where Nerzhin begins by voicing bitter complaints about the perversities and cruelties of Russian history, but quickly comes around to the view that he must share in the blame, since the merciless system that has ensnared him had been spawned, and has continued to be sustained, by the blind enthusiasm of people exactly like himself.

> We are quick to curse Mother Russia,
>
> ....
>
> But are we some kind of chance guests in the country?
> "Russia!" We have great sport with the word.
> But what about those of us who inhabit the land?
> Are not youths—just like me—to blame
> For inducing Russia to follow this evil path?

The Road ends as the prison van conveying Nerzhin wheels into the courtyard of Moscow's dread Lubyanka Prison.

The poetic text is followed by a brief prose afterword in which Solzhenitsyn asks the reader's indulgence for the technical inadequacy of his verse. He likens his poem to a tree that has taken root in a crevasse on the face of a cliff and has acquired a twisted and unnatural shape by virtue of its prodigious will to survive despite all odds. As an aesthetic judgment on the poem, the comparison is surely too harsh, but the fierce desire of the tree in Solzhenitsyn's analogy to retain its grip on life does reflect a vital aspect of the poem's meaning: The very act of composing the poem, the writer has stated, helped him survive both physically and mentally by allowing him to make sense of his life while also serving as a memory bank on which he would draw in future years. For readers and students of Solzhenitsyn, on the other hand, *The Road* can serve as the "mother-lode text" of the entire Solzhenitsyn corpus, providing excellent insight into Solzhenitsyn's developing moral vision.

Love the Revolution

The major part of this unfinished novel was composed in 1948 during Solzhenitsyn's stay in the Marfino *sharashka*. (The writer had to leave behind what he had written when he was shipped to Ekibastuz in 1950, but was able to retrieve this material when he returned from exile.) While the work has sometimes been referred to as a "prose sequel" to *The Road,* it is in fact focused on the period *preceding* the wartime episodes included in the autobiographical poem. The story begins on a Sunday morning in June 1941, when the protagonist, Gleb Nerzhin (the first name here differing from the "Sergei" in the poem), arrives in Moscow in order to enroll in a prestigious institute for the study of history, philosophy, and literature (MIFLI). As was true in *The Road,* the narrative is entirely autobiographical. And *Love the Revolution* discloses the same self-critical key familiar from the poem, with a heavy emphasis on Nerzhin's inflated opinion of himself and on the naïveté of his faith in the Marxist vision. Arriving in Moscow on the very day when Hitler launched his attack on the Soviet Union, Nerzhin not only feels ready to die for the ideals of the revolution but actually yearns for such a fate, and he is genuinely scandalized by individuals who have other priorities.

To his great frustration, Nerzhin had been classified as medically unfit for frontline duty, and when he is eventually called up, it is for service in a horse-drawn transport unit far from the fighting. Humiliated by this assignment, as well as by his inability to handle horses, and surrounded by middle-aged men who are almost totally indifferent to ideology, Nerzhin inevitably mellows a little, but nothing he experiences in this period is ultimately able to dampen his revolutionary enthusiasm. As Solzhenitsyn writes, "[Nerzhin] would for a short time be depressed by the waves of truth that washed over him, but some kind of inner resilience made sure that he was never moved to change his mind." It is likely that this is a fairly accurate reflection of Solzhenitsyn's own state of mind, for *The Gulag Archipelago* makes clear that it would take the body blow of arrest and incarceration to effect a permanent shift in his opinions.

Solzhenitsyn's original intent was for *Love the Revolution* to be an account of his entire military career; but his attempt to resume the narrative after returning from exile failed, and the work remains fragmentary. Yet even in this form, this earliest of Solzhenitsyn's known prose works stands as an impressive literary achievement. Especially memorable is the ironic yet warm portrayal of Nerzhin as he single-mindedly pursues his dream of serving the Revolution, despite the chaos of wartime Russia and in the teeth of bureaucratic obstacles. There are vivid descriptions of train travel to destinations unknown and unknowable in view of the countrywide blackout of scheduling information, sharply drawn character studies of individuals crossing Nerzhin's path, and clear-eyed commentary on the catastrophic situation that Nerzhin refuses to recognize as such. The narrative energy and pure esprit of the text are so great, in fact, that it is tempting to speculate that Solzhenitsyn may have found it impossible to finish the novel because of the unbridgeable contrast between the ebullient tone of this work and the tragic coloration of the equally autobiographical *The Road*, which had been completed several years before the writer tried to resume *Love the Revolution*.

Poems

As in the case of the two works discussed above, the poems composed in prison, camp, and exile provide much information that is directly autobiographical. This includes reminiscences of the early phase of the writer's incarceration, reflections on the complex relationship with his wife, and several lyrics on the frustrating way in which his desire for feminine companionship during the exile period conflicted with the need to protect the secret of his writing.

There are musings on incarceration as a special state of being, on the bitter irony of prisoners being forced to build more prisons,[5] on prison as a home that effects an irreversible change in the mentality of its inhabitants, and on the counterintuitive contrast between prison and the Stalinesque world outside the barbed wire ("I exchange prison, full of free and restless men / For freedom, inhabited by slaves immobilized by fear").

Several poems touch upon literary matters. In one, the writer names three masters to whom, he claims, he owes all that is good in his writing. He desires to be like Pushkin, "who spoke of darkness /

By casting light on the pain"; like Dostoevsky, "who beheld a glimmer of treasure / Amid the squalor of cramped lives" and who was "merciless only toward himself"; and, finally, like Tolstoy, who was "ever sensitive to the intricate patterns / Interwoven in another's soul."

But the most moving poems are dedicated to Russia.[6] The one and only right of a prisoner, he declares in a 1951 lyric, is "To be a wrathless son / Of the luckless Russian land." A 1952 piece is a tragic lament about the poet's inability to discover the "true Russia" among his "savage fellow-tribesmen":

> The birthmarks of Tartar patrimony,
> The foul red slime of Soviet years—
> On all of us! In all of us! May Russia
> Not be cursed by the world outside.

Solzhenitsyn's personalized and almost religious attitude toward Russia is revealed in a poem he wrote in December 1953 after being diagnosed with cancer and given only a few weeks to live. He here imagines looking back at the country from the mystical vantage point of one who has passed through death's door:

> I take it all in without anger or curse:
> The dishonor. The glory. The day-to-day stir.
> But no more shall I see you nailed onto the cross,
> No more shall I call you to rise from the dead.

Plays

The first of three plays that make up Solzhenitsyn's *1945* trilogy is *Victory Celebrations,* a drama in verse (subtitled "Comedy") which grew from a chapter of *The Road.* It seems probable that *Victory Celebrations* attained independent status because the plot departs from the highly autobiographical format of *The Road.* The play is a bitterly satirical work that revolves around the unexpected appearance of Lieutenant Gridnev, a representative of Soviet military counterintelligence ("SMERSH"), at a feast prepared by a group of Soviet army officers in celebration of their victorious advance through Eastern Prussia in early 1945. The SMERSH man poisons the festivities by voicing suspicions about a beautiful girl who has been invited to the party (and who has resisted his amorous advances), as well as by grilling the officer Gleb Nerzhin about his "social provenance." Solzhenitsyn's clear goal is to show the tension between the visceral dislike that Gridnev generates and the sinister power over everyone that he nevertheless wields. The tension is resolved when the Germans launch a sudden counterattack and Gridnev makes an ignominious exit.

The second part of the dramatic trilogy, *Prisoners* (subtitled "Tragedy"), was composed in camp in 1952 and memorized *in toto* before it could be written down a year later. It is set in a Soviet prison in mid-1945 and is based on Solzhenitsyn's experience of being thrown together with an incredibly diverse group of individuals as his incarceration commenced. The work communicates some of the intellectual tumult that Solzhenitsyn must have experienced then, and the mixture of poetry and prose seems an appropriate stylistic echo of the jumble of ideologies being voiced in the text. The *dramatis personae* include Soviet soldiers and officers liberated from German POW camps and promptly rearrested as alleged security risks, men who had fought with the Wehrmacht-directed Russian Liberation Army, Russian émigrés snatched from the streets of Western Europe, Christian believers, and a few diehard Communists. The arguments among these men are presented as a cacophonous mélange of clashing opinions. *Prisoners* also diverges in a particularly significant way from the strongly autobiographical tendency of Solzhenitsyn's other early works by lacking a protagonist who can be closely identified with the author. The most prominent character in the play is not the familiar Nerzhin but a former colonel in the tsarist army named Georgi Vorotyntsev, who had been fighting against the Soviet Union on the German side. The crucial point here is that Vorotyntsev is the main fictional protagonist of the *Red Wheel* epic, and *Prisoners* thus becomes, in a fascinating way, both the earliest inkling of the way Solzhenitsyn visualized *The Red Wheel,* his vast project-to-be, and an epilogue of sorts to a still unwritten cycle. (In the play, Vorotyntsev is sentenced to be hanged but refuses a chance to escape the gallows by committing suicide, arguing that the moral responsibility for his death must fall on his executioners, not on him.)

Solzhenitsyn got his first taste of forced labor soon after his sentence was pronounced in mid-1945, spending almost a year in camps of the "mixed" type, designated in this way for holding men as well as women and political prisoners together with common criminals. In the second volume of *The Gulag Archipelago,* the writer relates some of the difficulties and moral quandaries that bewildered and humiliated him during this period. Much of this experience has been condensed into the third play of his trilogy, *The Republic of Labor* (subtitled "Drama in Four Acts"), written in 1954. It is the story of a recently arrested frontline officer, Gleb Nerzhin, who is unexpectedly placed in a position of authority and tries to undo some of the flagrantly corrupt, unfair, and unsafe practices that characterize the camp's operation. Nerzhin's attempts at reform are shown to be hopelessly naïve, and by challenging numerous vested interests in the camp hierarchy, he soon generates enough hostility to be demoted and marked for transportation to a far more lethal labor-camp. He is saved from this fate by the intervention of a girl with whom he has fallen violently in love, but she is able to help only by a self-sacrificing act: She agrees—without Nerzhin's knowledge—to join the "harem" of the well-connected camp doctor.

All of Solzhenitsyn's early works show evidence of being shaped by the mind of a former true believer who has been shaken loose from his convictions by the impact of catastrophic events, and who is now engaged in an uncompromising search for truth, justice, and redemption. The works also function as valuable records of their author's personal experiences, as well as allowing the beginning writer to experiment in genre and structure as he searched for the form most appropriate to his message. And in terms of thematic focus and stylistic emphasis, they all point to the more mature works of a later period.

Texts and translations: *The Road (Dorozhen'ka)*, *Love the Revolution (Liubi revoliutsiiu)*, and the poems were first published in Aleksandr Solzhenitsyn, *Proterevshi glaza: sbornik* (Moscow: Nash dom—L'Age d'Homme, 1999). A chapter from *The Road* titled "Prussian Nights" appeared earlier as a separate publication: Aleksandr Solzhenitsyn, *Prusskie nochi* (Paris: YMCA Press, 1974); and also in a bilingual edition with an English translation by Robert Conquest: Alexander Solzhenitsyn, *Prussian Nights: A Poem* (New York: Farrar, Straus and Giroux, 1977). A different chapter from *The Road* translated into English appears in *The Solzhenitsyn Reader*, along with a translation of three poems. The dramatic trilogy first appeared in vol. 8 (1981) of Solzhenitsyn's Vermont-produced *Sobranie sochinenii*. A politically toned-down version of *The Republic of Labor (Respublika truda)* titled *Olen' i shalashovka (The Love-Girl and the Innocent)* appeared in 1969. This "lightened" version was translated by Nicholas Bethell and David Burg, and it accompanies the capable translations of *Victory Celebrations (Pir pobeditelei)* and *Prisoners (Plenniki)* by Helen Rapp and Nancy Thomas that together make up the volume: Alexander Solzhenitsyn, *Three Plays* (New York: Farrar, Straus and Giroux, 1986).

Miniatures

Solzhenitsyn has written thirty-two miniatures, none of which exceeds a page and a half in length. These texts have appeared under the rubrics "Prose Poems," "Etudes," and "Sketches," but the series title the author has chosen, *Krokhotki*, could be translated literally as "tinies." Seventeen of these miniatures were composed in 1958–60, often taking their inspiration from scenes the author discovered during cycling trips. Three years later, he added "A Prayer" ("Molitva") to this set. Starting in the mid-1990s, when he was once again on his native soil, he wrote fourteen new ones, including "A Prayer for Russia" ("Molitva o Rossii"). As he explained, "It was only when I got back to Russia that I found I could write them again; living abroad—I simply couldn't do it."[1] Continuity prevails between the two cycles of miniatures, even as the second cycle tends to articulate moral themes more overtly. For readers who associate the author's name with massive books and thundering voice, these diminutive works of art afford unexpected delights. They are delicate in design, gentle in spirit, pensive in mood, lyrical in expression, and exquisite in poetic language, in this sense providing ample evidence of Solzhenitsyn's mastery of a wide range of literary genres.

The miniatures typically move from a single episode or observation to a broad philosophical insight; from their genesis in Russian scenes, they expand in meaning to invite universal application. One recurring theme is the sheer joy of being alive. The simple involuntary act of breathing when out in nature is recognized as "the most precious of freedoms" of which prison deprives human beings. A puppy, too, when let off its leash, prefers freely frolicking to chewing on chicken bones. Praise of the life force at its most elementary level results from viewing a "weightless" little duckling, which humans capable of conquering space could not assemble even if given all the ready-made bones and feathers. The author's powers of minute observation of nature extend to ants that are so attached to their home in a rotten log that when it is tossed upon a fire, they will first flee but then return to it even if they perish there. Life surges in the plant kingdom, too, as a log of a sawn-off elm tree thrusts out a new shoot.

Another recurring theme is Solzhenitsyn's attachment to old Russian towns and domed churches dotting the rural landscape. A particular source of lamentation is the silencing of church bells that once sounded across the countryside according to rhythms of religious signification. On the other hand, when a dammed river swamps an ancient cathedral, the cross atop the bell tower keeps pointing straight up toward heaven, serving as a symbol that hope endures. Although Solzhenitsyn scrupulously avoids romanticizing old Russian ways, he does use them as a measuring stick for judging the sterility of modern Soviet society, which has, with willful disregard of nature and humanity, despoiled the nation's land and dehumanized its people. An implicit subtext running through many of the prose poems, and occasionally rising to the surface, is the contrast between Russia's traditional spirituality and Soviet materialism. The young people doing calisthenics in "Starting the Day" ("Pristupaia ko dniu") look from a distance as if they are at morning prayers, but their discipline extends only to matter, not to spirit. Modern disbelievers flee from thoughts of death and act as if "*We* Shall Live Forever" ("My-to ne umrem"). By contrast, the autobiographical "Growing Old" ("Starenie") of the 1990s shows the author contemplating death "as an organic link in the chain of life": Death comes best, he avers, "when advancing years guide us softly to our end"; and according to his personal testament in this miniature, "Growing old serenely is not a downhill path, but an ascent," for death does not end all. An elegiac note for perceived losses intensifies in the late prose poems, but such is the author's inveterate optimism that elegy, too, is suffused with hope.

Texts and translations: The Russian texts of all eighteen of the early miniatures and fourteen of the late ones are gathered in vol. 1 of the Moscow *Sobranie sochinenii*, titled *Rasskazy i krokhotki* (2006).

The most reliable translations of the early group are by H. T. Willetts, published in *Encounter*, March 1965, but that group includes only fifteen of the seventeen originally in the cycle (with the author adding "A Prayer" later). Michael Glenny translates sixteen early miniatures in Alexander Solzhenitsyn, *Stories and Prose Poems* (New York: Farrar, Straus and Giroux, 1971), but his versions are frequently untrustworthy. *The Solzhenitsyn Reader* (2006) contains all eighteen early miniatures, with fifteen translated by Willetts, two by Ignat Solzhenitsyn, and one by Michael Glenny as revised by Ignat Solzhenitsyn. Nine late miniatures, translated by Michael A. Nicholson, with Alexis Klimoff, appear in an appendix to Joseph Pearce, *Solzhenitsyn: A Soul in Exile* (Grand Rapids, MI: Baker, 2001). *The Solzhenitsyn Reader* contains all fourteen late miniatures, nine translated by Nicholson with Klimoff, four by Ignat Solzhenitsyn, and one by Stephan Solzhenitsyn.

The First Circle

The First Circle is Solzhenitsyn's first long work and the only one formally designated by him as a "novel." Its complex textual history has direct bearing on the work's meaning. Begun in 1955, by 1962 the novel was shaped into the ninety-six-chapter version that Solzhenitsyn considered complete at the time. Following the sensational appearance of *One Day in the Life of Ivan Denisovich* in a Soviet journal, the writer conceived the hope that *The First Circle* could also be published in the Soviet Union, and for that purpose prepared a politically toned-down eighty-seven-chapter version of the text. But efforts to bring the novel out in the USSR failed, and Solzhenitsyn released this shortened version (with some further revisions) to the West, where it appeared in 1968 both in Russian and in various translations. Meanwhile, Solzhenitsyn reconstituted the original ninety-six-chapter structure, introducing significant further changes. This text, which the writer considers final and canonical, appeared in Paris in 1978, but its English translation has not yet been published.

Solzhenitsyn's fictional works frequently originate in autobiography, and *The First Circle* is based on his incarceration in 1947–50 at a technical research institute staffed by prisoners—a so-called *sharashka*—located in Marfino (Mavrino in the version long available in English), an outlying district of Moscow. This *sharashka*, a former seminary building, serves as the principal setting for the novel. The "time compression" that is a characteristic feature of the writer's literary constructs is also on full display here: Solzhenitsyn's almost three-year-long stay in this *sharashka* has been compressed into four event-filled days, albeit interspersed with many episodes of flashback. The time frame of the main plot is December 24–27, 1949, the symbolically charged period of Christmastide that followed the extravagant celebrations of Stalin's seventieth birthday (December 21, 1949). The gallery of characters is huge, constituting a cross section of Soviet society. A substantial number of characters receive chapter-length treatment or more, including persons inside and outside the *sharashka*. Historical personages include Stalin, Minister of State Security Viktor Abakumov, even Eleanor Roosevelt.

The denizens of this *sharashka* are charged with developing a telephone encryption device. They enjoy adequate food, access to tobacco and books, space to walk, and time to talk, so that a prisoner newly arrived from the camps wonders if he has died and gone to heaven. But no, he has reached the "first circle" of hell, which in Dante's *Inferno* spared virtuous pagans the active torments of hell's lower circles. Employing understatement to highlight the deprivations of the gulag, Solzhenitsyn describes an almost good day in

One Day in the Life of Ivan Denisovich and an almost good prison in *The First Circle.*

Solzhenitsyn's own *sharashka* years had been a time of profound introspection, during which he reassessed his Marxist outlook and succeeded in constructing an alternative perspective to account better for what he had been experiencing and observing. This intellectual wrestling is prominent in Gleb Nerzhin, the author's alter ego, who, according to one of Solzhenitsyn's friends and fellow prisoners in the *sharashka*, is "an extraordinarily truthful and accurate picture" of Solzhenitsyn at that time.[1] Other major characters closely based on real-life individuals are Lev Rubin and Dmitri Sologdin, who represent Lev Kopelev and Dimitri Panin, respectively.

The First Circle features what Solzhenitsyn has called the "polyphonic" principle of construction. This is a method whereby sections of a work, typically a chapter or group of chapters, are presented from the point of view and in the language of a particular character, not necessarily a major protagonist. In each case the third-person format of the basic account is retained in combination with the subjectivity that would normally be a feature of the first-person mode. The technical term for this type of narrative is *erlebte Rede*, a German phrase that means "experienced speech" and that has sometimes been rendered in English as "narrated monologue." The "polyphonic" aspect simply points to the presence of a multitude of such individual viewpoints and voices within the text. This is a highly effective technique for bringing out the fundamental worldview of each character—as well as the clashes between worldviews—and one that seems to have been inspired by the methods of drama, the genre that had preoccupied Solzhenitsyn in the years preceding the writing of this novel.

The differences between the ninety-six-chapter and eighty-seven-chapter versions, significant though they are, should not be overstated. Characters remain recognizably the same in both texts. The basic structure of the detective-story plot remains the same, and the primary themes are unaltered. Still, the process of self-censoring that produced the eighty-seven-chapter version inevitably entailed an impoverishment of the text. Some major figures—most notably Innokenty Volodin, Dmitri Sologdin, and Gleb Nerzhin— are characterized more fully and deeply in the complete version, and a few noteworthy minor characters are present only in it. The central action that occurs in the opening chapter and sets the plot in motion is much more serious in the complete version. The "lightened" version also cuts other politically sensitive issues, including, most sensationally, the long-held suspicion that Stalin had served the tsarist secret police as a double agent. Further noteworthy differences between the two redactions have to do with literary form, involving such things as changes in chapter structure and numerous stylistic revisions. All in all, though, the most significant differences have to do with Solzhenitsyn's strongest suit as a writer of fiction, namely, characterization.

The sharpest contrast between the two versions of *The First Circle* comes with the characterization and actions of Innokenty Volodin. In the opening chapter, Volodin, a Soviet diplomat, makes a self-incriminating telephone call that is monitored and recorded. In the "lightened" eighty-seven-chapter version, he attempts to warn a doctor acquaintance against sharing an experimental drug with Western colleagues, since the authorities, in their paranoia, would consider this act a betrayal of Soviet science. This gesture of basic human decency greatly softens the overtly anti-Soviet act depicted in the definitive long version, where Volodin calls the American embassy in Moscow in an attempt to warn of an impending espionage operation in New York bearing on atomic-bomb technology. (A phone call of this very description was in fact made in 1949 by a Soviet diplomat, as we learn from the reminiscences of Lev Kopelev.)[2] In both versions, the authorities, wanting the crime solved, give a recording of this call to the *sharashka* prisoners who had been in the process of devising a scientific method of voice recognition and who are now instructed to identify the caller.

The much more radical act in the definitive ninety-six-chapter version needs significant justification, and Solzhenitsyn has dedicated considerable space to tracing the moral evolution of Volodin, a jaded member of the privileged Soviet elite, into an individual capable of the enormous risk involved in committing treason. A chapter titled "In the Open" depicts a summer trip into the countryside that for Volodin becomes a symbolic contemplation of the disfigured face of contemporary Russia. He is deeply moved by the boundless and majestic vistas, tragically besmirched as they are by abandoned villages and desecrated churches. Later, in another flashback, Volodin travels to visit his mother's brother, Uncle Avenir. He decides to make this trip after stumbling upon letters written by his now-dead mother. As a boy he had been thrilled by tales of his absent father's bold actions on the Bolshevik side of the Civil War, and he had considered his mother weak by comparison. But her letters reveal her to be independent-minded and knowledgeably dedicated to traditional Russian culture. Volodin hopes his uncle can illuminate him further. Avenir, who leads a reclusive life in an out-of-the-way village, has managed to accumulate a huge collection of old newspapers documenting the flagrant Soviet lies about the actual course of events in twentieth-century Russia. The list of cover-ups and deliberate misrepresentations is absolutely overwhelming, and Volodin is impressed by his uncle's thought that a regime capable of such massive deception must not have access to the atom bomb. Volodin's new insights propel him toward the previously unimaginable decision to make his momentous phone call. This moral choice leads eventually to his arrest and his initiation into the brutal world of the gulag.

Whereas both versions of the novel show clearly that Gleb Nerzhin is the author's principal alter ego in countless ways, including details of physical description, only from the complete version may readers observe the considerable extent to which Volodin, too, is a stand-in for the author. Solzhenitsyn's intellectual and moral evolution is paralleled in many stages of Volodin's development as he confronts the apparatus of a totalitarian state. Both the fictional character and his creator pass through an unthinking early phase of conformity with Soviet ideology. For both, a profound appreciation of the beauty of nature reinforces their love of country. Both find their minds opened by adversity, both grow through suffering, and both move through a philosophical phase of skepticism (which in Volodin's case centers on Epicurus's thought). And the manner in which Volodin is "processed" by the relentless system after his arrest unquestionably reflects the shock and disorientation experienced by the author in similar circumstances.

The thematic centrality of *The First Circle* is embedded in the complex interaction among Nerzhin, Rubin, and Sologdin, which readers of both versions can readily observe. However, the novel is enriched by the presence, available only in the ninety-six-chapter version, of a second similarly important locus of thematic import—the very sort of thematic reinforcement that the principle of polyphony fosters. In both loci, the primary thematic concern is essentially the same: The world depicted in the novel forces inescapable moral choices upon honorable persons. In distinction from the solo characterization of Volodin, divergent viewpoints come into play when the three *zek* intellectuals in the *sharashka* converse. Rubin argues for collectivism, Sologdin sides with individualism, and Nerzhin takes a middle ground between their antipodes, playing the role of skeptic even as he searches for a point of view that is anchored in a more positive philosophy.

Rubin remains stubbornly loyal to the state's Marxist ideology, mounting a fervent defense of the regime that has imprisoned him, all the while exhibiting genuinely humane instincts. That Rubin combines Marxism and humaneness serves to underline the moral appeal of Marxism, and one effect of this appeal is to heighten the drama of his friend Nerzhin's moral evolution away from Marxism. Rubin's contradictory tendencies also give rise to utopian visions. Thus, in order to imbue citizens of an atheist society with traditional morality, Rubin dreams of instituting compulsory attendance at "civic temples," which, despite his denials, are essentially "Christian temples without Christ," as Sologdin puts it.

The process of "lightening" the novel that significantly shortchanged Volodin's characterization did the same to Sologdin's. A brilliant engineer and powerful polemicist, Sologdin is Rubin's main ideological adversary, and he relishes reciting the evils of the Soviet system. In the shortened version, however, his critique of collectivism tends to make him sound more like an eccentric individualist, whereas in the complete version his iconoclasm stems from his Christian convictions. As the *zeks'* conversations proceed, Sologdin predicts that Nerzhin "will come to God"—by which he specifies that he means "a concrete Christian God," along with the full accompaniment of classic Christian doctrines. The characterization of Dmitri Sologdin is closer to the real-life prototype, Dimitri Panin, than the shortened version displays.

Nerzhin is a more dynamic character than either Rubin or Sologdin. Whereas they represent settled positions, he is on a search. He is fiercely committed to developing his own point of view, a goal that to him is "more precious than life itself." As he asserts, "Everyone keeps shaping his inner self year after year. One must try to temper, to cut, to polish one's soul so as to become *a human being*." This aspiration necessarily entails rejecting Rubin's doctrinaire collectivism; yet, as if to distinguish this viewpoint from Sologdin's proud elitism as well, Nerzhin immediately adds, "and thereby become a tiny particle of one's own people."

Nerzhin's quest for truth bears a striking resemblance to the depiction of Innokenty Volodin's movement toward enlightenment as Volodin attempts to break free of the suffocating mendaciousness of the world he inhabits. It is also Volodin who, at the very beginning of *The First Circle,* gives voice to a question that will resonate throughout the novel. Trying to bolster his resolve to go through with the warning phone call, he asks himself rhetorically, "If one is forever cautious, can one remain a human being?" Indeed, "humanity" functions as an ideal in the radically inhuman world depicted in *The First Circle.* The concept is understood to include both normal human desires and the kind of basic decency that needs no theoretical explanation. Positive characters either are drawn instinctively to this ideal or else, like Nerzhin, aspire to it consciously, while negative characters suppress it in themselves and wish to destroy it in others. It is not surprising, for instance, that in his nocturnal lucubrations, Stalin sees "people" as the principal impediment to his megalomaniacal fantasies. And it is precisely the paradoxical presence of authentic human instincts in the Marxist Rubin that makes him such an interesting character. Solzhenitsyn suggests that even when humanity is understood at the most rudimentary level, it can be a saving grace, as when the janitor Spiridon, despite his incredibly checkered life, retains moral stability by virtue of his unshakable love of family.

A chapter missing from the shortened version fills in a key step in Nerzhin's spiritual odyssey by making explicit that he has definitively broken with his youthful Marxism. In this chapter he denies that justice is relative or merely class-based, asserting instead that justice is "the foundation of the universe" and that human beings are "born with a sense of justice in our souls." This development prepares him to try "going to the people" not with Marxist shibboleths in mind but in the spirit of the longstanding Russian idea that the folk wisdom of the peasantry provides a reliable moral compass. He is drawn to the humble janitor, Spiridon, whose homespun but rock-solid moral sense provides a welcome contrast to the abstract philosophizing of Nerzhin's intellectual friends. When Nerzhin, after sufficient observation, concludes nevertheless that "the people" are not in all ways morally superior, he comes to see that the only route to becoming a fully actualized human being is to fashion his soul by thinking for himself. By virtue of his unrelenting search for moral absolutes, Nerzhin's odyssey carries him well beyond not only Marxism but also mere skepticism. His open-ended journey has brought him to the edge of religious belief.

Despite the positive moral and spiritual development in such major characters as Volodin and Nerzhin, the pitiless Soviet context can bring the ethical values associated with humanity into a heartrending conflict with natural human instincts. The system's way of brutally destroying human attachments is explored in considerable detail in the depiction of the relationship between Nerzhin and his wife, Nadya. As we learn, Nadya risks forfeiting her career prospects should it become known that she is married to a political prisoner. The rational—but emotionally distressing—way out is to file for divorce, and in a scene of great psychological subtlety, Nadya hesitatingly tries to broach this subject to an outwardly amenable but inwardly wounded Nerzhin. And even though Nadya sincerely wants to believe that the divorce would be a mere formality, later chapters suggest that this forced decision will inevitably lead to estrangement.

Nadya's brief meeting with Nerzhin also illustrates the important role that Solzhenitsyn has assigned to language in the novel. Language use is, after all, the most basic attribute of the human condition, and it is profoundly symbolic that the inhuman state described in *The First Circle* is bent on suppressing, distorting, and perverting all aspects of language. Volodin's warning phone call is cut off. Stalin commissions work on a device that will scramble speech. Everyone must constantly be on guard against potential informers who might be listening in on their talk. Harsh restrictions concerning what is allowed to be discussed during spouses' prison meetings aim to reduce the conversation between man and wife to little more than an exchange of platitudes, and Nerzhin and Nadya resort to hints and phonetic masking in an achingly insufficient attempt to communicate their complex feelings. The state even requires prisoners to pen optimistic lies to their loved ones. In fact, lies pervade all levels of the system, from the false reports presented to Stalin by his ministers, to the gross misrepresentations of Soviet propaganda about history and such things as the true contents of a truck conveying prisoners but labeled "Meat." The assault on language also amounts to a recognition of its crucial importance, and Stalin accordingly labors (fruitlessly) on an essay on linguistics. The same acknowledgment of the centrality of language can be seen in Rubin's attempts to buttress his Marxist faith with far-fetched etymological comparisons, as well as in Sologdin's equally eccentric project to purify Russian by inventing substitutes for foreign words. In contrast to these problematic undertakings, Nerzhin's fact-based study of phonetics is presented as scientifically valid, in this sense paralleling his sensible intellectual stance in other matters.

In a fine vignette that plays on the abuse and misuse of language, Nerzhin and Potapov entertain their fellow *zeks* with a hilarious improvisation portraying an imaginary prison visit by Eleanor Roosevelt (identified only as Mrs. R– in the eighty-seven-chapter version), who is caricatured as the prototype of a willfully blind Western "do-gooder." In this fable, incredulous prisoners, manipulative jailers, and self-deluding visitors all participate in creating an upside-down dream world where everything is a complete sham, including the hurriedly beautified prison cell, the extravagant amenities temporarily provided to the prisoners, and the wildly improbable crimes that are ascribed to them. Entirely taken in by this carnival of deception, Mrs. Roosevelt seems only too pleased to be duped by the preposterous façade erected for her benefit. "You have a magnificent prison!" she purrs as she sweeps out of the cell with her entourage of Quaker matrons.

Texts and translations: The eighty-seven-chapter version of *The First Circle* (*V kruge pervom*) was published in 1968 both in Russian (New York: Harper and Row) and in two English translations based on this version. The rendition by Thomas P. Whitney (New York: Harper and Row; reprinted in 1997 by Northwestern University Press) is superior to the one by Michael Guybon [pseud.] (London: Collins and Harvill). The Russian-language ninety-six-chapter version of the novel appears in vols. 1 and 2 of Solzhenitsyn's Vermont-produced *Sobranie sochinenii* (1978). A copiously annotated edition of this version, with notes featuring canceled texts and other important variants in the early drafts of the novel, appeared in the "Literaturnye pamiatniki" series produced by "Nauka" in Moscow in 2006. The full English translation by H. T. Willetts awaits a publisher, but excerpts appear in *The Solzhenitsyn Reader*.

One Day in the Life of Ivan Denisovich

Solzhenitsyn garnered world fame in 1962 through *One Day in the Life of Ivan Denisovich*. The work was published in exceptionally large press runs and immediately became the talk of the nation. Translations were rushed out around the globe. At home and abroad, *One Day*'s political impact was recognized immediately, and now it stands as the one work of fiction mentioned, along with Solzhenitsyn's nonfiction *The Gulag Archipelago*, as having made an indispensable literary contribution to the demise of the Soviet Union. *One Day* was also from the start adjudged hugely successful in purely literary terms, and this high estimate, too, remains in place (with some exceptions among academics).

The basic purpose of this work is to depict how prisoners experienced life in the gulag. The idea, the author reports, came to him during a dreary workday in the winter of 1950–51 as he toiled at Ekibastuz, a huge prison camp in central Kazakhstan, which he has described in *The Gulag Archipelago* and which is the setting for *One Day*. When in 1959 he finally sat down to write the work, he reports, it "simply gushed out with tremendous force"[1] and took only forty days to write.

Whereas Solzhenitsyn's long works of fiction explore several consciousnesses in depth, this story crystallizes attention on a single central character. The figure chosen for this representative, "everyman" role is not an alter ego for the educated author but a simple peasant. The focus on a particular individual is signaled by the author's original title, *Shch-854* (the depersonalizing number patched onto the protagonist's prison uniform), and by the presence of the protagonist's name in the final title (supplied by editor Aleksandr Tvardovsky). The name and mannerisms of Ivan Denisovich Shukhov are borrowed from a soldier who had served under Solzhenitsyn but was never imprisoned. The fictional Shukhov became a German prisoner of war, escaped back home, was falsely charged with being a Nazi spy (as was a common fate in reality), and was sentenced to a ten-year term in prison camp. Solzhenitsyn, adhering to his penchant for tight time frames, compresses the general experience of the gulag into a single day in 1951, from reveille to lights-out—a day that is as representative as is the individual who is the main protagonist.

A key element of the persuasive power of this book lies in its narrative point of view, technically known as *erlebte Rede;* it is a favorite device of Solzhenitsyn's. Third-person narration is present throughout. Since this mode is used to convey Shukhov's private thoughts, as would occur in a first-person account, as well as for objective descriptions that are normally associated with an authorial narrator, the usual distance between protagonist and narrator disappears almost entirely. With virtually everything filtered through the protagonist's mind and peasant idiom, his subjective outlook is expressed in unmediated form. This subtle, sophisticated narrative technique is particularly effective in transmitting Shukhov's astonishingly understated reactions to his brutal environment. A day that strikes readers as virtually unbearable he sincerely considers to have been "almost a happy one." The deprivations that he—with his limited perspective—evaluates primarily in terms of physical discomfort inevitably evoke much stronger reactions in readers, including pity, outrage, and exasperated wonder at Shukhov's stoic patience. How better than through understatement to press home one of the story's central concerns: "Can a man who's warm understand one who's freezing?"

Though down to earth and more cunning than saintly, Ivan Denisovich possesses admirable moral integrity. As he and his work brigade toil through a long day laying cinder blocks in the bitter cold for overlords toward whom they feel no loyalty, he paradoxically takes such pride in his work that he risks punishment by staying overtime to finish one last row of bricks in a way that will affirm his sense of self-worth as a skilled craftsman. Also cast in bare physical terms, as befits a man untrained in abstract speculation, are both the suffering he has endured through long years and his small successes on that particular day: He keeps his boots in good repair, sneaks through inspection a blade he can shape into a knife, wangles an extra portion of gruel, buys tobacco. But it is for his homespun morality that other prisoners respect him and readers honor him. He remains honest toward his fellow *zeks* and steadfast in maintaining his self-respect amid degrading circumstances.

Just as Solzhenitsyn's long fictions present a large cast of characters representing a cross section of society, so this short work shows humanity *in extremis* through the reactions of many characters. Fetyukov the pathetic scrounger is odious to all. An old man sitting ramrod upright during meals models rectitude in all aspects of life. Tough-minded Tyurin, arrested solely for belonging to a family classified as kulaks, rises to become the work-gang leader who makes hardheaded choices about how to live under tyranny. Captain Buynovsky the military commander and Tsezar Markovich the Moscow aesthete are Shukhov's intellectual superiors, but their blind spots about the camp world's reality leave them less able than he to cope with systemic evil.

The character who, next to Ivan Denisovich, receives the most attention is Alyoshka the Baptist. This selfless, helpful, meek man's serene faith in God provides a vocabulary that Ivan Denisovich lacks for explaining how the human spirit can triumph over unjust suffering. Ivan Denisovich respects Alyoshka and the other Baptists, who received twenty-five-year prison terms for no reason other than their faith, and he gives a sympathetic hearing to the Baptist's arguments on behalf of divine providence. But he cannot agree when Alyoshka says he is glad to be in prison because "here you have time to think about your soul." That Alyoshka articulates his Christian worldview near the work's culmination can be read as intimating the implicit religious foundation of the author's moral vision.

Yet to the end the focus remains on Ivan Denisovich. Some unarticulated life force carries him through prison's unrelenting degradations with his humanity intact, and the book's last paragraphs show him thinking of this single day in his life as, improbably, "an unclouded day." In the crowning piece of understatement, this man of concrete imagination numbers his sentence at 3,653 days, noting with finger-counting exactness the three extra ones for leap years.

Text and translations: *One Day in the Life of Ivan Denisovich* (*Odin den' Ivana Denisovicha*) was first published in the journal *Novyi mir*, 1962, no. 11, with some omissions and changes at the request of the powers-that-be. The canonical Russian text appears in vol. 3 of the Vermont *Sobranie sochinenii* (1978) and in vol. 1 of the Moscow *Sobranie sochinenii* (2006).

Six independent English versions exist, but only one, an excellent translation by H. T. Willetts (New York: Farrar, Straus and Giroux, 1991), is based on the canonical Russian text. The Willetts translation is also reproduced in the "Everyman's Library" edition (New York: Alfred A. Knopf, 1995), but there it has the misfortune of being preceded by an error-filled introduction by John Bayley. Of the five translations based on the censored *Novyi mir* text, the version by Max Hayward and Ronald Hingley is probably the best, although it cannot compete in quality with the Willetts rendition.

Matryona's Home

"**M**atryona's Home," written in 1959, is Solzhenitsyn's best-known short story, and some commentators consider it his most accomplished literary production. The domestic publishing window that had opened for Solzhenitsyn in 1962 with *One Day in the Life of Ivan Denisovich* would soon close. But before it did,

"Matryona's Home" appeared in the pages of *Novy Mir* in 1963. The story is thoroughly autobiographical, in this sense illustrating, along with many other works, that for Solzhenitsyn literature does not necessarily depend upon fictive invention and is not to be equated with it. As in the tradition established by his nineteenth-century literary forebears, the artistry entails selecting materials drawn from real life and shaping them into meaningful patterns. (Photographs exist of Matryona and her home.)[1] When Solzhenitsyn's sentence of "perpetual exile" was annulled in 1956, he moved from Kazakhstan back to Russia and located in a village named Miltsevo; this story is set there.

The narrator of this first-person account, referred to only by his patronymic, Ignatich, is, like the author, a former prisoner who has returned to European Russia after forced residence in Central Asia. Ignatich is looking for an authentic backwoods village. Having survived the batterings of prison and internal exile in an arid semi-desert, he yearns to find peace by losing himself in the Russian heartland of his nostalgic longings. Instead, he makes the melancholy discovery that most of the villagers, including a bearded elder of dignified and imposing appearance, turn out to be greedy, quarrelsome, and petty. Like Gleb Nerzhin, the authorial alter ego in *The First Circle,* Ignatich learns that "going to the people" offers no shortcut to virtuous living, for peasants are in moral terms no better and no worse than any others.

The one exception is Matryona, a poor and sickly middle-aged widow in whose house Ignatich has taken up residence. The story's center of gravity lies in Ignatich's observations of this worthy woman, in whom may be perceived symbolic aspects of long-suffering Mother Russia. Moral but not observably religious, Matryona has had a life filled to the brim with tragedy and suffering but has not become bitter. She accepts injustices with equanimity and does no one harm. With a sturdy work ethic not unlike that of Ivan Denisovich, but combined with an altruism that is all her own, she helps neighbors with their tasks whenever she is asked. With an unreflective natural piety, she respects the life-giving earth and loves animals, especially her lame cat. When she digs up potatoes for her neighbors simply for the pleasure of discovering big ones, her work ethic, altruism, and natural piety join in concord. The main plot element begins when her grasping relatives, needing wood for a construction project and heedless of her interests, dismantle part of her log cabin. As a result of slipshod work by the alcohol-impaired movers, the cart carrying the wood gets stuck on the railroad crossing, and a passing train smashes to bits the equipment and the load. And it kills Matryona, who, as usual, had been trying to help. Only an adopted daughter genuinely mourns her.

The story concludes by describing Matryona as "the righteous one without whom, as the proverb says, no village can stand. Nor any city. Nor our whole land." The proverb comes from a biblical text: Abraham's entreaty to God to spare the city of Sodom in Genesis 18.

Text and translations: The canonical Russian text of "Matryona's Home ("Matrenin dvor") appears in vol. 3 of the Vermont *Sobranie sochinenii* (1978), as well as in vol. 1 of the Moscow *Sobranie sochinenii* (2006).

The best English translation is by H. T. Willetts, available in various collections of Russian short stories, e.g., Clarence Brown's *Portable Twentieth-Century Russian Reader* (Penguin, 1985 and later editions); it is included in *The Solzhenitsyn Reader*. Note that the translations by Michael Glenny in Alexander Solzhenitsyn, *Stories and Prose Poems* (New York: Farrar, Straus and Giroux, 1971, and later editions) and by Paul W. Blackstock in Alexander Solzhenitsyn, *We Never Make Mistakes* (Columbia, SC: University of South Carolina Press, 1963, 1971), are both filled with egregious errors and must be avoided.

Incident at Krechetovka Station

This story was originally titled "Incident at Krechetovka Station" in both Russian and English, but in later editions Solzhenitsyn changed the place name to Kochetovka, the actual appellation of the locality. The narrative demonstrates the moral blinders that Soviet ideology imposes upon even the best of its adherents. Appearing in *Novy Mir* in 1963, it is the only prose work by Solzhenitsyn set in the World War II period that is available in English. After presenting the flavor of wartime in a slice-of-life manner,[1] the story peers inside the mind of the main character, Lieutenant Vasily (Vasya) Zotov, a seemingly exemplary product of the Soviet system who is second in military command at the eponymous railroad junction. This educated young Communist, who reads Marx's *Das Kapital* in his spare time, embodies many features of the positive hero extolled by Soviet propaganda. He is honest, earnest, energetic, and responsible in public and private affairs. Zotov is ashamed that he is not at the front, risking the ultimate sacrifice for his homeland—especially since, contrary to his ideological expectations, the war is going badly for his side. Choosing to be faithful to his pregnant wife, who is stuck behind enemy lines, he twice spurns other women's sexual advances.

But Zotov's consciously maintained and absolutely sincere ideological rectitude is subtly undermined by his physical appearance. He is nearsighted, a symbolically loaded trait in itself, and it is only his glasses and military cap (which he assiduously wears on duty) that give a stern air to his childish and kindly face. The subversive analogy is unmistakable: The Marxist faith that Zotov so ardently wishes to believe is, similarly, an external prop superimposed on his inborn human goodness.

The story's fateful, brief incident involves an actor named Tveritinov, who has accidentally lost contact with his military unit and now needs assistance in transit in order to catch up with it. Zotov is impressed by the man's refined bearing and cultural breadth and is genuinely touched by photographs of his family. When, however, Tveritinov asks what Stalingrad used to be called (it was named thus in 1925), Zotov's ideological guard goes up, and he concludes, falsely, that the ostensible soldier must be a spy, maybe a White émigré. As the suspicion ingrained in him by the Soviet system surges to the fore, overcoming his kind instincts, Zotov has Tveritinov arrested. Months later, unable to allay his misgivings about his action, he inquires about the man's fate, only to be told by the security officer, "Your Tverikin's being sorted out all right. We don't make mistakes." Given the bitter irony of this claim, in which the arrested man's name is garbled, it is no wonder that, as we are told in the next—and concluding—line, "Zotov was unable to forget the man for the rest of his life." As Zotov's case shows, the allegedly positive features of Soviet propaganda are false ideals, the pursuit of which leads directly to an otherwise decent human being committing a tragically unfair act.

Interestingly, Zotov's profound disquiet at the end of the story demonstrates the possibility of moral growth (encountered also in other works by Solzhenitsyn) when an instinctive moral protest against a serious transgression has a permanent and positive impact on the perpetrator's future behavior.

Text and translations: "Incident at Krechetovka/Kochetovka Station" ("Sluchnai na stantsii Kochetovka") appears in its canonical form in vol. 3 of the Vermont *Sobranie sochinenii* (1978) as well as in vol. 1 of the Moscow *Sobranie sochinenii* (2006).

The two best-known English translations, Michael Glenny's in Alexander Solzhenitsyn, *Stories and Prose Poems* (New York: Farrar, Straus and Giroux, 1971, and later editions) and Paul W. Blackstock's *We Never Make Mistakes* (Columbia, SC: University of South Carolina Press, 1963, 1971) are both deeply flawed, with instances of complete loss of meaning. No other translations are currently in print.

What a Pity

The short story "What a Pity" is a fictionalized treatment of factual information written up in *The Gulag Archipelago*.[1] A comparison of the two texts discloses Solzhenitsyn's habitual literary method of giving aesthetic shape to raw materials drawn from experience.

In real life Solzhenitsyn met an old engineer as both of them were being released from the gulag and heading into internal exile. In prerevolutionary times this engineer had begun developing a hydroelectric plant and irrigation system in the Chu Valley of Kyrgyzstan deep in Central Asia. The author was highly impressed by the serene self-control with which the man survived the deprivations and maladies inflicted by fifteen years of confinement on trumped-up charges of "sabotage." The account in *Gulag* also mentions that in Moscow the engineer's daughter came across a recent journalistic account about her father's achievements.

In "What a Pity" the old *zek* provides not a consciousness to be explored but an object for other characters to consider. The daughter, Anna, becomes the central consciousness. She tries to slip the newspaper out of its glass-front display case, since it is a dated issue no longer on sale. By this act of filial loyalty, Anna prepares for the day when her father is consigned to his location for perpetual exile and her mother can carry to him this public recognition of his engineering feat.

A policeman, however, espies her trying to pilfer the newspaper. His first assumption, when she explains whom the story is about, is that her father is being criticized, a likely guess in the Soviet context. No, she explains, he is being praised. When the policeman relents and lets her take the paper, he demonstrates—as other Solzhenitsyn characters sometimes do—that humaneness can win out over blind loyalty to the system, even among authority figures.

The third character whose consciousness is explored is the author of the newspaper article. In his florid account of a distant human-interest story, he follows the party line in interpreting a tragic life, blithely assuming that the engineer was treated badly by the tsarist regime but better by the Soviet authorities. "What a pity," the journalist writes in a sentence that provides the title to the story, "that the young enthusiast did not live to see the triumph of his brilliant ideas," namely, "the now transformed valley." The real pity, which the ideologically blinkered journalist cannot see, is that the Soviet regime mistreated the engineer throughout, unjustly incarcerating him, claiming his achievement as its own, and finally dispatching the man to a broken, isolated old age in exile.

The meaning of this realistic story is reinforced by a deft tinge of symbolism. The raindrops that Anna transfers onto her finger serve as mirrors, but as the jiggling drops change shape slightly, the mirror image becomes somewhat distorted. Point of view governs; and Anna, the policeman, and the journalist bring different perspectives to their observations of the old engineer.

"What a Pity" was finished in 1965, as Solzhenitsyn was about to concentrate on long literary forms. It was published in 1978. When he returned to short forms after moving back to Russia in 1994, he wrote several "binary" tales, of which this story, with its bipartite structure conjoining past and present events, can perhaps be seen as an early precursor.

> **Text and translation:** "What a Pity" ("Kak zhal'") was first published in vol. 3 of the Vermont *Sobranie sochinenii* (1978), and it is contained in vol. 1 of the Moscow *Sobranie sochinenii* (2006).
>
> An English translation by Robert Chandler came out in *Prospect Magazine*, January 2003, and was reprinted in Chandler's edition of *Russian Short Stories from Pushkin to Buida* (New York: Penguin, 2006). It is included in *The Solzhenitsyn Reader*.

Cancer Ward

*C*ancer Ward is based on Solzhenitsyn's personal knowledge of cancer, as is his short story "The Right Hand." The novel—which the author labels a "tale"—is set in the clinic in Tashkent, Uzbekistan, where Solzhenitsyn went for treatment in late 1953. Like *The First Circle* and *The Red Wheel,* it is polyphonic in structure, rich in characterization, tightly focused in time and place. A cross section of society is thrown together in a place of confinement—in this case a hospital. Although polyphony in fiction is designed to produce no main character, one person, Oleg Kostoglotov, towers over all others in importance. Various attributes of this rough-hewn, uneducated character are, in varying degrees, parallel to the author's. In fact, Solzhenitsyn has explained that Kostoglotov "arose by infusing the biography of a wartime acquaintance with the personal experience of the author."[1] A soldier in the great war, Oleg had been arrested for making injudicious remarks about Stalin, spent time in the gulag, was sentenced to perpetual internal exile, and carried his cancer into the Tashkent clinic. Other elements of Oleg's biography are similar but not identical to Solzhenitsyn's: Oleg was born in 1920 (not 1918 like Solzhenitsyn), contracted cancer in 1955 (not 1953), and lived exiled in the village of Ush-Terek (not Kok-Terek). Unlike Solzhenitsyn, he hails from Leningrad and is unmarried. In a novel in which themes are often reinforced through conversations, he speaks up frequently, and his views reflect the author's to the extent realistically allowable for a character of a different station in life. When Solzhenitsyn tried to follow up the success of *One Day in the Life of Ivan Denisovich* with the publication of a long work, he settled on *Cancer Ward* as the narrative most likely to get through the censors' sieve. But *Cancer Ward* was ultimately rejected, and the author was not to appear in print in the Soviet Union again until 1989.

Cancer patients, by the extremity of their plight, cannot avoid thinking about the ultimate issues of life and death. In this work, their thoughts turn public when a noisy habitual liar, Podduyev, reads Tolstoy's story "What Men Live By" and is jolted into realizing that he has lived unworthily. The broad question of how human beings should live is the thematic core of Solzhenitsyn's novel. Tolstoy's answer—by love—is the benchmark by which other answers are to be judged. When Podduyev asks his ward-mates what they think men live by, he receives shallow answers: rations, air, water, one's pay, one's professional skill. Patients loyal to Soviet ideology deal particularly poorly with life's big questions. The person most misshapen by ideology—and Kostoglotov's chief antagonist—is Rusanov, a self-important government functionary connected to the security agencies who loves "the People," but only in the abstract. The fact that he seems to be cured while better persons succumb underlines the theme of the mystery of suffering; for cancer, like the rain, falls on the just and the unjust alike. Another Communist, the young geologist Vadim, enters the clinic with all the optimism of the positive hero mandated by socialist realism, but his self-confidence ebbs as he confronts cancer. In several cases the cancers are aligned to comport with characters' identifying traits. Rusanov, who has denounced a neighbor in order to get his apartment, has cancer of the throat. A sexy teenager must undergo a mastectomy. Garrulous Podduyev dies from cancer of the tongue. Shulubin, an erstwhile Bolshevik who knowingly made one moral capitulation after another, must undergo a colostomy, which will result in a foul stench that he himself sees as symbolic of his moral degradation. But then, given the ultimately unpredictable way in which cancer strikes, the good Doctor Ludmila Dontsova develops the disease from the massive doses of radiation that she has tirelessly administered to others.

In conversations with Dontsova, Oleg achieves a breakthrough in self-understanding. Her ministrations have considerably ameliorated his cancer, but when he learns that hormone therapy makes a man impotent, he refuses to continue the treatments. Rejecting her "completely false position" that "nothing *depends* on me," he exclaims, "I don't want to be saved *at any price!*" Temporary reprieve from suffering is enough for one who is "not much of a clinger to life." In keeping with Solzhenitsyn's familiar assertion that the line dividing good and evil cuts through every human heart, Dontsova illustrates the "universal law" that "everyone who *acts* breeds both good and evil. With some it's more good, with others more evil." Oleg, for his part, illustrates that "a hard life improves the vision."

Issues of love and sex loom large in *Cancer Ward*. Solzhenitsyn consulted the plainspoken Mira Petrova, one of his "invisible allies," for help with "the specifically feminine point of view that I knew I lacked."[2] Two attractive women on the clinic staff draw Oleg's attention. The vivacious young nurse Zoya, of the "almost horizontal" breasts, is the one who tells Oleg what damage hormone therapy does. Seeing past his brusque exterior to the quality within, she daydreams of a stable life with a man, which her various sexual encounters have not provided. Vera Gangart—Vega—a slim-waisted "ethereal" doctor of Oleg's age, impresses him as not merely "professionally kind" but as "just naturally kind." Remaining faithful to the memory of the fiancé who perished in the war, Vega is now bereft of anyone "to advise her what to do or how to live." When Oleg expresses disdain for the Soviet sex manuals that reduce love to its physiological aspects only, Vega silently agrees. His habitual candor elicits reflections that she has never before shared with anyone. Despite disagreeing about the continuation of his treatments, they readily attain mutual appreciation and admiration.

Oleg leaves the clinic with his cancer abated but not eliminated. The final two chapters lyrically describe the coming of spring and his return to life. Their titles convey his initial exuberance ("The First Day of Creation . . .") and his resignation to life's hard realities (" . . . and the Last Day"). To his astonishment, both Zoya and Vega have offered him lodging before he leaves Tashkent for his home in exile and his friends, the Kadmins (who are based on real-life prototypes, as are Vega, Dontsova, and some other characters). He sets Zoya's sex appeal aside; and, overcoming a mirror's revelation of the shabby figure he cuts, he heads for Vega's residence, flowers in hand. He eventually decides that he should not impose his impotence upon a woman but should accept the path of renunciation. This decision is confirmed when on a trolley his body is crushed against that of a nubile girl and he experiences that "primeval" sensation which is now both "a happiness" and "a sorrow."

Although Solzhenitsyn's realism uses symbols sparingly, these last two chapters include several, starting with the "pink miracle" of a flowering apricot tree that represents Oleg's joyous revitalization. Symbolism surfaces, also, when he senses keenly his outsider status at a department store where a man knows not only his shirt size but also his collar size. He feels more at home at the zoo, where natural life is on exhibit. He attaches symbolic significance to the various animals. The motionless spiral-horned goat represents dignity; the squirrel running on its wheel but getting nowhere represents a contrasting, futile way of life. The fearless, trustful Nilgai antelope reminds him of Vega. The yellow-eyed tiger brings Stalin to mind. A sign at the cage for the Macaque Rhesus reports the senseless cruelty inflicted upon this creature, and the novel's final words linger on the moral dimension of human behavior: "An evil man threw tobacco in the Macaque Rhesus's eyes. Just like that."

Despite living under a dehumanizing regime, Oleg had arrived at the hospital with a mature humanistic vision. His highest compliment was, "He was a good man. A human being." His experience of cancer has not only prepared him psychologically to die but also has led him to "a state of equilibrium" by which to live. "And although you've never counted yourself a Christian, indeed the very opposite sometimes, all of a sudden you find you've forgiven all those who trespassed against you and bear no ill-will toward those who persecuted you." From the clinic, where all suffer but not all grow through suffering, Oleg leaves even better off, in moral terms, than he arrived. He has been enriched by his tiny sampling of human communion, most powerfully experienced in the love between a man and a woman. By an act of will, he overcomes despair, as physical renunciation yields spiritual liberation. It was precisely when established writers called *Cancer Ward* pessimistic and gloomy that Solzhenitsyn described himself as "an unshakable optimist."[3] And when they complained that the novel was political in character, he replied that the writer's task transcends political and economic issues and engages "more general and durable questions, such as the secrets of the human heart and conscience, the confrontation between life and death, the triumph over spiritual sorrow. . . ."[4] Whether or not Helen Muchnic overstates in calling Oleg Kostoglotov "the most complex of Solzhenitsyn's heroes,"[5] his spiritual achievement confirms once again the undeviating focus on moral values that animates Solzhenitsyn's fiction.

Text and translations: *Cancer Ward* (*Rakovyi korpus*), first published in 1968 (Frankfurt: Posev and other publishers), appears in vol. 4 of the Vermont *Sobranie sochinenii* (1979).

There are two English translations: by Nicholas Bethell and David Burg (New York: Farrar, Straus and Giroux, 1969) and by Rebecca Frank [pseud.] (New York: Dial Press, 1968). Both are quite good, with the former marginally the better of the two.

The Gulag Archipelago

*T*he Gulag Archipelago is a nonfiction historical work that points a brilliant spotlight at the existence and significance of the dehumanizing Soviet prison camp system. Few books ever written have rivaled it for its effect on the events of history, for it contributed signally to ending the Soviet experiment. Even unfriendly critics acknowledge that *The Gulag Archipelago* is *the* indispensable work about the distinctive character of the twentieth century—in quantitative terms, at least, the most murderous century ever.[1] It also is unsurpassed for expanding the understanding of the world among contemporary readers. Solzhenitsyn single-handedly introduced the word *gulag* to stand, alongside *Holocaust,* as a universally recognized linguistic emblem of the horrors of twentieth-century totalitarianism. The effectiveness of *The Gulag Archipelago* in discrediting Soviet communism at home and abroad verifies the adage that the pen is mightier than the sword.

By the mid-1980s *Gulag* had been translated into some thirty-five languages and sold more than thirty million copies.[2] Ironically, given *Gulag*'s influence, the author did not consider this his most important work but, rather, a boulder to be rolled out of his path so that he could proceed to completing *The Red Wheel.*[3] Solzhenitsyn wrote *Gulag* to discharge an obligation he felt toward the "*zek* nation" of which he was a member. He interviewed 227 witnesses and, having failed to enlist a coauthor, took upon himself the entire burden of transmitting "the many-throated groan, the dying whisper of millions, the unspoken testament of those who had perished."[4] Only when *Gulag* was finished did he attain "relief and peace of mind."[5] Solzhenitsyn was "sure" that the book "was destined to affect the course of history," and the initial reviews allowed him to state with satisfaction, "I am astonished to see how clearly its significance was realized."[6] For example, George F. Kennan, the foremost American diplomat of his generation, called *Gulag* "the greatest and most powerful single indictment of a political regime ever to be leveled in modern times," one sure to stick in "the craw of the Soviet propaganda machine . . . with increasing discomfort, until it has done its work."[7]

The Gulag Archipelago is a massive tome of eighteen hundred pages, which, though published in three volumes, is divided into seven parts. Efforts to pin down its genre fail; it is easier to say what it is not than what it is: "Neither objective history, nor personal memoir, nor political treatise, nor philosophical meditation, it is all of these at once, in an amalgam in which the whole is greater than the sum of its parts."[8] The main burden of the work is to tell the truth of history that the official Soviet record sought to erase or to distort. When Solzhenitsyn cannot corroborate eyewitness accounts, he meticulously says so and appeals to others to perfect the record. But he also seeks to tell the truth—as much of it as he has been able to collect—in such a compelling way that it will withstand all efforts to ignore or refute it. He eschews the usual chronological organization of history books, because any straightforward structuring would seem to impose rational order on a methodically perverse and nightmarish world. The work combines factual information with interpretive commentary in order to gain maximum effect in building a "case" against the ideological state that liquidated millions of its own citizens. Estimates of the number of victims of Soviet repression vary widely; Solzhenitsyn borrows an émigré demographer's figure of 66 million. In any case, the actual number of souls that perished within the gulag system may never be accurately determined.

Solzhenitsyn's daunting challenge is to make imaginable the magnitude of gulag's horrors; for the *zeks* themselves could not believe what was happening to them. Thus, he tries to draw readers into vicarious participation in various torments—as when, for instance, a *zek* lies spread-eagled and pinioned and "the interrogator (and women interrogators have not shrunk from this) stands between your legs and with the toe of his boot (or her shoe) gradually, steadily, and with ever greater pressure crushes against the floor those organs which once made you a man." Yet the compiling of many such snapshots risks the cumulative effect of mind-numbing imaginative overload. Solzhenitsyn repeatedly calls attention to this problem: "It is not I who am repeating myself, but Gulag." To keep readers engaged, he regularly shifts focus from chapter to chapter. Some chapters are historical, carrying the chronological account intermittently from Lenin's establishment of the gulag in 1918 through Stalin's expansion of it to Solzhenitsyn's exit from the system in 1956. Interspersed among these chapters are thematic chapters that provide generalized accounts of typical *zek* experiences, opening with arrest and mixing in interrogation, trial, transportation, camp rebellion, attempted escape, escape, death. Also scattered throughout are chapters on separate groups: interrogators, guards, thieves, informers, women, children, religious believers, imprisoned Communists. Among the work's heterogeneous materials are sections on show trials, autobiography, authorial speculation, and much more. The various juxtapositions from chapter to chapter create an aesthetic effect loosely akin to that of Solzhenitsyn's polyphonic novels.

As carefully as Solzhenitsyn takes his obligation to the historian's craft, *Gulag* differs from other historical works primarily in its use of literary elements. This difference is signaled by the unusual subtitle, *An Experiment in Literary Investigation.* The title itself, *The Gulag Archipelago,* shows in miniature how the author conjoins the historical and the literary. "Gulag" (or, more exactly, GULag) is an acronym for a real entity, the Chief Administration of Corrective Labor Camps. "Archipelago" transfers the term for islands in a sea to prison camps spread over the vast Soviet landmass, isolated from yet related to one another. Also, the Russian title, *Arkhipelag GULag,* carries a rhyme that is lost in translation. Imagery, a familiar poetic device, is copious in *Gulag* and enhances the work's vividness. Animal images appear particularly frequently to convey dehumanization. Prisoners are likened to easily scared rabbits and meek lambs; among other animal images used are goat, beaver, dog, worm, and insect (this one borrowed from Lenin). The long second chapter, titled "The History of Our Sewage Disposal System," describes the waves of innocents pulsing through the system's sewer pipes year by year. Cancer is evoked metaphorically, as in the chapter title "The Archipelago Metastasizes."

Just as Solzhenitsyn's fiction is strong on characterization, *Gulag* is packed with vignettes of individuals. The work indicts a whole abstract system not to advance some competing system but to attend to the fates of named and memorable persons who suffered the system's dehumanizing effects, one by one. Fourteen-year-old Zoya Leshcheva, who remained true to her family's Christian faith, claims responsibility for knocking down a statue of Stalin and putting feces in the broken-off head. Anatoly Fastenko, an old acquaintance of Lenin's, first puzzles Solzhenitsyn (new to the gulag and still a Leninist) by his coolness toward Lenin, then makes an impression with his insistent refrain, "Question everything." Anna Skripnikova, strong-willed and independent-minded, carries into her several sojourns in the gulag the same spirit of defiance of arbitrary authority that characterized her life on the outside. Two consecutive long chapters are given over to the efforts of a freedom-loving Estonian, Georgi Tenno, to escape. Among the many personages who are imprinted on readers' memories with novelistic force, the one most deeply imprinted is the one whose story the author knows best: his own.

The feature of literary art used to greatest effect in *Gulag* is the authorial voice. It is ever-present and commands an impressive repertoire of rhetorical strategies. This voice is the glue which holds together the huge and disparate text, in which masses of facts are presented with a running commentary that is by turns lively, sardonic, outraged, mordant, bitter, ironic, sorrowful, hopeful. The constantly shifting tone disturbs, challenges, or startles readers, making it difficult for them to preserve the stance of uninvolved observers in the face of the facts and images marshaled by the author. For example, when describing the transport of *zeks* to the camps, the voice explains the situation with a sentence that parodies logic and deflates the hope for a compensating factor that is teasingly implied by the structure: "They don't heat the car, they don't protect the [political] prisoners from the thieves, they don't give you enough to drink, and they don't give you enough to eat—but on the other hand they don't let you sleep either." Sarcasm is frequent, as when, remarking on the limited material available to him, Solzhenitsyn observes wryly, "We could not broadcast pleas for more on the radio." Among the many permutations of irony, a chapter on forced collectivization opens with a deliberately misleading understatement: "This chapter will deal with a small matter. Fifteen million souls. Fifteen million lives." The chapter "The Kids" narrates some particularly vile episodes of child torture, then concludes, "And let any country speak up that can say it has loved its children as we have ours!" The brisk and energetic language of the author's voice is at a far remove from the usual idiom of historical scholarship. Filled with parentheses and dashes, given to authorial asides, frequently elliptical in the extreme, and everywhere enriched with camp slang and folk speech, it is a blend that is designed to counter and sometimes to ridicule the stilted idiom of Marxist-influenced Russian.

In its unremitting indictment of the Soviet system, *The Gulag Archipelago* would seem to invite analysis in political terms. Yet Solzhenitsyn emphatically warns against that approach: "So let the reader who expects this book to be a political exposé slam its covers shut right now." He proceeds to explicate the moral vision that governs this book (as it does all of his writing). In a passage of supreme importance, he writes of "the line dividing good and evil," stating that this division passes not between good and bad classes of people, as Marxists and other ideologues would have it, but "through the heart of every human being." As this line shifts back and forth according to a person's actions, one is at times "close to being a devil, at times to sainthood." This moral principle applies to everyone, *zeks* and their keepers alike, up to and including Lenin and Stalin. When Solzhenitsyn describes the intentional sinking of barges with hundreds of *zeks* aboard, he pauses to comment that this episode "belongs to the history of *morals* [italics his], which is where everything else originates as well."

Solzhenitsyn fingers ideology as the ultimate culprit in *Gulag*. Although many use the word *ideology* as a neutral term synonymous with *worldview*, Solzhenitsyn restricts its reference to a sociopolitical program rooted in utopianism and committed to social engineering. Even so, he calls those who carry out the Soviet program not ideologues but "evildoers." Furthermore, he distinguishes between them and the villains of classic literature, such as Shakespeare's Iago, who "recognize themselves as evildoers" and "know their souls are black." Ideology relieves such self-condemnation by justifying evildoing. "Ideology . . . is the social theory which helps to make his acts seem good instead of bad in his own and others' eyes."

In contrast to ideology's fixation on group identities, Solzhenitsyn's commitment to the primacy of moral issues keeps attention trained on individuals. This personalism begins on the opening page of *Gulag:* "Each of us is a center of the Universe." According to this moral vision, the purpose of life, even when persons "keep getting banged on flank and snout again and again," is "to become, in time at least, human beings, yes, human beings." On the other hand, full humanity cannot be achieved in isolation but requires solidarity with others. A fulfilling human communion is to be distinguished from its parody in the collectivism imposed by Marxist ideology; there is a good use of the pronoun "we": "Yes, that word which you may have despised out in freedom, when they used it as a substitute for your individuality ('All of us, like one man!' Or: 'We are deeply angered!' Or: 'We demand!' Or: 'We swear!') is now revealed to you as something sweet: you are not alone in the world! Wise, spiritual beings—*human beings*—still exist."

The work's moral vision reaches its clearest expression in the luminous chapter titled "The Ascent." This chapter contains the last words of Dr. Boris Kornfeld, a testimony of his Christian faith spoken the night before he is mysteriously killed and addressed to his patient, Solzhenitsyn. Kornfeld's words lie upon Solzhenitsyn as a burden and "an inheritance," spurring him toward his personal regeneration. Imprisonment, for all its attendant cruelties, can provide the occasion to reconsider everything in one's previous experience, and some *zeks* grow through their suffering. Solzhenitsyn himself comes to declare, "*Bless you, prison,* for having been in my life." Nevertheless, this apotheosis is immediately followed by an acknowledgment of the extraordinary fortune that allowed him to reach this quintessentially Christian conclusion—and to be able to tell about it: "But from the burial mounds I hear a response: 'It's very well for you to say that—you who've come through alive.'"[9] This qualification is an archetypal example of Solzhenitsyn's resolutely unsentimental view of the world as well as of the inner dialogue that energizes the entire text. In fact, the chapter following "The Ascent" is titled "Or Corruption?" and describes odysseys not of ascent but of descent.

"The Ascent" is located in the memorably titled section "The Soul and Barbed Wire," the fourth and midway part of the seven parts of *Gulag*. This placement hints at a crucial organizational principle, namely, the movement of emotional response from grief to hope. The long recitation of misery in the early parts provides readers little relief from a sense of depression. Lying ahead, however, is the climactic celebration of hope. To miss this salute to the enduring human spirit is to miss the work's apex. *Zeks* pursue escape; whole prison camps stage strikes and uprisings; individuals achieve spiritual regeneration. *Total*itarianism fails in its attempt at *total* control of everyone's inner and outer life. Ending on the note of hope is a constant feature of Solzhenitsyn's writings, whether fiction or nonfiction, and it is unquestionably an organic by-product of his religious convictions. *Gulag,* though rife with horror, is in fact a hopeful book. In Solzhenitsyn's own words, "the main goal, the main sense of *Archipelago* [is] a moral uplifting and *catharsis*" [italics his].[10]

The Gulag Archipelago is monumental in every sense. However history ranks his various works, this one alone is enough to ensure that the name of Solzhenitsyn will endure.

Text and translation: *The Gulag Archipelago* (*Arkhipelag GULag*) was first published in Paris by YMCA Press in three volumes, 1973–76. In somewhat augmented form the work appears in vols. 5–7 of the Vermont *Sobranie sochinenii* (1980). An edition produced in 2007 (Ekaterinburg: U-Faktoriia) identifies all of Solzhenitsyn's witnesses and includes a full name index complete with brief biographical information on each entry.

The English translation is based on the original Paris edition and was published (in three volumes) by Harper and

Row in 1974–78. Vols. 1 and 2 appear in the translation of Thomas P. Whitney; vol. 3 was translated by H. T. Willetts. The Whitney translation has numerous flaws; the Willetts rendition is excellent. In 1985 Harper and Row published a one-volume abridgment of the work, edited by Edward E. Ericson, Jr., reprinted in 2002 in the Perennial Classics series of HarperCollins.

Nobel Lecture

The *Nobel Lecture* is Solzhenitsyn's most sustained statement on the meaning and function of literature. Solzhenitsyn attached high importance to this lecture and expended great labor in preparing it. The highly charged atmosphere in which it was composed, however, was not conducive to the theoretical reflection needed to organize and clarify his complex thoughts, so that the text was completed only after considerable delay.

In "Nobeliana," a forty-five-page chapter in *The Oak and the Calf,* Solzhenitsyn describes in gripping detail the role that his receipt of the 1970 Nobel Prize in Literature played in his ongoing duel with the Soviet regime. Reaction to the announcement of his award fell along predictable Cold War lines, with foreigners nearly unanimous in approval and the unending domestic press campaign of vilification against him rising toward a crescendo. Uncertain that the Soviet government would allow him to return home if he traveled to Sweden to accept his medal in person, he was granted the award in absentia.

The Nobel committee's citation honored Solzhenitsyn "for the ethical force with which he has pursued the indispensable traditions of Russian literature." And, true to those traditions, the lecture begins with a spiritual and moral validation of art and moves along to an exposition of the social purposes that art can advance.

The opening section contrasts two kinds of artists (with literary artists chiefly in mind). One kind starts with his own subjective experience and seeks to create "an autonomous spiritual world" in any given literary work. This preference for "withdrawing into self-created worlds or into the realms of subjective whim" develops out of the Enlightenment concept of the autonomous self. In Solzhenitsyn's view, this approach, which has many practitioners among contemporary writers, is futile, for it ignores those perennial, universal concepts that unite all of humanity. Standing in sharp contrast to Solzhenitsyn's vision of the moral universe, this fixation on subjectivity divorces literature from life by abandoning the principle that the moral laws governing the real world of human experience apply equally to human actions in a literary work. Thus, it can be not only futile but dangerous, for it can "surrender the real world into the hands of profit-seekers, of non-entities, or even of madmen."

The other kind of artist views himself as "a humble apprentice under God's heaven." He seeks no autonomy of the self from the higher power above him. A writer's creative powers are imbued in him by divine creation. He "develops his gifts only partially by himself; the greater part has been breathed into him ready-made at birth." His creation of a literary world imitates in microcosm the original Creator's making of the real world. Having "no doubts about [the] foundations" of the world in which he lives and works, this sort of writer accepts that his task is "to sense more keenly than others the harmony of the world, the beauty and ugliness of man's role in it—and to vividly communicate this to mankind." Embedded in these deceptively simple words are the basic Christian teachings about God's creation of the world and man's fall into sin—exactly what Alexander Schmemann so shrewdly perceived in Solzhenitsyn's literary art before the *Nobel Lecture* was written.[1] "Harmony" refers to the orderly goodness of the original creation; "beauty" and "ugliness" refer to the full range of effects that human actions add to the picture.

When the composing process reached the point of the pivot to art's social function, Solzhenitsyn found himself at an impasse. His efforts to "*combine* the two themes" of art and society, he has explained, "didn't come off. The two overstrained shafts sprang apart again and would not be bent into line."[2] Two years elapsed before he aligned the two themes to his satisfaction.

The exposition of the social purposes that literature and art can fulfill starts with a description of the contemporary world. It is, as the published title of Solzhenitsyn's Harvard address put the matter, "a world split apart." Different cultures have different "scales of values" for making moral judgments. Unwilling to give cultural relativism the last word, he asks whether any agency can coordinate these scales and "give mankind a single system of evaluations for evil deeds and for good ones." His answer is yes: "It is art. It is literature." Because literature is capable of transmitting "incontrovertible condensed experience" from generation to generation and from nation to nation—across time and across space—Solzhenitsyn thinks of world literature as "one great heart which beats for the cares and woes of our world." This faith hinges on the crucial assumption that true art "carries its verification within itself" and that in this sense it is completely irrefutable, prevailing in a world where clashing value systems seem to exclude any hope of mutual understanding. Furthermore, Solzhenitsyn is much taken by Dostoevsky's celebrated formulation that "Beauty will save the world," by which he understands that even when ethical values are mocked or considered relative, aesthetic ones can still have universal impact. This high view of literature's potential also embraces the currently unfashionable belief that there is such a thing as "timeless human nature" and thus that "the growing spiritual unity of mankind" is a legitimate aspiration. And he has world literature in mind as he adds (echoing the words of Dostoevsky), "The salvation of mankind lies only in making everything the concern of all." This view also takes the concept of truth seriously: It recognizes that there are lies that art can vanquish and there is truth that art can communicate. For, as a Russian proverb has it, "One word of truth shall outweigh the whole world."

Although his selection as a Nobel laureate set off a discussion about its political ramifications East and West, the lecture itself, to Solzhenitsyn's surprise, "raised not an eyebrow among our masters, and it produced no big shift of opinion, no shock of realization, in the West." He was disappointed because "it seemed to me that I had said a *very* great deal, said all that really mattered."[3] It is of course possible that this *Nobel Lecture* has attracted more appreciative readers than its author has had any way of knowing.

Text and translations: "The Nobel Lecture" ("Nobelevskaia lektsiia") was first published in the Nobel Foundation yearbook, *Les Prix Nobel en 1971* (1972). It has been reprinted many times, including in vol. 9 of the Vermont *Sobranie sochinenii* and vol. 1 of *Publitsistika*.

The lecture has been translated by F. D. Reeve (in a bilingual edition: Alexander Solzhenitsyn, *Nobel Lecture* [New York: Farrar, Straus and Giroux, 1972]) and by Alexis Klimoff (included in the collection edited by John B. Dunlop, Richard Haugh, and Alexis Klimoff, *Aleksandr Solzhenitsyn: Critical Essays and Documentary Materials*, 2nd ed. [New York: Collier, 1975]). The latter translation is reproduced in Aleksandr I. Solzhenitsyn, *East & West* (New York: Perennial Library, 1980) and in *The Solzhenitsyn Reader*.

Lenin in Zurich

*L*enin in Zurich appeared in 1976 at the height of the controversies that engulfed Solzhenitsyn. This volume pulls together the eleven chapters on Lenin written for *The Red Wheel*, all of which also remain in their proper places in the constituent fascicles—*August 1914*, *November 1916*, and *March 1917*—and can now be read in their intended contexts. Publishing the Lenin chapters early was a way for Solzhenitsyn to press his case against the many historians who respected Lenin's historical contribution and blamed Stalin for corrupting Lenin's allegedly pure revolutionary ideals. This character study of Lenin parallels that of Stalin in *The First Circle*; but, at three hundred pages, it is considerably more detailed, since Solzhenitsyn considered Lenin the more historically important figure as well as a more multifaceted personality.

The portrayal of Lenin is a classic example of how Solzhenitsyn subsumes history into literature. Relying on extensive research to fulfill his role as historian, Solzhenitsyn scrupulously endeavors to recount external events accurately. Then, as a literary writer, he seeks to imagine his way into Lenin's inner being—in this aspect, too, working diligently to remain faithful to the evidence. Internal monologue is the main literary technique he employs for this purpose. The goal is to present "Lenin as a psychological type, his character, his inner life and day-to-day behavior."[1]

Solzhenitsyn's Lenin changed the world and may be the most important actor on the stage of twentieth-century history, but he also misread many events, leading him to miscalculate which steps to take and when. He failed to anticipate the outbreak of World War I, speculated that world revolution might well begin in Switzerland, and concluded that a German victory would pave the way for revolution in Russia. Only after Russia's revolution in February 1917 did he decide to return to the land of his birth, yet he was able to achieve state power in a matter of months by dint of his one-track, even monomaniacal mind. He had few close friends, treated women shabbily, and was a committed schismatic: "Split, split, and split again!" Consumed by ideology, he despised Russia and thought that "nothing in his character, his will, his inclinations made him kin to that slovenly, slapdash, eternally drunken country." He was arrogant, obsessive, cold, difficult, alienated—and successful. In sum, Solzhenitsyn's Lenin is a fully realized, three-dimensional character with believable motives who bears moral responsibility for bringing much evil into the world.

Some Western critics claimed that Solzhenitsyn and Lenin had similar personalities, but the parallels are superficial. The one serious quarrel with Solzhenitsyn's treatment of Lenin came from Boris Souvarine, a French historian who had known Lenin personally. Souvarine focused his criticism entirely on matters of historical methodology, faulting Solzhenitsyn for his choice of sources and for erring on certain historical details. In reply, Solzhenitsyn defended his factual accuracy. He also noted that Souvarine ignored the literary nature of the portraiture and thus did not challenge its faithfulness.

Text and translation: *Lenin in Zurich* (*Lenin v Tsiurikhe*) was published in Paris by YMCA Press in 1975 and has not been separately reprinted because it consists of chapters dispersed among three "knots" of *The Red Wheel*.

An English translation by the redoubtable H. T. Willetts appeared in 1976: Alexander Solzhenitsyn, *Lenin in Zurich* (New York: Farrar, Straus and Giroux).

From under the Rubble

O n February 12, 1974, at the very moment that Solzhenitsyn
was arrested and prepared for his involuntary exile, he was
conferring with a colleague, Igor Shafarevich, about a communal
manifesto-in-progress to which they and their collaborators attached great importance. This group effort, edited by Solzhenitsyn, was titled *From under the Rubble*. It was published in Paris in
1974, shortly after Solzhenitsyn's exile, and brings together eleven
essays by seven hands, three of the essays authored by Solzhenitsyn.
The collection takes as its model a 1909 gathering of essays, titled
Vekhi (*Landmarks*), in which formerly radical intellectuals argued
against adopting post-Enlightenment ideologies from the West and
in favor of reinvigorating Russia's traditional spiritual values. *From
under the Rubble* is titled *Iz pod glyb* in Russian, which is a phonetic
echo of *Iz glubiny* (*De Profundis*), a 1918 sequel to *Vekhi*. As the *Vekhi* group sought to warn Russia away from the socialist revolution
looming on the near horizon, so the cohort led by Solzhenitsyn,
anticipating the end of the Soviet parenthesis in Russian history,
seeks to point the way forward for Russia by appealing to the same
spiritual traditions that imbued *Vekhi*.

According to the essays in *From under the Rubble*, the way forward lies not in political action but in a moral revolution: "To create a good and just society we must first become good people."[1]
In his opening essay, "As Breathing and Consciousness Return,"
Solzhenitsyn uses Christ's own words to show the "secondary
significance" of the state structure: "'Render unto Caesar what is
Caesar's'—not because every Caesar deserves it, but because Caesar's concern is not with the most important thing in our lives."
Although we dare not render unto Caesar what is God's, "the absolutely essential task is not political liberation, but the liberation
of our souls from participation in the lie forced upon us." In "The
Smatterers," Solzhenitsyn aims to show that all too many contemporary intellectuals lack the spiritual and intellectual resources to

guide Russia wisely. For the wisdom that Russia needs, Solzheni-tsyn hopes for the development of a *"sacrificial elite,"* and he be-lieves that people with "a thirst for truth" and "a craving to cleanse their souls" are already surfacing.

"Repentance and Self-Limitation in the Life of Nations," which Solzhenitsyn considers one of his most important essays, lays out basic principles that could guide Russia's emergence from its Soviet shackles. Nowhere are the Christian foundations of his thought set forth more explicitly than in this long essay. His argument is rooted in a "transference of values" from individual to nation, since na-tions are answerable to the same divinely generated moral princi-ples that apply to individuals. Russia needs to repent for the crimes of the Soviet era—or, in the biblical language he borrows, for "the sins of the fathers" that are visited upon the children. Repentance, "which perhaps more than anything else distinguishes man from the animal world," remained the leading theme in the speeches Sol-zhenitsyn gave upon returning home in 1994.

After repenting, the nation should practice self-limitation. This concept stands in contrast to "the Western ideal of unlimited free-dom," which depends upon "the concept of *infinite progress,* which we now recognize as false." It also contrasts with "the Marxist con-cept of freedom as acceptance of the yoke of necessity." In the pe-rennial paradox that makes sense to the religious mind, self-limita-tion makes operational "the true Christian definition of freedom. Freedom is *self-restriction!* Restriction of the self for the sake of others." Thus, the nation must eschew imperial expansionism and direct its energies toward internal development. This emphasis on limitedness contradicts the common opinion that Solzhenitsyn is a "nationalist." He considers himself a patriot, and he defines pa-triotism as "unqualified and unwavering love for the nation, which implies not uncritical eagerness to serve, not support for unjust claims, but frank assessment of its vices and sins, and penitence for them." That Russia has not repented for its Soviet transgressions against humanity but simply swept them under the historical rug is demonstrated, Solzhenitsyn would surely argue, by the flawed and deficient manner in which it has been emerging from under the rubble.

Text and translation: *From under the Rubble* (*Iz pod glyb*) was published by YMCA Press in Paris in 1974.

The English translation, by several hands and under the direction of Michael Scammell, was released by Little, Brown and Co. in 1975.

Letter to the Soviet Leaders

The *Letter to the Soviet Leaders,* dated September 5, 1973, is Solzhenitsyn's attempt to give practical advice to the Soviet rulers about what they should do with their power in the immediate future. With admittedly only a small hope that, amid the country's deepening stagnation, the leaders might take his counsel to heart, he wrote in a spirit of compromise and seeking common ground, all the while tinkering with the tone to avoid sounding too "conciliatory."[1] Conceding that the current leaders would not willingly relinquish the levers of state power, he recommended simply that they abandon the platform of Marxist ideology, a faith which they showed no sign of believing anymore. Were they to agree, they would be free to consider the letter's other, more specific proposals for reforming Russian society. This proposition to the leaders dovetailed with his roughly simultaneous statement to the Soviet citizenry titled "Live Not by Lies!" which urged them to leave the falsehoods of ideology behind. The letter's outline of possibilities for the first stage of Russia's post-Soviet future, which Solzhenitsyn saw on the horizon as did few others, was the harbinger of the short-term and long-term proposals that were to come a quarter century later in *Rebuilding Russia*.

The leaders never reacted publicly to this letter,[2] but when it was published in the West in early 1974, many commentators did react—and most unsatisfactorily. Many misperceptions arose by leaving out of account the intended audience and thus regarding the letter as an abstract treatise laying out the author's political ideals. Since Solzhenitsyn had just then embarked upon his Western exile, commentators scanned the text for clues of what he thought about the West, and a common reaction, despite the paucity of textual evidence to that end, was that he disapproved of democracy and Western liberalism. Critics also expressed incredulity that anyone could be so utopian as to conceive of a Russia without Marxism in the foreseeable future. If the reactions of Western critics are any guide, a too-conciliatory tone was the last thing Solzhenitsyn needed to worry about. Indeed, nothing damaged Solzhenitsyn's reputation so much as did the myopic misreadings of his *Letter*, and even the death of the Soviet Union has not fully repaired the injury.

The letter's main burden is to urge the Soviet leaders to focus on internal development. The West, having lost its spiritual moorings, has become too weak of will to take Cold War advantage of this redirection of energies, and Soviet military might may therefore be reduced to the level needed only to defend against possible Chinese encroachments. With a not untypical "green" cast of mind, Solzhenitsyn offers such proposals as husbanding increasingly scarce natural resources according to the insights of the then-prominent Club of Rome, shifting from an economy of unsustainable expansion to a zero-growth economy of conservation, developing new small-scale technologies to undo the ecologically disastrous effects of typically gigantic Soviet enterprises, and opening up the nearly uninhabited Russian Northeast to the construction of new towns built to human scale. The letter's explicitly political suggestions are moderate and gradualist in nature, reformist rather than revolutionary. Without the prop of ideology, totalitarianism will give way to authoritarianism, which can serve as a tolerable intermediate arrangement during the course of an increasing liberation for individuals and a decentralizing of political institutions. No national reinvigoration can come about, however, until Marxism's monopoly on state power is cast off.

The passage of time has been kind to this *Letter*. It sounds much more sensible and moderate in the post-Soviet era than it initially sounded to its detractors. In general terms, the transition from the Soviet Union to post-Soviet Russia that Solzhenitsyn envisioned has come to pass.

Text and translation: *Letter to the Soviet Leaders* (*Pis'mo vozhdiam Sovetskogo Soiuza*) was originally published in a separate brochure by YMCA Press in Paris in 1974. The Russian text has been reprinted in vol. 9 of the Vermont *Sobranie sochinenii* and vol. 1 of *Publitsistika*.

The English translation by Hilary Sternberg appeared in 1974, published by Index on Censorship in association with Harper and Row. This translation is reprinted in *Aleksandr I. Solzhenitsyn, East & West* (New York: Perennial Library, 1980).

Harvard Address

W hen Harvard University invited Solzhenitsyn to deliver the address for its commencement ceremony on June 8, 1978, he took the celebratory occasion—and the notoriously dull genre of graduation speech—as an opportunity to lay out his understanding of the problems of the contemporary West and his counsel for remedying them. The advice with which he concluded his address was fundamentally spiritual in nature, and the generally secular orientation of his audience effected a mismatch that virtually assured incomprehension. The profuse—and often obtuse—commentary on this speech fixed in the popular mind the opinion that Solzhenitsyn simply did not understand the West.

After opening with an expression of friendship, Solzhenitsyn spends the first of his two rhetorical movements describing defects in contemporary Western society. These include various cultural epiphenomena: invasive commercial advertising, "TV stupor," "intolerable" popular music, the ready availability of pornography, excessive litigiousness—in sum, the evidence of mediocrity in public life often lamented by Westerners themselves. These attention-getters are lodged within his critique of larger targets, especially a prevailing uniformity of judgments among journalists and a decline of courage among the intellectual and ruling elites. The faults that Solzhenitsyn identifies suggest to him that the problem lies not in current practices alone but in the view of life and the world that underlies them. This view proclaims that "man—the master of this world—does not bear any evil within himself, and all the defects of life are caused by misguided social systems, which must therefore be corrected." The real problem is, in a word, secularism; and its source is the Enlightenment.

The second of the speech's two movements, which, oddly, received less attention than the first, further delineates this heritage of the Enlightenment and supplies his remedy for the West's malaise. The mistake "at the root" can be called "rationalistic humanism or humanistic autonomy: the proclaimed and practiced autonomy of man from any higher force above him." This "anthropocentricity" leads to a materialism that shrinks the soul and a libertarianism that passes into libertinism. In early American democracy, "all individual human rights were granted on the ground that man is God's creature," and "freedom was given to the individual conditionally, in the assumption of his constant religious responsibility." Since then, however, "a total emancipation occurred from the moral heritage of Christian centuries with their great reserves of mercy and sacrifice." The secular liberalism of the West and the Marxism of the Soviet bloc share "an autonomous irreligious humanistic consciousness"; both of them have "lost the concept of a Supreme Complete Entity which used to restrain our passions and our irresponsibility." Thus, "the split in the world," a phrase that was turned into the title of the published text of the speech,[1] "is less terrifying than the similarity of the disease afflicting its main sections." The corrective that Solzhenitsyn offers, far from being anti-Western, is for the West to be more fully the West by embracing the full range of its rich inheritance, not merely the thinking of the preceding two centuries.

Solzhenitsyn's concluding call is for nothing less than "reassessing the fundamental definitions of human life and human society." Even when the surface topic is political, he is probing the perennial issues of the human heart. Is there a God above us or not? Should we live according to material or spiritual principles? Solzhenitsyn posits that we have "reached a major watershed in history, equal in importance to the turn from the Middle Ages to the Renaissance," and that the time has come to redress imbalances in the general orientations of prior epochs. The Middle Ages undervalued our physical nature, and the modern era undervalues our spiritual being. A new, balanced synthesis would establish proper harmony between body and soul.

To ask in one speech for secular listeners to adopt a perspective that is ultimately rooted in religious values was to hope for too much, as the reactions to the speech showed. To hope that auditors would understand what the speaker was saying, however, was not unreasonable.

Text and translation: The Russian text of the *Harvard Address* (*Rech' v Garvarde*), earlier published as *A World Split Apart* ("Raskolotyi mir"), first appeared in several émigré serials, e.g., *Vestnik RKhD*, no. 125 (1978). The text is republished in vol. 9 of the Vermont *Sobranie sochinenii* and in vol. 1 of *Publitsistika*.

The English translation, by Irina Alberti (under the title *A World Split Apart*), was published by Harper and Row in 1978. In slightly edited form, this translation appears in *East & West* (New York: Perennial Library, 1980), and in *The Solzhenitsyn Reader*.

The Oak and the Calf

*T*he Oak and the Calf is Solzhenitsyn's account of his life as a writer in conflict with the Soviet regime. It covers his activities from 1961, when he began plotting how to have his works legally published, to 1974, when he was expelled to the West. Thus, it is the indispensable source for information about his most hectic and heroic years. As his relationship with officialdom soured in early 1967, Solzhenitsyn started keeping a record of events for purposes of self-defense in case the authorities decided to move against him. Soon he turned his notes into "these scrappy memoirs," for which his term is "sketches." Then he added supplements in 1967, 1971,

1973, and 1974, the last section of his "agglomeration of lean-tos and annexes" being written in Switzerland. A fifth supplement, which named helpers of his, was withheld until after the Soviet Union expired, then appeared in the form of a serial publication (published in the West as a separate book, *Invisible Allies*); it has since been folded into an expanded edition of the Russian *Oak and Calf*.

The title image, drawn from a Russian proverb, alludes to the boisterous little calf (Solzhenitsyn) that keeps butting its head against a mighty oak (the regime) in a manifestly silly effort to knock the tree down. The self-deprecating title is ironic in that, despite the apparently insuperable odds against the calf, Solzhenitsyn does not in the least consider his efforts doomed to failure. Rather, he deems himself "an unshakable optimist." By the book's conclusion, "The oak has not fallen—but isn't it beginning to give just a little?" At any rate, "The calf has proved no weaker than the oak." Recurring military imagery reinforces the sense that the outcome of the battle is uncertain. After the demise of the Soviet Union, these sketches can be read as tracing one memorable strand in the chronicle of its collapse.

Solzhenitsyn identifies *Oak* as "*secondary* literature," or "literature *on* literature," and thus seems to suggest that it is of a lower order than primary literature. Yet the work's focus is in fact much more on life experiences than on literature per se. Thus, *Oak* invites the same literary strategies as does his fiction. And literary artistry is precisely what has led critics to rate *Oak* high among his corpus.

The volume starts with "The Writer Underground," writing "for the drawer" in tiny script to facilitate hiding. In the next chapter, he comes "Out of Hiding" and transmits the manuscript of *One Day in the Life of Ivan Denisovich* through intermediaries to Aleksandr Tvardovsky, esteemed editor of the leading Soviet journal, *Novy Mir*. Once "On the Surface" (chapter 3), Solzhenitsyn says he makes blunder after blunder, delaying when he should have pressed forward, denying he had anything else to submit when in fact his drawer was full, not guessing how quickly his publishing window would close. In the fourth and final chapter of the original installment, he describes himself as "The Wounded Beast," as the conflict between his integrity and the establishment's imperatives intensifies and a large cache of his papers is seized by the KGB.

As events keep cascading, Solzhenitsyn adds supplements to his record. Trying doggedly to parlay the sensational success of *One Day* into additional approved publications, he goes through ceaseless rounds of struggle with the literary and political authorities. He keeps a record of contentious meetings with members of the Soviet Writers' Union. Meanwhile, in every spare moment he continues to compose fresh text. Throughout, he remains acutely conscious of his mission as a truth-telling writer and equally aware that one false step could imperil his mission and even his life. Alternately, he revels in his successes and mercilessly admits his failures. In a chapter titled "Asphyxiation," he relates his expulsion from the Writers' Union. Then comes his wish fulfillment of receiving the Nobel Prize in 1970, the last year he says it could have been tactically useful. The excitement of "Nobeliana" leads into the "Encounter Battle" of his last years before his forced exile. Even as official wrath against him mounts, he feels stronger than ever, and he exults that "*for the very first time*, I can walk upright and shout aloud as I go out to do battle. . . . In *my* life, this is the great moment, this struggle, perhaps the reason why I have lived at all." Imagining himself "a sword made sharp to smite the unclean forces," he prays, "Grant, O Lord, that I may not break as I strike! Let me not fall from Thy hand!"

Solzhenitsyn's arrest and deportation climax the calf-and-oak story and launch one more supplement. Having outmaneuvered the authorities for years, he is caught completely off-guard by the brutally simple knock on the door. He describes himself unsparingly as "in a state of witless shock." Sitting in his cell on that night between his arrest and his forced expulsion on a flight to Germany, he quickly regains his equanimity, musing defiantly, "*You Bolsheviks are finished—there are no two ways about it.*" And he reviews his life "with detachment, as though it were already finished. I was content. It had been worthwhile." He had wanted to finish *The Red Wheel*. "But I praised God for what I had been able to achieve." This rousing fourth supplement is the book's emotional high point.

One other personage besides Solzhenitsyn receives three-dimensional characterization, namely, Aleksandr Tvardovsky; this portrait offended some of Tvardovsky's friends. In Solzhenitsyn's reckoning, relations between author and editor are sometimes rocky, but their mutual admiration is genuine. Solzhenitsyn values Tvardovsky's editorial skills and rates him "Russia's number one poet," with "a refined poetic taste" superior to the author's own. Also, Solzhenitsyn "love[s] the peasant core of the man." On the other hand, Tvardovsky's penchant for taking over all decision-making rankles Solzhenitsyn, and the editor's uncontrollable alcoholism bewilders the austere author. The main reason why Solzhenitsyn kept Tvardovsky at arm's length, however, is the editor's divided soul. He is "a poet, but also a Communist." His loyalty to the Party provides him power and luxuries, but it also turns him pusillanimous in pursuing his loyalty to Russian literature. Solzhenitsyn's Tvardovsky is a truly tragic figure.

Eighty-two pages of appendices round out the volume. These include invaluable letters, statements, interviews, and transcripts of meetings.

Text and translation: *The Oak and the Calf* (*Bodalsia telenok s dubom*) was published by YMCA Press in Paris in 1975. An expanded version, containing the material that makes up *Invisible Allies* (*Nevidimki*) and other emendations, appeared in Moscow in 1996, produced by the "Soglasie" publishing house.

The excellent English translation by H. T. Willetts (based on the Russian edition of 1975) appeared in 1980 under the Harper and Row imprint. The English translation of *Invisible Allies* was published separately.

The Mortal Danger

In 1980 Solzhenitsyn inserted himself into the scholarly discussion among America's Soviet experts with a substantial article published in the journal *Foreign Affairs* and titled "How Misconceptions about Russia Are a Threat to America." The article was promptly published as a book titled *The Mortal Danger*. A second edition of the book appended six responses and a reply by Solzhenitsyn called "The Courage to See." These responses, including a couple by established Sovietologists, were either sharply negative or angrily overwrought, except for one by an English teacher. Following hard on the heels of the tumult over the Harvard commencement address, this episode widened the chasm between Solzhenitsyn and American opinion-shapers.

Having written much about "the failure to understand the radical hostility of communism to mankind," Solzhenitsyn devotes this essay to "a second and equally prevalent mistake," which is to locate the source of contemporary Russia's travails in alleged defects in the primordial Russian character. He locates it not in nationality but in ideology. And this ideology—Marxism—is not indigenous to Russia. Out of this root error grow other errors. Westerners use "Russian" and "Soviet" interchangeably, whereas in Solzhenitsyn's view "'Russia' is to the Soviet Union as a man is to the disease afflicting him." The West sees Russians as the ruling nationality in the USSR; Solzhenitsyn sees Russians as the chief victims of the Soviets. He also castigates the scholars' "complete disregard for the spiritual life of the Russian people and its view of the world—Christianity." He spends a full section on Western reactions to *Letter to the Soviet Leaders*, which he says "simply astonished" him. His against-the-grain argument emphasizes discontinuity between tsarist Russia and the Soviet regime (though not in order to advocate tsarism) and continuity from Lenin to Stalin. The scholars' misconceptions, he argues, stem from hostility toward Russia and have contributed to blunders in American policy toward the Soviet Union.

Solzhenitsyn showed himself to be conversant with American scholarship, commenting on numerous Soviet specialists by name. But his characteristically plainspoken rhetoric displeased other members of the scholarly fraternity, who leaped to the defense of their peers. Given the academic forum, his blunt, irascible tone offended more than ever. His no-holds-barred rejoinder in "The Courage to See" was not meant to assuage wrath, and it culminated in his despair of engaging in fruitful dialogue with Western experts.

Texts and translation: The Russian text of "How Misconceptions about Russia Are a Threat to America" ("Chem grozit Amerike plokhoe ponimanie Rossii") and the rejoinder to critical comments, "The Courage to See" ("Imet' muzhestvo videt'"), first appeared in the Paris periodical *Vestnik RKhD*, nos. 131 and 132 (1980). The texts appear in vol. 9 of the Vermont *Sobranie sochinenii* and vol. 1 of *Publitsistika*.

The English translation, by Michael Nicholson and Alexis Klimoff, appears in *Foreign Affairs* (vol. 58, no. 4, and vol. 59, no. 1, both 1980), and also as a book titled *The Mortal Danger* (New York: Harper and Row, 1980). It was republished in 1982 in a second edition containing Solzhenitsyn's polemical exchange with several critics.

Templeton Lecture

The "Templeton Lecture" is Solzhenitsyn's most explicit state-ment of his Christian faith. He delivered it in London in 1983 upon receiving the Templeton Prize for Progress in Religion, an award established by financier John Templeton to fill a perceived gap in the roster of Nobel prizes. As Solzhenitsyn explains in *The Little Grain*, he had long avoided giving religious testimonies, preferring to let his faith "flow silently but incontrovertibly." His decision to overcome his reticence for this occasion grew in part from being impressed by the aptness with which the Templeton Foundation's invitation cited passages of his that comported with the purposes of the prize. Notable among these citations was his "Prayer," which, to his initial consternation, had been released without his permission by an impetuous confidante, Elizaveta Voronyanskaya. Later, as the widely circulated prayer generated many appreciative responses, he came to feel gratitude, concluding that by her willful act "she had served as an instrument of God's will." Precisely because writing about religion was unfamiliar to him, this composition had the happy effect of serving "as a step toward greater understanding for myself." In particular, he sharpened his "view of our earthly life as a step in the development of life eternal."[1] This growth in religious self-awareness is of a piece with the impact on him of Father Al-exander Schmemann's 1970 essay characterizing Solzhenitsyn as a "Christian writer" whose works were imbued with the theological "triune intuition" of creation, fall, and redemption. Solzhenitsyn remarked that this essay "explained me to myself" and "formulated important traits of Christianity which I could not have formulated myself."[2]

Even in the "Templeton Lecture," Solzhenitsyn eschews inti-mate revelations, focusing on the general human condition in the twentieth century. He proposes a "determined quest for the warm hand of God," rather than merely emphasizing his own personal quest. His understanding of God is neither deistic nor pantheistic but biblical and orthodox. God's providence is personal: "The Creator constantly, day in and day out, participates in the life of each of us." It is also universal: "And in the life of our entire planet the divine Spirit surely moves with no less force." Although the meatiest content comes in the culminating five paragraphs of the lecture, the most memorable part comes in the opening movement. The author recalls that as a child he heard his elders explain "the great disasters that had befallen Russia" in four simple words: "Men have forgotten God." Now, in adulthood, he uses the same four words to identify "the principal trait of the *entire* twentieth century." The whole world suffers from "the flaw of a consciousness lacking all divine dimension." For the Marxist-Leninists governing his homeland, "hatred of God is the principal driving force, more fundamental than all their political and economic pretensions." The West, too, he asserts, "is experiencing a drying up of religious consciousness" and "is ineluctably slipping toward the abyss." Characteristically, amid his warnings Solzhenitsyn injects a note of hope, in this case insisting that communism, though formidable, "is doomed never to vanquish Christianity." The spiritual insights distilled in this speech constitute the bedrock of Solzhenitsyn's worldview.

Text and translation: The Russian text of the lecture ("Templtonovskaia lektsiia") appeared first in *Vestnik RKhD*, no. 139 (1983). It is reproduced in vol. 1 of *Publitsistika*.

The English translation, by Alexis Klimoff, appeared in *The* [London] *Times*, May 11, 1983, p. 10b, and was widely reprinted on both sides of the Atlantic. It is reprinted in *The Solzhenitsyn Reader*.

Rebuilding Russia

*R*ebuilding Russia is Solzhenitsyn's effort in 1990 to advise his nation about how to manage what he perceives is its fast-approaching post-Soviet condition. Published in two mass-circulation periodicals based in Moscow, *Komsomolskaya pravda* and *Literaturnaya gazeta*, and distributed in some 27 million copies, the essay was the first Solzhenitsyn work since 1966 to make its initial appearance in his homeland. (As mentioned in the "Life" chapter, a few works had been republished in the preceding two years.) Given that its genre is a sketch of a pragmatic political program, *Rebuilding Russia* is a sequel to the 1973 *Letter to the Soviet Leaders,* though the audience addressed is now the citizenry at large, as was the case with "Live Not by Lies!" While even in 1990 very few expected the Soviet Union to collapse, Solzhenitsyn was counseling how to avoid being crushed beneath the rubble of the crumbling system. His counsel is reformist rather than revolutionary, as is conveyed by the title's operative term *obustroit',* which intimates "fixing up" or "refurbishing." Drawing upon a lifetime of study and reflection, he shows himself open to learning from the West but eager to find usable models within Russia's own historical experience. A calm, earnest tone shows his respect for his audience and comports with the fundamental moderation of his proposals.

The essay's two halves address immediate and long-term needs, respectively. Faced with the impending breakup of the union of fifteen republics that made up the USSR, Solzhenitsyn quickly plunges into the tangled question of nationalities. He suggests that the East Slavic peoples—Russians, Ukrainians, and Belorussians—join in a new union. The other republics must become independent. Ownership of land must be privatized, though gradually. The economy must be transformed from central control to free enterprise, but with an accompanying social safety net. The state should encourage "normal families," with special attention paid to the "disastrous plight of women." The schools are of "equally urgent concern." The first half closes with an application of the author's familiar themes of repentance and self-limitation to the transition to a free Russia.

The primary long-term concern discussed in the essay's second half is the form of government. Solzhenitsyn chooses democracy over monarchy or authoritarianism ("aristocracy"). But democracy can take on many guises, and Solzhenitsyn painstakingly sorts through various options in search of the form that would best suit Russia. Solzhenitsyn sees democracy not as an end in itself but as a means to achieving freedom. Thus, democracy should be developed from the bottom up, not imposed by fiat from above, and the outcome should be the decentralization of power. Also, the new democracy should be implemented gradually. Direct representation ought to occur within the smallest political units, where voters know the candidates personally. The old *zemstvo* system provides a native model of grassroots democracy to emulate. Locally elected officials would then choose their best members to represent them at the next tier up, until after perhaps four siftings the national level is reached. The indirectness of this representation has much in common with early American practice, though Solzhenitsyn outdoes the American model in terms of democracy *per se* by advocating direct popular election of the nation's president. In all, Solzhenitsyn shows himself to be a cautious, even reluctant democrat in the vein of Churchill, who famously described democracy as the worst form of government except for all the others. Unlike apostles of the religion of democracy, he sees that democracy needs to be safeguarded, so far as possible, from the human nature that can corrupt it.

This essay was Solzhenitsyn's first step in immersing himself in the new Russia's public life, with more to follow upon his return home. Western responses to this essay fell along predictable lines, predetermined by the commentators' political views and their attitudes toward the author. Russian reactions were profuse; *Komsomolskaya pravda* received more than a thousand letters of response. Not all commentators, at home or abroad, read the essay carefully; Mikhail Gorbachev even claimed that it propounded monarchy. On the other hand, numerous other Russians engaged the text seriously and sometimes enthusiastically. But the initial flash of interest faded rapidly amid the hectic tumble of events in the early 1990s. While regional and local leaders showed considerable interest in decentralization when they met with Solzhenitsyn, the essay has not had the influence he had hoped for.

> **Text and translation:** Apart from the serial publications mentioned (both dated September 18, 1990), *Rebuilding Russia* (*Kak nam obustroit' Rossiiu?*) appeared in brochure form published by YMCA Press in Paris in 1990. It is reprinted in vol. 1 of *Publitsistika.*
>
> The English translation, by Alexis Klimoff, appeared under the title *Rebuilding Russia* in 1991 (New York: Farrar, Straus and Giroux).

Playing upon the Strings of Emptiness

This speech, composed by Solzhenitsyn for the National Arts Club of New York City, is one of his two forays into literary theory, the other being the *Nobel Lecture.* In January 1993 this exclusive club, established in the nineteenth century to promote public interest in the arts, bestowed upon him its medal of honor for literature. The writer's wife accepted the medal on his behalf, his son Ignat read the text, and the *New York Times* affixed to its printed version the coarse and clumsy title "The Relentless Cult of Novelty and How It Wrecked the Century." (Later, the author supplied his own preferred title.) The speech focuses on the role of literature in society and demonstrates the author's grasp of contemporary cultural currents.

Solzhenitsyn advises artists to avoid extremes, whether that of disdainfully rejecting tradition or that of dully imitating the classics. With the same spirit of moderation that prompts him to encourage taking a middle way in politics, he promotes for literary art a middle way that retains "the necessary equilibrium between tradition and the search for the new." (Solzhenitsyn's approach is akin to T. S. Eliot's in "Tradition and the Individual Talent.") The twentieth century has repeatedly upset the desired equilibrium by indulging in "a falsely understood 'avant-gardism'" that has typically nurtured destructiveness. Early in the century, Russia's "futurists," with their manifesto titled "A Slap in the Face of Public Taste," had first foretold and then joined "the most *physically* destructive revolution of the twentieth century." Now, late in the century, the same nihilistic impulse manifests itself in the cultural phenomenon known as postmodernism. The century's "spiritual illness" afflicts both the art and the life of the whole world, East and West. Art cannot aspire to be good or pure, and life cannot be based on high moral and ethical ideals, so long as society accepts that "there is no God, there is no truth, the universe is chaotic, all is relative." Although humanity seems to be on a "downward slide," Solzhenitsyn's characteristic optimism brings this speech to the hopeful conclusion that a new generation may well reinvigorate "the great cultural tradition of the foregoing centuries" and thereby contribute to resuscitating society's spiritual health.

> **Text and translation:** The Russian text of what Solzhenitsyn originally titled "Acceptance Speech at the Award Ceremony of the National Arts Club" ("Otvetnoe slovo na prisuzhdenii literaturnoi nagrady Amerikanskogo National'nogo Kluba Iskusstv") was first published in *Novyi mir*, 1993, no. 4. It is reproduced with the current title ("Igra na strunakh pustoty") in A. I. Solzhenitsyn, *Na vozvrate dykhaniia* (Moscow: Vagrius, 2004).

The English translation, by Ignat and Stephan Solzhenitsyn, appeared in the *New York Times Book Review*, February 7, 1993. It appears in *The Solzhenitsyn Reader* under the title the author came to prefer, "Playing upon the Strings of Emptiness."

We have ceased to see the Purpose

When Solzhenitsyn traveled to Europe in 1993 to say his farewells to the West, he delivered his most substantial valediction to the International Academy of Philosophy, a small Roman Catholic institution in Liechtenstein. In part, this speech revisits major themes presented fifteen years earlier at Harvard University, but the tectonic geopolitical rearrangement wrought by the Soviet Union's disappearance relaxes the tense urgency of the tone exhibited at Harvard. For the rest, a speech that begins with attention to politics and intellectual history finishes with reflections on meaning in individual lives as offered by a man in his mid-seventies. (These reflections govern the after-the-fact choice of title.) As one (Orthodox) Christian speaks to other (Catholic) Christians about the "eternal questions," notably including how to approach death, the tone becomes fittingly mellowed. All in all, this is a good essay for Solzhenitsyn neophytes to read first.

As at Harvard, so at Liechtenstein, Solzhenitsyn takes aim at the Enlightenment. One error of that project that he dwells on is the tendency to detach political activity from the imperatives of morality. The resulting human catastrophes of the twentieth century reveal the folly of this decoupling. These same "cannibalistic horrors," along with today's awareness of the earth's limited natural resources, point to the failure of the Enlightenment's doctrine of infinite progress. These criticisms were, however, not part of a wholesale attack on Western values. Solzhenitsyn singles out for special praise the West's "historically unique stability of civic life under the rule of law—a hard-won stability which grants independence and space to every private citizen." Still, who could have imagined that the optimism of the Enlightenment would issue in totalitarianism? Only Dostoevsky foresaw this end. And the anthropocentric humanism that lies at the root of the Enlightenment project as a whole fosters a sense of "helplessness" and "intellectual disarray" at "the loss of a clear and calm attitude toward *death*." As a way forward, Solzhenitsyn proposes that we recover "the golden key of Self-Restraint," a concept of premodern provenance. The theme of self-limitation, which he has sounded for some thirty years, becomes ever more insistent in his late essays. This theme is flatly at odds with the idea of progress as defined by the Enlightenment, but it can be invoked in a way that actually redefines progress by shifting its ground from man-centeredness to a renewed "awareness of a Whole and Higher Authority above us—and the altogether forgotten sense of humility before this Entity." In that case, the "one true Progress" is "the sum total of the spiritual progresses of individuals; the degree of self-perfection in the course of their lives."

In sum, the Liechtenstein speech knits together themes found in other Solzhenitsyn essays: the failure of the Enlightenment project asserted in the *Harvard Address*, the value of self-limitation propounded in "Repentance and Self-Limitation in the Life of Nations" (in *From under the Rubble*) and also in *Rebuilding Russia*, and the need to acknowledge God above, formulated with especial clarity in the "Templeton Lecture."

Text and translation: The Russian text, originally titled in the published version as "Speech at the International Academy of Philosophy" ("Rech' v Mezhdunarodnoi Akademii Filosofii") was published in *Komsomol'skaia pravda*, September 17, 1993.

It is reprinted with the current title ("My perestali videt' Tsel'") in A. I. Solzhenitsyn, *Na vozvrate dykhaniia* (Moscow: Vagrius, 2004).

The English version, translated by Yermolai Solzhenitsyn, appears in the same binding with the writer's *"The Russian Question" at the End of the Twentieth Century* (New York: Farrar, Straus and Giroux, 1995). It is included in *The Solzhenitsyn Reader.*

"The Russian Question" at the End of the Twentieth Century

“*The Russian Question" at the End of the Twentieth Century* is a succinct statement of how Russia has arrived at what Solzhenitsyn calls "the Great Catastrophe of the 1990s" and how it can best emerge from it. Composed in March 1994, a mere two months before Solzhenitsyn returned home, this essay is designed to help the nation get its bearings during a turbulent time. It does not make programmatic proposals for Russia's post-Soviet future, that task having been done in *Rebuilding Russia* four years earlier. And whereas Solzhenitsyn devoted more than six thousand large pages of *The Red Wheel* to scrutinizing Russian history in the four fateful years of 1914–17, in *"The Russian Question"* he allots only a hundred small pages to a broad-brush sketch of four centuries of that history. This essay presupposes substantial familiarity with the sweep of Russian history and is thus probably inappropriate for neophytes in this subject, despite the importance of its themes.

Although Solzhenitsyn had reason to feel vindicated by the demise of the Soviet Union, he considers the 1990s calamitous in that

Russia was emerging from under the rubble of communism in the worst possible way. In his view, Russia is now enduring its third "Time of Troubles," the others being the seventeenth-century turmoil for which the label was invented and the troubled time centered on 1917. The thesis of Solzhenitsyn's polemic is that Russia, if it is to recuperate from its nearly fatal sickness, needs to attend to its internal development. This process will require prolonged, undistracted calm, a condition that Russia has never enjoyed. Again and again, its leaders have embroiled the nation in foreign adventures, unfailingly to Russia's disadvantage. Along the way, Russia has adopted foreign concepts and models, such as Marxism, with disastrous consequences. The most melancholy of these consequences has been what Solzhenitsyn labels "counterselection," the systematic liquidation over three generations of the best of Russia's human capital. Soviet rule has left Russia's civic resources severely depleted. With the schools in disarray, with government officials ineffectual at best and openly criminal at worst, with life-expectancy and birth rates plummeting, the demoralization of the citizenry is so profound that "the Russian question" has now coalesced into stark alternatives: "Shall our people *be* or *not be?*" Yet despite all, Solzhenitsyn believes that a nucleus of spiritually healthy people has survived, and to them he addresses his closing exhortation: "We must build a *moral* Russia, or none at all—it would not then matter anyhow."

> **Text and translation:** *"Russkii vopros" k kontsu XX veka* first appeared in *Novyi mir*, 1994, no. 7. It is reprinted in *Publitsistika*, vol. 1.
>
> *"The Russian Question" at the End of the Twentieth Century*, translated by Yermolai Solzhenitsyn, appeared in 1995 under the Farrar, Straus and Giroux imprint.

The Little Grain

While the subtitle of Solzhenitsyn's memoir of his twenty years in the West, "Sketches of Exile," is a straightforward indication of its contents, the title needs some comment. In Russian, the memoir is named *Ugodilo zërnyshko promezh dvukh zhernovov*, an aphorism whose folksy tone might be rendered by "As luck would have it, the little grain landed smack between two millstones."[1] (*The Little Grain*, then, can serve as the provisional English heading for this still-untranslated work.) The "little grain" is a metaphor for the autobiographical protagonist who is subjected to harsh criticism in the West while at the same time being vituperated in the Soviet Union. There is an element of self-irony here, since the image suggests naïve unawareness of the difficulties ahead. Some self-deprecating notes had also been sounded in the title of Solzhenitsyn's earlier autobiographical sketches, published in English as *The Oak and the Calf*. That title is an abbreviated version of another Russian aphorism, which, translated literally, reads "A calf butted an oak," thereby evoking an image of a rambunctious but foolishly immature creature knocking against the colossus of Soviet power in the silly hope of bringing it down.

Despite the common aphoristic provenance, however, the two titles exhibit a difference of emphasis that is remarkably consistent with the respective orientation of each text. In *The Oak and the Calf*, the image of the sprightly young "calf" is in playful tension with the vigorous and crafty tactician depicted on its pages. In contrast, the image encapsulated in *The Little Grain* (once we consider the full original phrasing) suggests naïveté combined with a sense of unjust injury. And, indeed, Solzhenitsyn's text features more than a few bitter pages on the avalanche of uninformed, sharply hostile, and at times deliberately malicious Western criticism that he had to endure in the two decades between his expulsion from and return to Russia. It was one thing to be attacked by the Soviet state, from which he could expect nothing better, but quite another when—simultaneously—gross misrepresentations of his views were offered by influential Western commentators, and when the Western media mindlessly recycled charges of Solzhenitsyn's alleged "dangerous nationalism," "opposition to democracy," and "theocratic tendencies." Even the US Senate got into the act in 1985, holding short-lived hearings on a report that US-financed Radio Liberty was contributing to anti-Semitism by broadcasting a reading of *August 1914*. (The charge was quickly dropped as devoid of substance.) Criticisms of this kind, together with dismay at Michael Scammell's biography, which, in the writer's opinion, presented a seriously distorted picture of him and his works, constituted the essence of the second—Western—"millstone" grinding away at his good name. Though he reports on much of this with the sarcastic verve familiar to readers of *The Oak and the Calf*, it is clear that the attacks rankled.

Yet throughout this entire period, Solzhenitsyn, as *The Little Grain* testifies, exhibited a genuine appreciation for most aspects of the West. He admired the smooth functioning of local self-government in Switzerland as well as in New England, expressed deep reverence for the infinitely rich cultural legacies permeating the European countries he crisscrossed, and had high praise for the energetic efficiency he witnessed in America. It was this admirable—but, in his view, vulnerable—West that he wished to warn against the dangers of encroaching Soviet influence. But his admonitions fell on deaf ears, at least in his opinion, and *The Little Grain* documents a gradual decline of Solzhenitsyn's faith in his ability to influence his Western contemporaries. In any case, Solzhenitsyn is explicitly on record in *The Little Grain* to the effect that he could no longer subscribe to the ringing assertions about the power of literature to transmit experience across time and space which he had himself formulated in his *Nobel Lecture*.

The Little Grain is a rich conglomerate of many themes, and in some respects it resembles a diary that chronicles the major events in which Solzhenitsyn played a part after 1974. Sections of the text are pure travelogue, with vivid descriptions of journeys to various

North American locales and to assorted countries in Europe and the Far East, in most cases related with panache and occasional flashes of humor. There are fascinating descriptions of one-on-one meetings with prominent individuals, including British Prime Minister Margaret Thatcher (1983) and Pope John Paul II (1993), detailed accounts of public speeches at occasions such as the Harvard University commencement (1978) and the Templeton Prize ceremony (1983), comments on TV appearances in which Solzhenitsyn took part, and explanations of the circumstances that led to the writing of particular works. Some of the important speeches and statements he produced during this period are discussed in detail elsewhere in the present volume, while in *The Little Grain* Solzhenitsyn frequently gives direct information on the themes he wished to emphasize. There are also passages on "domestic" matters, such as the efforts made to assure a proper education for the writer's three sons, and numerous accolades to his extraordinary wife, Natalia Dmitrievna, who has been able to combine the roles of wife, mother, and household manager with the functions of literary adviser, editor, and typesetter,[2] apart from the burdens of heading the Russian Social Fund and acting as Solzhenitsyn's public representative in numerous contexts.

Much space is allotted in *The Little Grain* to Solzhenitsyn's evolving views of the processes that led to the collapse of the Soviet Union. His attitude passed from skepticism about Gorbachev's early steps, to hope that the reforms were for real, to growing apprehension that the movement would become as chaotically destructive as the February Revolution in 1917, and finally to near despair at seeing his worst fears realized. In this connection one can undoubtedly speak of a challenge to Solzhenitsyn's view of his role as writer. While he may have abandoned his hope of affecting the West, his relationship to Russia was different. In Russia, after all, he had achieved a truly massive effect through works such as *One Day in the Life of Ivan Denisovich* and *The Gulag Archipelago*. But now, amid the clamorous chaos of the Gorbachev era, the reforming potential of literature, that special power that had made it possible for "one word" to "outweigh the whole world" (to quote the ending of Solzhenitsyn's *Nobel Lecture*), seemed suddenly to have become impotent. A reading on the Voice of America (in the late 1980s) of *March 1917*, the third "knot" of *The Red Wheel*, specially abridged for the occasion by Solzhenitsyn in the hope of warning his compatriots of the dangers ahead, evoked only minimal response. Perhaps even more disappointing to the writer, his "Rebuilding Russia" essay (1990) was ignored or dismissed as irrelevant despite its enormous distribution. In *The Little Grain* Solzhenitsyn confesses that for him this particular disregard served to confirm the rightness of his decision to forswear Russian politics: "What I could not attain by my pen, I would never be able to achieve by shouting orders." Nothing—and no effort of his—seemed capable of impeding Russia's slide into its "third Time of Troubles," and it is this realization that casts a gloomy shadow over the closing chapters of Solzhenitsyn's work.

> **Text:** *Ugodilo zërnyshko promezh dvukh zhernovov* was serialized in seven installments in *Novyi mir* between 1998 and 2003. A book edition has been promised, but no English translation has yet appeared.

Invisible Allies

W hen Solzhenitsyn published *The Oak and the Calf*, the autobiographical account of his writing career, he omitted a substantial section in which he named helpers of his who would be in jeopardy if the Soviet authorities knew of their activities. This material was serialized under the title *Invisible Allies* after the Soviet Union disappeared, and in 1996 it was included in an expanded edition of *The Oak and the Calf*, where it takes its rightful place as the Fifth Supplement. The definitive biography of Solzhenitsyn, whenever it is written, will draw heavily on this information. With its revelation of previously unknown episodes and the *dramatis personae* engaged in them, *Invisible Allies* significantly enhances the sense that the man's life, in and of itself, took on the contours of a work of art. Among the correctives, this account puts to rest the notion that Solzhenitsyn operated as a lone wolf.

Invisible Allies comprises fourteen sketches, in most cases one person per sketch. All told, these accounts pay homage to more than a hundred helpers, with forty persons in the second echelon of the network of allies presented in a single chapter. As a novelist, Solzhenitsyn has always been especially strong at creating characters, with the plot usually playing a secondary role. The plot line handed to him by his conflict with the regime needed no heightening here, however. And since he was moving among people who would lay down their life for a friend, he had rich material upon which to exercise his powers of characterization. In *Invisible Allies* he sketches personalities with quick, assured strokes, leaving out all inessentials, yet with a keen eye for those telling idiosyncrasies that bring a literary portrait to life. Participants in his network of support were involved in all phases of his work. They typed out his long manuscripts with as many carbon copies as the typewriter could accommodate, in order to generate enough copies to ensure safekeeping. Then came the transporting, the hiding, the tracking of the typescripts. Then there were the emendations and additions—

and more typing and retyping. What now is done with a keystroke on a computer took weeks and months. And every step had to be out of view of the Unsleeping Eye of the KGB. Meanwhile, the author kept turning out fresh text. In addition to the making, there was sometimes the unmaking. If copies became obsolete or a potential leak was feared, a given cache had to be destroyed. Once a conduit opened to the West, more purging of duplicate copies would follow. The light of fires runs like a leitmotif through the book, as manuscripts were burned. Yet the whole of Solzhenitsyn's large corpus survives.

Most of Solzhenitsyn's helpers were women. They were fearless and dedicated. (The reader can be forgiven for wondering how many of them loved Solzhenitsyn, for in some way they all did.) The longest sketch describes the author's right-hand intimate, Elena Tsezarevna Chukovskaya, granddaughter of the famous critic and writer of children's literature, Kornei Chukovsky. Their collaboration entailed the pain of gradually discerning a serious conflict in their worldviews; but the complicated friendship of these two indefatigable workers, though stretched thin, did not break. One of the helpers, Natalia Dmitrievna Svetlova, became the author's second wife. The highly discreet narration of their love story is among the book's most memorable sections. Some of the personages are real-life prototypes of such fictional characters as Potapov in *The First Circle* and the Kadmins of *Cancer Ward*. Others are old gulag friends, most notably two Estonians, Arnold Susi and Georgi Tenno, who helped provide a safe haven in a house in the Estonian countryside for composing *The Gulag Archipelago*.

The writer himself is necessarily the volume's central character, and one of the highlights is the intensely dramatic story of his furtive work on *Gulag*, his most dangerous book. At his Estonian "Hiding Place" during the winters of 1965–66 and 1966–67, the ever-driven author outdid himself in the feverish pace of his writing. The cumulative 146 days of labor—and it is typical of him to specify the number exactly—marked for him "the highest point in my feelings of victory and of isolation from the world." Never once during the composition process was the whole manuscript sitting available on his desk—for fear that if the KGB would confiscate that cache, he would never be able to reconstruct the whole work. Despite the high stakes entailed in his underground life, Solzheni-tsyn boyishly relishes the conspiratorial game. The exhilaration of outwitting deadly but lumbering foes creates an uncommon camaraderie among all of his intimates. Commentators on the Harvard commencement address were baffled by Solzhenitsyn's insistence that he could not recommend the West as a model to his own country because people back home had "been through a spiritual training far in advance of Western experience."[1] The characters depicted in *Invisible Allies* are the kind of people he had in mind. The network expanded to include foreigners, journalists among them. They, too, maintained the trust, and their fidelity amplifies a phenomenon mentioned in *Gulag* that was curious even to the author. Some almost mystical "spiritual relay," or "sensor relay," unerringly guided him in choosing confidants during seventeen years of prison, exile, and underground operations. "I recklessly revealed myself to dozens of people—and didn't make a misstep even once."[2]

Reading *Invisible Allies* is greatly enriched by reading in tandem *The Solzhenitsyn Files*, the now-declassified records of the efforts by top Soviet officials to handle the recalcitrant author. These two volumes chart the same confrontation from opposite sides—versions written by the calf and by the oak, as it were. Among the many perverse pleasures the regime's files afford is the realization of how successfully Solzhenitsyn's allies remained invisible, as the writer and his confederates outfoxed the befuddled authorities.

Invisible Allies ends with a sensational appendix containing the reminiscences of a repentant KGB man who participated in a failed operation to assassinate Solzhenitsyn in 1971.

Text and translation: *Invisible Allies* (*Nevidimki*) was originally serialized in *Novyi mir* in 1991. With some further additions it was incorporated into a new edition of *Bodalsia telenok s dubom* (*The Oak and the Calf*), Moscow: Soglasie, 1996.

The English translation, by Michael Nicholson and Alexis Klimoff, is based on the *Novyi mir* text. It appeared in the US in 1995 (Washington: Counterpoint) and in the UK in 1997 (London: Harvill Press).

The Red Wheel

Solzhenitsyn has always viewed his multivolume epic on the Russian Revolution as the most significant undertaking of his writing career, one that in his eyes outranked in importance the works on the camp-and-prison theme that had brought him world fame. As Solzhenitsyn makes clear in *The Oak and the Calf,* he looked upon his writings on Soviet repression as a compelling moral obligation, and in the particular case of *The Gulag Archipelago* as his "duty to the dead," but at the same time he believed it to be a digression from what he saw as his main task. The point is made with a striking metaphor. The earlier works, he writes, were "a burden that had grown as I had rolled it along year by year," a burden that Solzhenitsyn very much yearned "to heave over the hill" so that nothing more would lie between him and what he deemed "the most important thing in my life: *R-17.*"[1]

R-17 (clearly an abbreviation for something like "Revolution 1917") was Solzhenitsyn's working title for what eventually came to be named *The Red Wheel.* His plan to undertake a detailed study of the causes and consequences of the Russian Revolution began to take written shape back in 1937, when the teenaged Solzhenitsyn, at the time a student in his first year of university and a fervent convert to Marxism, resolved to investigate what he then considered to be the most significant—and salutary—event in world history. He set out with research on the catastrophic defeat of a Russian army corps at the outset of World War I, producing a text so thorough that it proved useful to the mature author more than three decades later. University studies, service in the army, arrest, imprisonment, exile, and a near-fatal bout with cancer followed, all contributing to a radical shift in Solzhenitsyn's views. These experiences also prevented him from turning his full-time attention to his chosen project, yet in no way did they attenuate his desire to delve into what he now viewed as a malevolent and calamitous rupture in Russian history. The subsequent decade was largely consumed by his tense and risky struggle with the regime and the writing of the works he would later categorize as his duty to the fallen. And even though Solzhenitsyn collected materials and made substantial notes throughout the years,[2] it was only in June 1968, when he received word that a microfilm copy of *The Gulag Archipelago* had been safely carried across the border to the West, that he judged himself finally free of his obligations and ready to devote his full energy to the long-delayed undertaking.

The Red Wheel is a cycle of historical narratives, encompassing ten volumes and totaling some six thousand pages in the Russian edition. To say that it is based on prodigious research is to understate the matter. Solzhenitsyn, whose capacity for work is legendary, spent many years scouring the available printed sources, interviewing surviving witnesses, and (during his American decades) searching archives and collecting unpublished memoirs as well as making much use of the Inter-Library Loan system in order to obtain rare editions and microfilms of period newspapers. The majority of this historical material he has transmuted into a mode that is distinctly literary, essentially in the tradition of the historical novel, albeit with substantial peculiarities that will be discussed presently.

The cycle is subtitled "A Narrative in Discrete Periods of Time." As was true in the case of the subtitle to *The Gulag Archipelago*, Solzhenitsyn's wording points explicitly to the methodology he adopted in structuring the cycle. The key principle involves rejecting any attempt to portray the full sequence of historical events. Instead, Solzhenitsyn has focused, in extraordinary detail, on relatively brief and sharply demarcated segments of historical time, making no effort to fill in the gaps between these discrete periods. The text allocated to each temporal segment is designated a "knot" (*uzel*), a term derived from the mathematical concept of "nodal point," and in the present context referring to intervals in historical time when the interconnected issues of the day become aligned in a manner that proves decisive to the course of events.[3]

The initial plan for the cycle envisaged five acts subdivided into twenty knots and covering the period between August 1914 and the spring of 1922, with the latter date marking the final consolidation of Bolshevik rule. In addition, five epilogues were to bring the story up to 1945. This plan proved to be vastly overambitious, however, especially in view of the detailed approach that characterizes Solzhenitsyn's method, and he decided to call a stop after producing four knots in ten volumes. The first three knots together constitute Act I of the narrative (with the series title *Revolution*) and focus on events that prepared the ground for the Bolshevik coup: Knot I—*August 1914* (2 vols., 1983),[4] Knot II—*November 1916* (2 vols., 1984), and Knot III—*March 1917* (4 vols., 1986–88). This is followed by Act II (series title *Democracy*),[5] represented by Knot IV—*April 1917* (2 vols., 1991), with the last of these volumes containing an appendix with a detailed outline of the originally planned twenty-knot sequence.

Like *The Gulag Archipelago* before it, *The Red Wheel* tests the limits of conventional genre classification. While parts of it, especially in Knots I and II, are presented in the traditional format of the historical novel, a significant—and in the case of Knots III and IV, predominant—proportion of the text steps outside the standard canons of that genre to focus at length on historical figures who exhibit no narrative links to the fictional characters. They include Tsar Nicholas II and his strong-willed wife, Lenin, Alexander Kerensky, and dozens of actual military and political actors of the day, all of whom are presented in terms of what might be designated as dramatized history. These sections, moreover, have no fictive intent whatever, with the actions, words, and thoughts of each of the depicted individuals being grounded in the research that had occupied Solzhenitsyn for decades. Yet even this mode proved incapable of absorbing the immense amount of material that Solzhenitsyn wished to present, and the writer repeatedly digresses into densely written third-person excursuses on historical and political circumstances that he considers crucial to an understanding of the state of affairs. There is, finally, the telling fact that in the last two knots, the fictional characters introduced in the earlier knots become almost peripheral to the narrative. The general movement away from all fictional constructs is actually consistent with the approach stated in Solzhenitsyn's subtitle, for the unbridged chronological gaps between the knots are in fundamental conflict with the literary demands of character development.

In stylistic terms *The Red Wheel* exhibits features characteristic of Solzhenitsyn's earlier work but includes some new literary devices. A prominent example of the former is the "polyphonic" technique, whereby individual characters are given the opportunity to carry the narrative point of view in the section (usually chapter) of the text where they are the principal actors. This device is used throughout Solzhenitsyn's historical cycle and has an especially striking effect in Knot III, where shifts of perspective follow one another in rapid succession due to the brevity of most chapters, thereby accentuating the rising tide of disruption and chaos that is the key ingredient in Solzhenitsyn's vision of revolutionary turmoil.

Among the stylistic innovations of *The Red Wheel,* the most significant is the manner in which the writer has interspersed his prose with diverse materials that are visually set off from the main text—documents in boldface, historical retrospectives in eight-point font, collages of excerpts from the press of the time set in a variety of styles and sizes, "screen sequences" arranged in columns of brief phrases intended to mimic cinematic effects, transcripts of Duma sessions in condensed form interspersed with authorial comment, and Russian proverbs printed entirely in capital letters. Solzhenitsyn demonstrates special fondness for these pithy verbal constructions, and some chapters of *The Red Wheel* conclude with free-standing proverbs that provide a kind of "folk judgment" on the preceding text. A case could be made for comparing the effect produced with that of the chorus in Greek tragedy.

The major thematic concerns of *The Red Wheel* can be stated summarily. Central to the cycle is the question of whether one loves Russia. On one side are those whose sense of organic connection to the land and people causes them to take an active role in helping and defending their increasingly embattled homeland, whether on the level of Prime Minister Stolypin's struggle to institute desperately needed systemic reforms or in such instinctive acts as the decision of a would-be pacifist to enlist at the outset of World War I because he "feels sorry for Russia." On the other side are individuals obsessed by ideology-induced hatred or blinded by self-interest who willingly or unwittingly contribute to the Russian catastrophe. The further the cycle progresses, the less resistance is offered to the surging forces of revolution that Solzhenitsyn has linked with the title image of a wheel. The wheel is conceived in almost cosmic terms,[6] but in physical descriptions it is reinforced by images of actual wheels, as when (in a screen sequence) a wheel tears loose from a careening field ambulance and speeds threateningly toward the camera, growing larger and larger and seeming to "crush everything in its path."[7]

August 1914

Knot I is a study in the manifold weaknesses of the ancien régime, and the writer has chosen to focus the text on two specific historical tragedies, the annihilation of a Russian army corps in 1914 in the battle of Tannenberg, and the assassination of Prime Minister Stolypin three years earlier. In Solzhenitsyn's view, these events were profoundly symptomatic and therefore crucial to an understanding of Russia's slide toward the catastrophe of 1917. Indeed, he posits a direct link to later historical developments, asserting that the military debacle in East Prussia had a baleful psychological impact on the Russian army's subsequent performance in the war and that the death of Stolypin deprived Russia of the one statesman who could have kept the country from getting involved in the disastrous conflict in the first place.[8] Solzhenitsyn's polemic with Tolstoyan fatalism comes to the fore in this context. As the writer has taken pains to document in minute detail, the disaster suffered by the Russians at Tannenberg could easily have been prevented or even reversed at many points in the course of engagement, were it not for the stubborn obtuseness and scandalous irresponsibility of the military command. In similar fashion he shows that the murder of Stolypin could have been averted without great difficulty if the professional level of the security organization had been up to barest minimum standards. Nothing was inevitable, history was perfectly open-ended, and everywhere actions (or non-actions) of concrete individuals determined the development of events.

August 1914 indicates very explicitly that the major contributing factor to the malaise permeating Russian life was the corrupting influence of the court, where a well-meaning but weak-willed, shortsighted, and hopelessly tradition-bound tsar had allowed or even encouraged suave nonentities to rise to positions of great responsibility. As Solzhenitsyn sees it, nepotism and favoritism had become so engrained in the upper echelons of power that a fine general like Martos seems to be a rare exception, and the emergence of an outstanding statesman like Stolypin is referred to as a "miracle of Russian history."

In Knot I, as elsewhere in the *Red Wheel* epic, Solzhenitsyn dwells bitterly on the unrealized hopes and missed opportunities that have figured with heartrending frequency in twentieth-century Russian history. The failure in war of General Samsonov, an admirably honest and well-meaning man who is at the same time humiliatingly ineffectual, and who is shamefully abandoned by his superiors, epitomizes the failings of the national machinery in which he plays his tragic part. Samsonov embodies many of the honorable values of traditional Russia, but also some of its faults, and thus his suicide symbolizes the imminent end of the old order. The author's palpable frustration over Russia's national breakdown is personified to a considerable extent in a fictional character named Georgi Vorotyntsev, a colonel in the Russian army. Presented as a witness of many of the attitudes and events that are contributing to the country's drift toward the revolutionary precipice, Vorotyntsev is somewhat like a visitor to the past who emerges from a time machine but is incapable of changing the events that history has recorded. For although Vorotyntsev is not explicitly armed with the historical hindsight of the author, he is nevertheless the direct bearer of Solzhenitsyn's distress, even despair, at the events described. The tension between what did not have to happen and what did in fact happen energizes the whole narrative and gives it its tragic coloration.

November 1916

Knot II picks up the story after a more than two-year-long hiatus. The time interval addressed in the knot is a period in which there are no military or political events as dramatic as those described in Knot I, although the scandal set off by a scurrilous attack on the Empress in Pavel Milyukov's Duma speech has serious consequences. Still, the primary focus is on the listlessness and foreboding that accompany the anticipation of some imminent disaster. Squeezed by war abroad and revolutionary ferment at home, Russia needs action in its defense, but no one takes the requisite initiative. Intrinsic to this knot is the burden of writing compellingly about a period in which not much happens. In rendering the atmosphere of oppressive stagnancy, Solzhenitsyn is once again making the point that the revolution was not inevitable. Inactivity has its consequences; the action needed to save Russia was not taken, but it could have been.

Solzhenitsyn juxtaposes the unresolved political and social tensions of the time with the equally inconclusive and dispiriting marital crises and destructive amorous entanglements that constitute a major part of the fictional parts of the novel. The principal one involves Vorotyntsev, who had come to Petrograd in order to meet with a powerful politician who is as frustrated as Vorotyntsev by Nicholas II's ineffectual leadership and is considering a possible coup. But Vorotyntsev is deflected from the meeting and virtually immobilized by an intense adulterous liaison that brings chaos into his married life. This is paralleled by the obsessive relationship between the writer Fyodor Kovynev and one of his former students. The final chapter of *November 1916* focuses on this young woman, Zinaida, a second-level character whose memorable story contributes to the explicitly Christian tone of this volume. Her baby, born out of wedlock, sickens and dies while she is distracted by her disastrous affair; grieving inconsolably, she finds her almost-accidental way to a church, where, upon confession, she experiences unconditional divine forgiveness. Her story is emblematic of the repentance and spiritual healing that Russia herself needs. Beyond the realm of fiction, the effect of private affairs on public life is echoed in the depiction of the unhealthy dominance that Empress Alexandra exerts over the compliant Nicholas II.

The nonfictional sections of the knot are mostly presented in the dramatized-history mode typical of the entire cycle. However, this knot stands out for the unusually large number of excursuses on historical and political matters that the author deemed necessary to include. In a note at the beginning of *November 1916*, Solzhenitsyn offers the following defense for what he acknowledges to be an awkward feature in his epic: "The recent history of our country is so little known, or taught in such a distorted fashion, that I have felt compelled, for the sake of my younger compatriots, to include more historical matter in this Second Knot than might be expected in a work of literature."[9]

The educational purpose envisaged by the author could not have been more clearly enunciated. But one must immediately add that Solzhenitsyn is being far too modest in assuming that only his "younger compatriots" need to be enlightened. For there surely cannot be many readers of any age, historians specializing in early-twentieth-century Russian history excepted, who could be assumed to know much, if anything, about such significant historical characters of the time as Dmitri Shipov, the proponent of local self-government, or the prominent Kadet politician Andrei Shingarev, or the mysterious revolutionary Parvus. Together with dozens of others, these individuals make their appearance in contexts that leave no doubt that Solzhenitsyn intends to present a historically authentic version of events.

March 1917

Knot III overwhelms by its sheer size (656 chapters, almost three thousand large pages), as well as by the seemingly endless cascade of events and personalities presented from constantly shifting narrative perspectives. In contrast to the tension-filled stagnation permeating *November 1916*, the third knot radiates frenetic energy as it chronicles the chaos and feverish activity in the period immediately preceding and following the so-called February Revolution of 1917.[10]

In a 1987 interview, Solzhenitsyn revealed that he had not appreciated the tremendous significance of the February events until he had immersed himself fully into a study of the period.[11] Specifically, he became convinced that what had occurred was *the* revolution, that unique set of circumstances which set in motion the destructive rotation of the metaphorical wheel. In comparison, the writer argues, the Bolshevik takeover was a rationally executed coup d'état, an entirely different type of act.

While all the principal stylistic features of the earlier knots are represented in *March 1917*, two points deserve notice. First, despite the four-volume length of Knot III, it contains only four historical excursuses (two are very brief) of the type that are so prominent in Knot II. In this connection, furthermore, the author removed four summary essays that were intended to be placed at the end of each of the four volumes. (They have been published separately.)[12] One must conclude that Solzhenitsyn decided to let the material speak for itself.

Second, apart from the already mentioned effect produced by the shortness of most chapters, Solzhenitsyn has in addition broken a number of them into brief segments, some no more than a sentence or two in length, with each offering a snapshot-like glimpse of the Petrograd street scene. For example:

> A hatless woman galloped past, her face set in mindless jubilation. Her locks fluttered in the wind.

Or:

> On Theatre Street two men with ugly mugs were pulling along a small sled. A corpse of a policeman was tied to it, face up. Of the passers-by, some were stopping and asking with a laugh how the "flatfoot" had been killed. And two boys of about fourteen ran behind and were trying to insert a cigarette into the dead man's lips.

A barrage of such striking but disconnected images deepens the impression of catastrophic disorder that is the dominant theme of *March 1917*.

The picture of anarchy in the streets is paralleled by a description of the mushrooming political turmoil. The tsarist regime, Solzhenitsyn shows, was afflicted by something far more serious than mere incompetence: It was paralyzed by an organic unwillingness to take the decisive actions that alone could have saved the day. But after its ignominious collapse, the political cacophony only increases in volume with the emergence of two competing centers of power, the Provisional Government and the Petrograd Soviet of Workers' and Soldiers' Deputies. Solzhenitsyn provides examples of the tangled polemics and frenzied activities of socialist and Marxist ideologues in the Soviet, and of the astonishing lack of realism among the leaders of the Provisional Government, especially visible in the loquacious extravagances of Alexander Kerensky.

But Knot III also contains sections where time slows and the writer provides leisurely and finely nuanced psychological observations. A tour de force of this type is the chapter relating the tsar's abdication. Solzhenitsyn, who holds the tsar primarily responsible for Russia's descent into the revolutionary maelstrom, here presents a profoundly moving description of the disarmingly helpless Nicholas confronted by men whose brusque or dishonest manner is morally offensive. Another section depicts the nighttime departure from the Winter Palace of Grand Prince Michael, the tsar's younger brother, due to the perceived danger of remaining in the essentially unguarded building. During Michael's long walk through the darkened halls of the Hermitage, past the priceless treasures collected by his mighty ancestors, he ruminates about the fate of the dynasty which, the reader knows, is about to be extinguished forever.

April 1917

Knot IV begins some three weeks after the conclusion of Knot III and to a certain degree represents an ironic echo of the unnaturally rapid capitulation of the ancien régime that was played out in *March*. While it was already clear toward the end of *March* that the new Provisional Government was in danger of being outflanked on the left, this becomes obvious in *April*, Kerensky's oratorical talents notwithstanding. The crucial new element is the arrival of Lenin in Petrograd (April 3, O.S.) and his immediate efforts to cut short the discordant signals emanating from the Petrograd Soviet. Solzhenitsyn, who has spent a lifetime studying the biography and writings of the future leader of the Soviet Union, shows Lenin as a totally committed Marxist who is at the same time a clever opportunist adept at maneuvering in the uncertain conditions of the day, in this sense easily outclassing Kerensky, who tends to mistake his oratorical constructs for reality. And when Trotsky arrives toward the end of the knot and joins the Petrograd Soviet, it becomes clear, Solzhenitsyn suggests, that the Provincial Government stands little chance of survival.

Meanwhile, the fictional characters of the cycle, including Georgi Vorotyntsev, are only faintly visible amid the dramatic historical events described by the writer. However, the very last chapter of Knot IV features Vorotyntsev's musings on future developments in Russia, and his decision to take an active part in a conference of frontline officers groping their way toward some kind of counterweight to the political forces tearing Russia apart. It is obvious that this will be the germ of what would later become the White movement, and Solzhenitsyn is here signaling the envisaged future direction of his protagonist's fictional life.

This is textually confirmed in an unusual way. In Solzhenitsyn's 1953 play, *Prisoners,* the main protagonist is Georgi Vorotyntsev, who has fallen into Soviet hands in 1945 after having fought on the German side with the Russian Liberation Army. In a conversation with his SMERSH overseer, he confirms that he had fought in the Civil War on the White side.[13] But much more interesting is the extraordinary information this suggests about *The Red Wheel* cycle as a whole. It shows, specifically, that some two decades before the first knot was completed, Solzhenitsyn had projected the overarching trajectory of the epic to which he hoped to dedicate his life. There cannot be many examples in world literature where an epilogue to a projected work is composed decades before the main text is even begun.

Outline of Unwritten Knots

Equally unprecedented in the annals of literature is an author's decision to publish outlines of works that were not brought to completion. It is clear that Solzhenitsyn was moved by the hope that these summaries would make the truth of history he has sought to reveal more accessible to future citizen-readers seeking to understand the grievous events of the Russian past.

The 135-page appendix presents a summary account of the political and military developments that Solzhenitsyn intended to address in his original twenty-knot plan. The outlines for Knots V through IX are all focused on 1917 and include substantial detail, especially the almost sixty-page summary of Knot VIII (on October–November 1917), while the knots dealing with later periods typically receive only single-page write-ups.

Texts and translations: *Krasnoe Koleso* (*The Red Wheel*) was first published in vols. 11 through 20 of the Vermont *Sobranie sochinenii* (1983–91). As the present book goes to press, the entire cycle is being produced in newly edited form as part of the thirty-volume *Sobranie sochinenii* launched in 2006 by Moscow's "Vremia" publishing house. Earlier, the ten *Krasnoe Koleso* volumes (in the Vermont-produced version) were reprinted in Moscow by Voenizdat in 1993–97. The first two "knots" (in the Vermont redaction) are available in the excellent English translation of H. T. Willetts, published in New York by Farrar, Straus and Giroux: Aleksandr Solzhenitsyn, *August 1914* (1989) and *November 1916* (1999).

In 2001 the writer also published (Ekaterinburg: U-Faktoriia) three separate selections of chapters from the *Red Wheel* cycle: (1) *Stolypin i Tsar'* (*Stolypin and the Tsar*), containing chapters from *August 1914*; (2) *Lenin: Tsiurikh—Petrograd* (*Lenin in Zurich and Petrograd*), containing chapters from all four knots; and (3) *Nakonets-to revoliutsiia* (*The Revolution at Last*), a two-volume compendium of chapters from *March 1917*. In these volumes Solzhenitsyn has chosen to present only sections bearing on historical figures and events, removing all reference to his fictional characters.

Selected chapters from *March 1917* and *April 1917*, translated by Michael A. Nicholson, appear in English for the first time in *The Solzhenitsyn Reader*.

Two Hundred Years Together

I n *Two Hundred Years Together* Solzhenitsyn broaches one of the great vexing issues of Russian history, the troubled relationship between Russians and Jews. The title reflects the fact that Russia's "Jewish Question" attained importance only in the latter part of the eighteenth century, when territories with substantial Jewish populations were incorporated into the Russian Empire as a result of the three partitions of Poland in 1772, 1793, and 1795. Prior to this period, the Jewish presence in Russia was not statistically significant.[1]

As Solzhenitsyn states at the outset of this work, the idea of writing *Two Hundred Years Together* came to him in the course of his intensive research on the Russian Revolution, upon which his *Red Wheel* is based. The material bearing on Russian-Jewish interaction during the decades leading up to 1917 was so abundant, Solzhenitsyn writes, that he needed to separate it out from the main narrative to retain clarity. The book was therefore conceived in the context of Solzhenitsyn's all-consuming focus on Russia's slide toward the revolutionary precipice, and it very much needs to be seen in that light. For it is the writer's central contention that the troubled relationship between Russians and Jews was destined to become an important contributing factor to the historical cataclysm that engulfed the nation in 1917. Yet despite the importance that the writer clearly assigns to this theme, and despite the statements made (in *The Oak and Calf* and elsewhere) to the effect that a full description of the Russian Revolution constitutes the principal task of his life as a writer, Solzhenitsyn admits that he approached the issue of Russian-Jewish relations with considerable hesitation. As he explains it, he decided to proceed with this project only because no one else had stepped forward with a balanced analysis that took the concerns of both sides into sympathetic consideration. And that, in the words of the book's preface, is precisely the spirit in which he attempts to illuminate this difficult question.

The first volume, which takes the story up to the eve of the Revolution, is a more or less chronological account of the heavy-handed, frequently counterproductive, and mostly failed attempts of the tsarist government to bring its Jewish subjects into the sphere of state control, and of the growing confluence between accumulating Jewish resentments and the indigenous Russian revolutionary movement. Solzhenitsyn points out that the trend toward Jewish radicalization was by no means typical, and that, furthermore, the "renegades" from traditional Jewish values must be compared to the far greater number of Russian "renegades" who similarly rejected their national and religious roots. For in the case of both Russian and Jewish communities, the revolutionary radicals were a distinct minority, yet their choice set the pattern that, tragically, was fated to triumph in historical terms.

Solzhenitsyn has been criticized by some reviewers for relying heavily on mainline sources like encyclopedias in volume 1 of this work, but this objection certainly does not apply to the crucial chapters bearing on the late nineteenth and early twentieth centuries. Immersed as he has been in a close study of this period for many years, he demonstrates unparalleled knowledge of the interplay of social, political, and ideological forces of the time, and of the role of the Jewish factor in the multiple crosscurrents of the day. Meanwhile, the tsarist government, as Solzhenitsyn shows, seemed hopelessly incapable of responding to or even understanding the Jewish-related issues before it, illustrated (as Solzhenitsyn suggests) by its mind-boggling obtuseness in not foreseeing the damage that would be done to its credibility and reputation by initiating the infamous Beiliss trial,[2] or the massive consequences generated by its decision to deport all Jews from the potential war zone in western Russia during World War I.

The second volume begins with an account of the Jewish participation in the February Revolution, followed by a similar review of the subsequent phases of Russian and Soviet history. As a number of commentators have noted with a degree of awe, Solzhenitsyn is here treading on the equivalent of a minefield. He himself prefers to speak of the thankless task of trying to keep to what he calls the "middle line"—a position that acknowledges the reasonable arguments on both sides and rejects all extreme accusations. Thus, he scorns the dog-eared anti-Semitic bromide according to which "the Jews" ushered in the Revolution, emphasizing, instead, the prime responsibility of Russians in the fateful events of 1917. At the same time, Solzhenitsyn documents the vigorous supporting role played by Jews in revolutionary developments. Proceeding to the early post-1917 period, Solzhenitsyn tackles the equally thorny issue of the energetic Jewish participation in upholding the young Bolshevik regime and implementing its radical policies. The prominence of Jewish names among Soviet functionaries and enforcers during the regime's first two decades in power is a historical fact that has too often been passed over in silence.[3] For Solzhenitsyn, who considers the resurrection of the full truth about the past his paramount goal as a writer, such oblivion is as incomprehensible as it is unacceptable. Absolutely unsparing in the depiction of his own failings in *The Road* and *The Gulag Archipelago*, pitiless in scourging the fatal weaknesses of old Russia in *The Red Wheel*, and filled with despair at the destructive behavior of revolutionary Russian masses in 1917 and beyond, Solzhenitsyn asks that Jews also acknowledge their contribution to the human and historical calamity of the Russian Revolution and the subsequent Bolshevik assault on traditional Russia. He ends, as he began, with hope for a genuine Russian-Jewish reconciliation, one based on a mutual recognition of responsibility for past wrongs against each other.

> **Text:** *Two Hundred Years Together* (*Dvesti let vmeste*) was published in Moscow by "Russkii put'" in 2001 (vol. 1) and 2002 (vol. 2). The work constitutes the seventh volume in the series *Issledovaniia noveishei russkoi istorii* (*Studies in Modern Russian History*). There is as yet no full English translation, but substantial excerpts appear in *The Solzhenitsyn Reader*.

Russia in Collapse

Russia in Collapse (1998) is Solzhenitsyn's fourth major essay addressing the social and political problems of contemporary Russia. The work's predecessors in this genre are *Letter to the Soviet Leaders* (1973), *Rebuilding Russia* (1990), and *"The Russian Question" at the End of the Twentieth Century* (1994), but none of them approach the grim darkness that is characteristic of the 1998 essay.

"I am writing this book," Solzhenitsyn states on the first page of his essay, "as merely one of the witnesses and victims of Russia's infinitely cruel century, in order to record what we have seen and what we are now seeing and experiencing." This self-definition of chronicler inevitably brings to mind the very similar introductory remarks in *The Gulag Archipelago*. And just as the *Gulag* epic was born of numerous meetings with former inmates of the Soviet prison and forced-labor camps, so too, some three decades later, *Russia in Collapse* takes its primary impulse from the writer's experience of meeting with people from all walks of life in the course of his extensive travels throughout the land after he returned to Russia in 1994. The impressions gained from face-to-face dialogues were reinforced by the countless letters from anguished citizens that came to Solzhenitsyn in the 1990s. Excerpts from these texts take up several pages of *Russia in Collapse*.

These letters make painful reading. We hear an immense chorus of dismayed, despairing, and grief-stricken voices pleading for help, crying of injustice, lamenting ruined lives, and sinking into hopelessness. Yet the myriad concerns being expressed in this litany of grief and distress are ultimately similar, Solzhenitsyn argues, since all derive from the new regime's grossly irresponsible, not to say criminally negligent, attitude toward the welfare of the people it ostensibly represents.

An analogy with *The Gulag Archipelago* is appropriate here as well. Just as that work, to quote George F. Kennan, must be considered "the greatest and most powerful single indictment of a political regime ever to be leveled in modern times," so *Russia in Collapse* is certainly the most damning critique of the Yeltsin years yet published. For the bulk of Solzhenitsyn's essay is a detailed catalogue of the incompetence, miscalculations, and total unconcern for consequences that characterized the public actions of a regime that seemed focused only on personal gain as it careened from one crisis to another, all the while continuing to enjoy benevolent encouragement from the West.

The book includes bitter comments on the opportunities missed in 1991, when Yeltsin failed to move decisively against entrenched Soviet interests that were then ready to yield, gives an account of the massively corrupt process of "privatization" carried out by the new regime, details Russia's pathetic kowtowing to the West in direct contradiction of its national interests, and laments the fate of millions of Russians who woke up to find themselves unwelcome foreigners in the "near abroad" after the breakup of the Soviet Union and who were thereupon betrayed by a Russia that offered them neither help nor protection. Solzhenitsyn excoriates the government's policies in Chechnya, both before and during the (first) Chechen war, and condemns the regime's unbelievable lack of concern for the collapse of medical services, the disastrous lack of support for schools and scientific institutions, and the well-nigh total deterioration of the army.

But Solzhenitsyn does not limit himself to viewing the narrow range of years associated with Boris Yeltsin's time in power; he goes on to ponder the larger questions of Russian history. In particular, he notes the major shifts that had occurred in what he calls the Russian national character in the two or three decades preceding 1917. He also points to the analogy and probable direct link between the prerevolutionary intelligentsia's implacable hostility to the old regime and the new elite's similarly single-minded opposition to all manifestations of genuine Russian patriotism.

And yet, despite the overwhelmingly negative picture that he has presented in *Russia in Collapse*, Solzhenitsyn retains hope for the future. It is, he believes, incarnated in the multitude of earnest, talented, and energetic individuals whom he has met in Russia's vast provincial areas. He ends his book with an appeal to all Russians to dedicate themselves to a life of peaceful construction of the society and country that Russia deserves.

Text: *Russia in Collapse* (*Rossiia v obvale*) was published in Moscow in 1998 by the "Russkii put'" publishing house. There is as yet no full English translation, but substantial excerpts appear in *The Solzhenitsyn Reader.*

Short Stories of the 1990s

A fter winding up his work on the *Red Wheel* cycle, Solzhenitsyn turned to shorter forms of literary prose, in the process introducing a new genre that he christened "binary tales" (*dvuchastnyi rasskaz*). Texts of this type consist of two distinct (always numbered) parts that are related thematically in some manner, all the while exhibiting a significant shift that permits the two parts to be juxtaposed. This shift can be a gap in time, a switch of narrative mode, or even a change of fundamental subject matter.[1] Eight such stories appeared in *Novy Mir* between 1993 and 1999, with the two most effective ones having grown out of materials Solzhenitsyn had gathered—but not used—in the originally envisaged part of *The Red Wheel*. The context, specifically, is the 1920–21 peasant rebellion in the Tambov region—the last significant armed challenge to Bolshevik rule in the wake of 1917.[2]

"Ego," the first of the two tales set in this period, builds on the actual biography of Pavel Ektov (nicknamed "Ego"), a Tambov-based proponent and organizer of peasant-run cooperatives who finds himself drawn further and further into the rebellion. But Ektov was eventually captured, and part 2 of the story is the painful account of how he was pressured by his captors to betray his fellow resisters. "On the Edge" (*Na kraiakh*), a particularly effective example of the "binary" genre, begins with the early biography of Georgii Zhukov, the future Soviet marshal of World War II fame, focusing on his role as an ambitious officer in the Red Army units sent to crush the Tambov rebellion. (Fully in line with the methodology of *The Red Wheel*, Solzhenitsyn inserts several historical documents into this part of the text.) In the second part of the tale, readers enter the mind of the aging Zhukov, now retired and in ill health, as he reviews the past in the process of composing his reminiscences. Solzhenitsyn's text is here based on Zhukov's actual memoirs, as well as on a multitude of other materials made available in recent years. The iron marshal emerges as an intellectually and morally limited man who is sincerely—because unthinkingly—loyal to the Communist cause, yet whose native leadership talent is feared by the Soviet regime.

Three binary tales are set in the Soviet 1920s and '30s. In "The Upcoming Generation" (*Molodniak*), a hopelessly slow student, a member of the newly privileged proletarian class, is promoted by a professor out of charity and social duty. Some years later, the professor finds himself confronting the same person, except that the professor is now under arrest and his erstwhile student serves as an interrogator in the security services.

"Nastenka" compares the separate fates of two young women with this name, which is a diminutive of Anastasia. The story is a study in the catastrophic deterioration of social and moral norms experienced by individuals who had led orderly lives before the revolutionary upheavals. The first Nastenka becomes the victim of brutal sexual exploitation that brings about a virtual destruction of her personhood. The other Nastenka manages to preserve her identity through sheer luck and dogged perseverance, but at the cost of intellectual compromise. Despite these losses, it seems symbolic that the moral anchor which allows the second Nastenka to survive amid the fanaticism, squalor, and destruction that surround her is her love of Russian classical literature.

Literature also plays a key role in the excellent binary tale entitled "Apricot Jam" (*Abrikosovoe varen'e*). The story begins with a letter from a desperately ill prisoner to a famous writer, appealing for help and relating the horrific injustices he has suffered as the son of a deported kulak family. In an aside, he recollects that his mother used to make wonderful jam from the fruit-bearing apricot tree that was cut down as punishment for his family's kulak status. Part 2 switches to the luxurious dacha of the recipient of the letter. (Although his name is not specified, biographical data and bibliographic hints make clear that this writer is Aleksei N. Tolstoi, the same individual whom prisoners in *The First Circle* mockingly called Aleksei Non-Tolstoi.) The crucial episode occurs at the end, when the writer picks up a spoonful of translucent, gold-colored apricot jam and proclaims to a visitor that the duty of Soviet writers is to aim for this kind of clarity and beauty in their prose. In this regard, he continues, he is particularly proud of having examined seventeenth-century transcripts of interrogations under torture. In circumstances of extreme duress, he asserts, men express the very purest kind of Russian, and he goes on to cite several phrases from the letter that makes up part 1 as examples of such prose. Needless to say, for the established writer the letter holds merely linguistic interest, and responding to it, to say nothing of helping its despairing author, has not even entered his mind.

Two binary tales touch upon the post-Soviet scene. In part 1 of "It Makes No Difference" (*Vse ravno*), an overzealous World War II lieutenant receives the advice encapsulated in the title when he contemplates taking serious action against several soldiers who have committed a minor infraction of the rules. Part 2, set a half century later, depicts a high-ranking official of the new regime who quotes the title phrase to himself in order to rationalize his decision not to try stopping a mindless construction project that will have dire ecological and social consequences.[3]

"On the Fractures" (*Na izlomakh*) traces the life stories of two men trying to find their footing in the treacherous new world of slashed government funding and cutthroat capitalism.

The last binary tale to have appeared thus far (first published in *Novy mir,* 1999, no. 3) is purely autobiographical in character. In part 1 of "Zheliabugskie Vyselki" (a place-name), Solzhenitsyn gives a vivid description of several frontline days experienced by his sound-ranging unit during the Soviet Army's mid-1943 offensive. This section ends with the unit's political officer promising the collective farmers of the war-ravaged area that life after the end of hostilities will be infinitely better than anything they have ever known. Part 2, in bitter contrast to this rosy prediction, presents Solzhenitsyn's first-person account of his 1995 visit to the same area, and his joyless observations of the utter poverty and shocking lack of social services available to the aged survivors who still linger in a few remaining huts.

In 1999 Solzhenitsyn also published "Adlig Schwenkitten" (another place-name), a short-story-sized text, subtitled "A Tale of 24 Hours," which relates the circumstances of a particularly dramatic military engagement involving Solzhenitsyn's unit in late January 1945.[4] Related in twenty-four short chapters roughly corresponding to the time frame, it is the story of a highly unconventional surprise attack on overexposed Soviet positions by German units that seemed to materialize out of the mists of a moonlit winter landscape. Interestingly, the text includes no direct mention of Solzhenitsyn's own role in this episode—the narrative is presented from the point of view of a collective "we"—and the particulars of his personal involvement are known only from a detailed account given in *The Little Grain.*[5] As Solzhenitsyn writes there, he was due to receive a decoration for having rescued the unit's sound-ranging equipment in the heat of battle, but his arrest for disrespectful comments about Stalin (which occurred only a few days later) cut short this process forever.

Texts: All eight binary tales, along with "Adlig Schwenkitten," are included in vol. 1 of the Moscow *Sobranie sochinenii* (2006).

Only one of these nine texts has been translated into English (see note 3).

Literary Collection

L iterary Collection is the series title of a large number of sketches in which Solzhenitsyn offers extensive comments on various Russian authors and specific literary works. In a brief preface to the inaugural publication (*Novy Mir*, 1997, no. 1), Solzhenitsyn refers to this series as notes he originally made for himself as he was reading certain works in the late 1980s, when his decades-long labors on *The Red Wheel* were beginning to wind down. He was persuaded to publish these sketches, he writes, when he became aware of the extent to which the memory of many notable Russian books had faded among his countrymen.

This desire to preserve the memory of certain books is clearly of a piece with the driving force that animates his epic attempt to resurrect a true vision of the Russian past by means of the *Red Wheel* cycle. What is more, the timing of the series—its birth at the end of Solzhenitsyn's immersion in historical research—could not help shaping his approach to these literary productions. This is evident, for example, in his focus on the depiction of historical *realia* and social attitudes, as well as on the attitude toward Russia expressed in the texts, in this sense reflecting the methods and concerns of *The Red Wheel*.

Of the twenty-two sketches that have appeared in print between 1997 and 2005 (more are said to be in the pipeline), about half deal with writers and works that are presented as especially important for revealing vital aspects of social and historical reality not recorded elsewhere. In Solzhenitsyn's view, writers such as Panteleimon Romanov and Aleksandr Malyshkin have left invaluable records of mores, attitudes, and social conditions characteristic of the Soviet 1920s and '30s, Ivan Shmelev's *Sun of the Dead* reveals the terrifying scale of the Bolshevik repressions in post–Civil War Crimea, Felix Svetov portrays the overheated identity crises that roiled Moscow intellectual circles in the 1970s, Vasily Belov and Evgeny Nosov have preserved authentic images of the traditional village life that has vanished forever, Georgy Vladimov provides a profoundly authentic perspective on World War II, and so on. In all these cases, it must be emphasized, Solzhenitsyn has focused on works that he deems not only informative but significant in purely literary terms.

This issue comes up with particular force when Solzhenitsyn comments on the portrayal of prerevolutionary life. In his view, many celebrated authors have chosen to approach this topic in an astonishingly hackneyed fashion. This is true, he avers, of Boris Pilnyak, Yuri Tynianov, Andrei Bely, and many others. The "brilliant" Evgeny Zamiatin is deemed incapable of seeing anything beyond "total swinishness" in old Russia. Even Chekhov is seen as slavish to the tediously predictable canons of this attitude. Yet the two last-named writers garner the greatest praise of all the authors Solzhenitsyn discusses. What Solzhenitsyn admires most is their ability to be succinct, and he is particularly taken with Zamiatin's imagery, citing dozens of examples that he deems strikingly successful. While Solzhenitsyn greatly regrets Zamiatin's views of Russia, his radical atheism, and his seemingly "unextinguishable" sympathy for Bolshevism, he nevertheless considers him one of the greatest masters of Russian prose.

An important aspect of Solzhenitsyn's approach to the works he has chosen to examine, one that is directly linked to his overarching concern about preserving memory, is the close attention he pays to the purely lexical quality of the works surveyed. It is a concern driven by his belief that the Russian language has experienced a massive lexical impoverishment in the twentieth century.[1] Consistent with this view, virtually every sketch includes a list of words and expressions that in Solzhenitsyn's opinion can and should enrich the Russian lexicon. (Yet this does not become an aesthetic criterion of primary importance, and the greatly admired Chekhov is credited with perhaps the shortest list of lexical innovations.)

In a sketch on the features of the epic genre exemplified by the works of Mark Aldanov and Vasily Grossman, Solzhenitsyn reveals a great deal about his own methodology in the *Red Wheel* cycle. Here is his understanding of the term "epic" [*epopeia*] as applied to a narrative structure:

> This is a prose form next in order of magnitude after the novel. The individual fortunes of the protagonists are here not at the center of attention as in a novel. They are not even very important, because the field of vision is not limited to them, rising instead to a different level: to a depiction of the events of an era, of an entire nation, of individuals who are no longer fictional, and of their actions in real historical circumstances.

With this definition in mind, Solzhenitsyn criticizes Aldanov's *Origins* for the undue space assigned to the fictional part of the plot, but he praises the author for including surveys of newspapers, a device he has himself often employed. Solzhenitsyn proceeds to a close analysis of Grossman's epic of the Stalingrad battle, *For the Right Cause,* and its posthumously published sequel, *Forever Flowing,* concluding that this "dilogy" represents a very substantial contribution to Russian literature. It is notable that here again Solzhenitsyn's literary and aesthetic judgment diverges sharply from his political and moral evaluation, which is presented in a separate sketch.

Considerations central to *The Red Wheel* are also likely to have affected the inclusion of two otherwise unlikely works in Solzhenitsyn's list: Aleksei K. Tolstoi's dramatic trilogy on the circumstances leading up to the early-seventeenth-century "Time of Troubles," and Leonid Borodin's recent novel on Marina Mniszek, a tragic participant in the events of that chaotic period. It would seem that Solzhenitsyn chose to focus on these particular works by reason of the perceived analogy between the historical calamities loosed by 1917—a period to which Solzhenitsyn has on several occasions referred as Russia's "second Time of Troubles"—and the similarly destructive chaos of three centuries earlier.

Of the several sketches on poets, the one on Joseph Brodsky stands out for its severely critical tone. Solzhenitsyn acknowledges Brodsky's virtuosity and admires many of his poems, but he chooses to emphasize what he considers the poet's too-frequent use of prolix and self-indulgent language. He judges Brodsky's trademark irony and mocking tone difficult to bear, connecting it to the metaphysical revulsion Brodsky often reveals in contemplating life and human activity. And Solzhenitsyn ends his most angry sketch by skewering Brodsky's grossly unfair comments about Russia and Eastern Orthodoxy.

In another piece Solzhenitsyn fulfills a promise he had made to the widow of Mikhail Bulgakov to name the Soviet critics who had hounded Bulgakov mercilessly in the 1920s and '30s, all but baying for his blood. He enumerates them, quotes from them, and follows this "list of dishonor" with a harsh review of a recent collection of articles on the great novelist.

Texts: Twenty-two sketches in the *Literary Collection* (*Literaturnaia kollektsiia*) series have appeared in *Novyi mir* between 1997 and 2004. None have been translated into English.

Beliefs

While it is common, and correct, to call Aleksandr Solzhenitsyn a moral writer, it is equally common for critics not to look beyond that level of generalization. Yet leaving the matter there results in an impoverished and inadequate understanding of a moral vision that has emanated from, and that continues to be sustained by, explicitly religious wellsprings. The present chapter addresses the issue of Solzhenitsyn's core beliefs and the manifold ramifications of these views for his thought and works.

The Textual Evidence

In a 1989 interview with American journalist David Aikman, Solzhenitsyn stated that he had been "raised by my elders in the spirit of Christianity" and that, while in school, he "had to conceal this from others." But, he continued, within a number of years the powerful "force field of Marxism" that he experienced in his Soviet schooling undermined these views. The social environment "has such an impact that it gets into the brain of the young man and little by little takes over," so that "from age seventeen or eighteen, I did change internally, and from that time, I became a Marxist, a Leninist, and believed in all these things." In prison, however, he met various people with differing viewpoints, and "I saw that my convictions did not have a solid basis, could not stand up in dispute, and I had to renounce them. Then the question arose of going back to what I had learned as a child. It took more than a year or so. Other believers influenced me, but basically it was a return to what I had thought before." Next, he fell into the grip of cancer, from which he was told he could not recover, and "the fact that I was dying also shook me profoundly."[1]

The Aikman interview, granted when the author was seventy years old, emphasizes the end result of the odyssey and skimps on the stages along the way. Other works by Solzhenitsyn fill in some gaps. As the above summary indicates, in early adulthood, and especially during the years of university study and army service, Solzhenitsyn was a committed Communist. Yet we know from *The Road,* his early and largely autobiographical narrative poem, that his observations and experiences during the war raised serious challenges to his faith in Marxism-Leninism, challenges that were then magnified by his arrest and incarceration. The gathering doubts gradually ushered in a period during his time in prison when skepticism was his dominant intellectual mood. This philosophical position is on clearest display in the portrayal of Gleb Nerzhin, the substantially autobiographical protagonist of *The First Circle.* A renewal of religious belief followed in the phase of Solzhenitsyn's incarceration spent at the Ekibastuz prison camp starting in 1953. These changes of mind, first in one direction and then in another, entailed an evolving process; his is not the story of a sudden conversion. The actual positions to which Solzhenitsyn adhered at various times are clearer and better defined than are the processes and exact timing of the shifts involved. And in this connection it should be added that there is nothing novel or idiosyncratic about his Christian beliefs; Solzhenitsyn has not indulged in speculative theologizing.

Since a writer's beliefs about ultimate concerns necessarily frame his thoughts and words, to read Solzhenitsyn with full understanding requires an awareness of his religious cast of mind. Often he settles for broadly theistic, rather than pointedly Christian, expressions, because that degree of specificity suffices for the topic being treated or the audience being addressed. He has no interest in driving needless wedges between himself and non-Christian theists. Still, he is not "merely" a theist (a term he does not use); he is a Christian theist. The religious idiom that he knows from the inside is Christian, and references to the Bible and Christian thought run like a leitmotif throughout his corpus. Many of these references are presented obliquely to serve literary purposes immediately at hand, but others are presented quite directly and stand as clear textual evidence that his religious framework is specifically Christian. Yet, strangely, little focused attention has been paid to this clear and abundant evidence. In part this is so, no doubt, because some of the strongest evidence appears in little-known texts. For instance, *Candle in the Wind*, a play written in 1960 and originally titled *The Light That Is within Thee* (borrowed from Luke 11:35), argues for Christian faith and against hedonism and scientism.[2] Calling attention to such evidence sets the table for the more important issue of how the writer of literature deploys his religious beliefs in his texts.

Solzhenitsyn has shown an active church member's engagement with ecclesiastical matters. In his open—and, to many, highly contentious—"Lenten Letter" of 1972 addressed to Patriarch Pimen of Russia, he mentions presenting his son for christening, showing in the process his ready familiarity with the Bible by citing Christ's parable about the one lost sheep and the ninety-nine "safely in the fold." More broadly, he points out that the church hierarchy's craven submissiveness to the Soviet regime makes the church complicit in the fact that Russians "are losing the last traces and signs of a Christian people." And he takes note of the crowning irony: "A Church ruled dictatorially by atheists—this is a spectacle unseen in two thousand years."[3] "The Easter Procession," a story written in 1966, depicts the beleaguered situation of practicing Christians, by then mostly old women, bereft of protection from menacing young toughs with sacrilege in their hearts. The plight of fellow believers is part of the backdrop for the letter to Pimen.

Solzhenitsyn has also expressed his personal religious devotion in his writing. Shortly after he came to fame in 1962 with the publication of *One Day in the Life of Ivan Denisovich,* he penned "A Prayer," the opening lines of which show his unforced manner in addressing God: "How easy for me to live with you, Lord! / How easy to believe in you!" The rest of the prayer reflects gratefully on God's guidance in the past and expresses trust that God will continue to direct his journey. Then, in 1994, as he returned to his homeland, he composed "A Prayer for Russia," imploring God, "Our Father All-Merciful" and "Lord Omnipotent," not to abandon "long-suffering Russia / In her present daze, / In her woundedness, / Impoverishment, / And confusion of spirit."[4] Solzhenitsyn prays this prayer daily.

These two prayers had a number of antecedents in Solzhenitsyn's oeuvre. Apart from the description of the early phase of his religious odyssey that is given in *The Road,* he provides even more intimate glimpses into his spirituality in lyric poems written during 1952–53. In one particularly moving piece, "Acathistus,"[5] written immediately after a seemingly successful surgery for his cancer, he contrasts the apparent meaninglessness of his past life with the new possibility of living purposefully and concludes, "Oh great God! I believe now anew! / Though denied, you were always with me. . . ." When, several months later, the cancer's recurring ravages caused his doctors to give him only two weeks to live, he composed a poem about death. In it he views death not as a chasm but as a crest, or ridge, onto which the road of his life has now ascended. Meanwhile, "Up in the black sky that shrouds my deathbed / Gleams the White Sun of God." The dying man accepts the prospect of his death with remarkable equanimity and shifts his "otherworldly gaze" to "crucified" Russia, with a note of sad yearning for his beloved country.[6]

The Gulag Archipelago, with its luxuriant growth of subjects, themes, and characters, also conveys Solzhenitsyn's explicit Christian affirmations. Solzhenitsyn lavishes attention on the gulag's Christians, whose vibrant witness impressed him profoundly. For instance, when at one point he had dismissed a prayer by President Roosevelt as hypocrisy, young Boris Gammerov asked why a political leader might not sincerely believe in God. Solzhenitsyn realized right then that "I had not spoken out of conviction but because the idea had been implanted in me from outside." So he merely murmured in return, "Do you believe in God?" And Gammerov "tranquilly" answered, "Of course."[7]

Part IV of *The Gulag Archipelago* has as its epigraph I Corinthians 15:51, a reference to resurrection signaling that, at the midpoint of the seven-part work, the downward emotional movement of lament has reached its nadir and is giving way to the upward, religiously tinged movement of consolation. The first chapter of part IV is fittingly titled "The Ascent," and at the heart of this remarkable chapter is a vignette about Solzhenitsyn's own spiritual ascent, for which his surgeon, Dr. Boris Kornfeld, served as the human intermediary by telling his patient the story of his conversion to Christianity. This chapter is where the poem "Acathistus" first appeared in print.[8]

The "Templeton Lecture," delivered by Solzhenitsyn in 1983, is his most detailed articulation of the role he assigns to faith in God both in his own life and in history. As he has explained in his reminiscences, formulating these thoughts required overcoming a psychological barrier. "Throughout the years," he had "avoided speaking directly about faith because it is immodest, and it grinds on the ear. Instead of noisy proclamations, faith should be allowed to flow silently but incontrovertibly." But when he was selected as the recipient of the Templeton Prize for Progress in Religion, the public ceremony called on him to present a lecture, and he understood clearly that "what was being asked of me now was precisely a speech on a religious theme"—the very style of utterance that until then (at this point he was sixty-four) he had sidestepped. While being struck by "the newness of the task," he was aided in dropping his accustomed reticence by the way the Templeton invitation was phrased. He found "more profound than I had expected" the importance that the decision-makers attached to the issue of "the viability of the Orthodox spiritual tradition in Russia." He was also impressed by the "great efforts" they had undertaken in "combing through my works in order to select passages appropriate to the award," and he believed that they were "absolutely correct" in emphasizing the importance of "A Prayer" and "Acathistus." After the fact, Solzhenitsyn remarked with satisfaction that "this speech served as a step toward greater understanding for myself."[9]

True to form, in this speech Solzhenitsyn approaches his subject not through the categories of abstract theology but by placing his beliefs within the context of concrete history—specifically, history as experienced by himself, by those immediately surrounding him, and by his nation. He begins the address by asking what the chief defining characteristic of the twentieth century is. In his answer he rehearses the explanations he heard in his childhood from his elders when they commented on "the great disasters that had befallen Russia" by saying, "Men have forgotten God; that's why all this has happened." If asked now to state succinctly "the main cause of the ruinous Revolution that swallowed up some sixty million of our people," he could do no better, he continues, than to repeat that judgment, for "unbridled militant atheism" lies at the core of Bolshevism. "And," he further generalizes, "if I were called upon to identify briefly the principal trait of the *entire* twentieth century, here too I would be unable to find anything more precise and pithy than to repeat once again: 'men have forgotten God.'" Indeed, Solzhenitsyn sees the calamities of the modern world as directly linked to "the flaw of a consciousness lacking all divine dimension." Yet even amid the surrounding wreckage stands a steadfast faith in the active role of divine providence in human affairs: "Material laws alone do not explain our life or give it direction. The laws of physics and physiology will never reveal the indisputable manner in which the Creator constantly, day in and day out, participates in the life of each of us. . . . And in the life of our entire planet the Divine Spirit surely moves with no less force. . . ."[10]

In Solzhenitsyn's account of the knowledge and wisdom available within the Christian tradition, he joins other Christians through the ages in witnessing to "the faith once delivered unto the saints"[11] and in applying those unchanging affirmations to particular historical times and social contexts. The latitude of expressions he has used, moreover, invites believers of non-Christian religions to join him at many points.

Sampling explicit, or overt, religious references is only the first step in considering the role that Solzhenitsyn's beliefs play in his writings. This step, however, does put readers on the alert for implicit, or oblique, references, which are more numerous and pervasive. Before turning to such examples, we proceed to a brief survey of Solzhenitsyn's more theoretical pronouncements.

Beyond Politics to the Moral Universe

Acknowledging Solzhenitsyn's religious heart puts readers on guard against the most widespread error that Solzhenitsyn critics have committed, namely, approaching him as a primarily political writer. Aware of this common misconception, Solzhenitsyn has gone out of his way to dissuade commentators from viewing him through the prism of politics. Indeed, he has flatly denied that politics is his "framework" or "task" or "dimension."[12] He forcefully steers readers away from approaching even *The Gulag Archipelago,* surely a work with profound political implications, in exclusively political terms: "[L]et the reader who expects this book to be a political exposé slam its covers shut right now."[13]

In "As Breathing and Consciousness Return," the lead essay in *From under the Rubble,* Solzhenitsyn succinctly consolidates the case for subordinating politics to morality. Politics cannot have primacy precisely because "the state structure" itself "is of secondary significance." (In this he is merely rephrasing Christ's teaching about rendering unto Caesar what is Caesar's, but not surrendering unto Caesar that which is God's.) With the Soviet context in mind, Solzhenitsyn asserts that this sense of priorities is crucial. "[T]he absolutely essential task is not political liberation, but the liberation of our souls from participation in the lie forced upon us." Such liberation "requires from each individual a moral step within his power—*no more than that.*"[14] Politics matters, but morality matters more, simply because morality trumps politics. Elsewhere, he notes with approval that "Erasmus believed politics to be an ethical category" and that the Russian philosopher Vladimir Solovyov "insisted that, from a Christian point of view, moral and political activity are tightly linked, that political activity must a priori be *moral service,* whereas politics motivated by the mere pursuit of *interests* lacks any Christian content whatsoever."[15]

As the reference to Solovyov indicates, Solzhenitsyn leaves plenty of room to explore political themes; he is particularly attentive to politics in its broadest sense of organizing human interrelationships for the benefit of all. His interest in politics is intense; in fact, he has acknowledged that "political passion is an inborn characteristic of mine," and when in the 1970s he believed that the balance of world power was in danger of tipping toward tyranny, he vigorously sounded the alarms. At that time in particular, he felt caught in an "eternal contradiction: to write or to fight."[16] It should be noted, however, that even when in the fighting mode, he saw the conflict not in economic terms (capitalism versus socialism), nor in immediately political terms (democracy or its absence), but in the moral categories of good and evil. Gradually, "to write" won out over "to fight"—in some measure because of his sense of futility about altering the thinking of the ruling elites, but even more because his lifelong mission of writing literature could not be suppressed for long. More than one good book could be written—and at least two by political scientists have been—bringing suitable nuances and balance to the discussion of Solzhenitsyn's politics.[17]

If religious beliefs can be viewed as the framework for Solzhenitsyn's writings, what is the picture inside the frame? It is, in a phrase, the moral universe. This term signifies that human life is carried on against the panorama of a universe that is ordered by moral principles. Such a universe operates according to two axioms. First, actions and consequences are integrally, not randomly or arbitrarily, connected. Actions carry their consequences within themselves and are not completed until their effects are played out. Or, stated the other way around, consequences are not detachable subsequent events; rather, they are extensions of actions. What seems to have been done in a moment actually stretches out over time, and there is no more possibility of altering these unfolding developments than there is of keeping seeds from growing into plants. The most forceful articulation in Solzhenitsyn's texts of the nexus between actions and consequences comes from Dr. Boris Kornfeld's last words to Solzhenitsyn as the writer lay in a postoperative haze:

> [O]n the whole, do you know, I have become convinced that there is no punishment that comes to us in this life on earth which is undeserved. Superficially it can have nothing to do with what we are guilty of in actual fact, but if you go over your life with a fine-tooth comb and ponder it deeply, you will always be able to hunt down that transgression of yours for which you have now received this blow.[18]

The correlation of actions and consequences has almost endless ramifications. As actions are linked forward into their consequences, they are also linked backward into their motivations. Turning motives into deeds is the very stuff of character development in literature. A certain movement of heart and mind precedes, and transmogrifies into, actions taken. Actions have a social dimension, affecting not only the actor but others in his environment, whether nearby or far off. In this social dimension the consequences of actions spread through time as well as space. Thus, Solzhenitsyn picks up on the biblical dictum that the sins of the fathers are visited upon the children unto the third and fourth generations: "How, you may ask, can we repent on their behalf—we weren't even alive at the time! . . . But the saying is not an idle one, and we have only too often seen and still see children *paying* for the fathers."[19] The "sins of the fathers" theme surfaces explicitly in *The Road, The First Circle, Cancer Ward,* and *The Gulag Archipelago.* Furthermore, the tie between actions and consequences applies to corporate entities, or social groupings, as well. Solzhenitsyn's term for this move from the one to the many is "the transference of values," a process that comes naturally to persons of "religious cast of mind" but is practiced just as "readily and naturally" by persons "without a religious foundation." Judging social groups and organizations as "noble, base, courageous, cowardly, hypocritical, false, cruel, magnanimous, just, unjust, and so on" is done by "even the most extreme economic materialists, since they remain after all human beings."[20] They, too, inhabit the moral universe, even if not they do not acknowledge it.

The second axiom of the moral universe, as Solzhenitsyn sees it, is that actions can and should be measured according to the traditional standards of good and evil. In their essence, good and evil are not socially constructed or culturally conditioned; they are simply part of the nature of things and apply universally. To speak of greater or lesser good or evil is not to define the terms as relative but only to speak of degrees of falling short of those absolute standards. Human beings have an innate sense of what is good and what is evil and an innate ability to choose between them correctly, if they only will. The instrument for distinguishing between good and evil is known as conscience; one traditional image for it is an umpire. At every moment, a person chooses either good or evil by following or violating the dictates of conscience.

One of the best-known passages in all of Solzhenitsyn's work, from *The Gulag Archipelago,* expounds upon the line dividing good and evil and places that line not between groups of people but within every human heart. No sooner does Solzhenitsyn pinpoint the human heart as the battleground where good and evil compete than he observes that "all the religions of the world" agree on the "struggle with the evil *inside a human being* (inside every human being)."[21] As a proponent of moral universals, Solzhenitsyn speaks on behalf of a religious worldview that extends beyond any denominational boundary. At the same time, he acknowledges that moral universals are no longer universally accepted, and that the very "concepts of Good and Evil [have] become a subject of ridicule."[22] In particular, communism "rejects all absolute concepts of morality" and "considers morality to be relative."[23] Moral relativism thrives among many Western intellectuals, and Solzhenitsyn has accused certain Sovietologists of failing "to acknowledge [communism] as the quintessence of dynamic and implacable evil" precisely because they insist on viewing "evil" as "an unscientific concept, almost a four-letter word, for instead of 'good' and 'evil' there exists only a multiplicity of opinions, each one as valid as the next."[24]

In Solzhenitsyn's view, the reality of the moral universe is a fact unaffected by modern disbelief, and one can identify the main thematic elements that constitute this world. The moral themes that figure most prominently in Solzhenitsyn's writings are justice, freedom, repentance, hope, and truth. As will be seen, generalizations that pertain to the moral universe as a whole also pertain to its parts.

Solzhenitsyn describes justice as one of those lasting concepts valid for all mankind. It is "the common patrimony of humanity throughout the ages." As is true of the overarching concept of the moral universe, "justice," as one of its parts, "exists even if there are only a few individuals who recognize it as such." Furthermore, "There is nothing relative about justice, as there is nothing relative about conscience. Indeed, justice *is* conscience, not a personal conscience but the conscience of the whole of humanity."[25] In the ninety-six-chapter version of *The First Circle,* Gleb Nerzhin summarizes, "Justice is the cornerstone, the foundation of the universe! . . . We were born with a sense of justice in our souls."[26]

Freedom is another staple of Solzhenitsyn's moral vision. The world initially celebrated him precisely as a fearless freedom fighter. Prison itself cannot prevail against the freedom that matters most, inner freedom. As Bobynin, a minor character in *The First Circle,* declares, the person who has been deprived of everything is "free all over again."[27] Carefully discriminating among competing conceptions of freedom, Solzhenitsyn defines this concept in explicitly Christian terms. He sets "the true Christian definition of freedom" in contrast to both "the Western ideal of unlimited freedom" and

"the Marxist concept of freedom as acceptance of the yoke of necessity"—each rooted in Enlightenment thinking. On the contrary, he asserts, "Freedom is *self-restriction!* Restriction of the self
for the sake of others!"[28] This formulation may sound jarring to
modern ears; but, as Solzhenitsyn observes, this paradox underlies
the Golden Rule. The "meaning of liberty," which, Solzhenitsyn
charges, post-Enlightenment Europe has been forgetting, once was
"a sacred concept stemming directly from the old religious world,"
according to which "liberty pointed the way to virtue and heroism." But, he laments, as he addresses the generalized West in the
person of his interviewer, "Time has eroded your conception of liberty. You have retained the word and manufactured a new conception: the petty liberty that is only a caricature of the great, a liberty
devoid of obligation and responsibility, which leads, at best, to the
enjoyment of material possessions. Nobody is prepared to die for
that."[29]

An aspect of Solzhenitsyn's moral vision that is even less likely
to resonate with modern readers is repentance. Solzhenitsyn has
long proclaimed this theme; it is the leading note in one of his most
important essays, "Repentance and Self-Limitation in the Life of
Nations." It is, he declares in that essay, repentance that "perhaps
more than anything else distinguishes man from the animal world."
He believes that nations, as communities of individuals, inevitably
bear collective responsibility for the political and military actions
of their nation-state, and that as a result citizens cannot escape paying "for the sins of their fathers." And since, furthermore, "a nation
can no more live without sin than can an individual," the destiny of
each nation is common repentance.[30] Recalling in 1990 the contri-
tion expressed in West Germany after Nazism passed, he imagines
the catharsis if the old Soviet leaders still alive in the 1990s were to
follow suit, but he anticipates that "we won't live to hear a word of
repentance from any of them."[31] The call to repentance was the chief
message that Solzhenitsyn propounded to his countrymen when he
returned to Russia in 1994. However, he was painfully aware that,
by and large, this call was falling upon deaf ears. "Cleansing only

comes about through repentance. . . . We need to repent. But no one wants to."[32]

Hope is yet another constituent element of Solzhenitsyn's moral vision. The conventional opinion that he is a Jeremiah figure is grossly misguided. Any attentive reader can confirm that Solzhenitsyn repeatedly adopts the rhetorical structure of movement from lament or warning to hope. Concluding on the note of hope is not empty rhetoric or wishful thinking to a believing Christian. It is, rather, an assertion that human history is neither meaningless nor incomprehensible. Good ultimately triumphs over evil. This view is encapsulated in the title of Dante's *Divine Comedy*. Comedy in its richest literary sense ends its story with a resolution into harmony and wholeness. For such a story hope is the proper final word.

Solzhenitsyn has all along been honored for his dedication to truth. He was honored for bravely and boldly exposing the mendacity of the Soviet regime. Indeed, the respect he earned for demolishing official lies was the emotional core of his early reception. He also deserves recognition for the meticulous effort he has put forth in his literary works to treat historical events and the lives of historical personages with scrupulous accuracy, part of his titanic effort to counter decades of Soviet lies about the past. But beyond this project stands the positive aspect of his worldview, for truth and falsehood are moral issues just as surely as are good and evil. There is a truth to be known about human nature and about the nature of things in general, and every step in Solzhenitsyn's endeavor to tell the truth is in this sense an effort to approach the essence of reality.

Solzhenitsyn has expressed confidence that in the end truth will win out over falsehood in open battle. Noting that "the favorite proverbs in Russian are about *truth*," he ends the Nobel lecture with one of them: "*One word of truth shall outweigh the whole world.*"[33] In the final analysis, then, truth is best understood as more than simply one additional constituent element of Solzhenitsyn's moral vision. Truth is the sum of all the parts of Solzhenitsyn's moral vision and is coterminous with it.

Solzhenitsyn's passion for truth does not lead him into abstract theorizing about the concept; rather, he devotes his indefatigable efforts to establishing the concrete truth about the tragic history of his country. This commitment to truth compels him to embark on a mission of memory, the specific goal of which is to resurrect a reality that had been "crushed, trampled, and maligned" during the Soviet decades.[34] He has typically expressed this aspiration in terms of *restoring memory*. In a 1976 interview he spoke of what had animated his drive to evoke a truthful picture of the camps, just as it had energized his research into the Russian Revolution: "My desire was to fulfill the function of memory. The memory of a people that had suffered a great misfortune."[35] The same basic point was formulated at another time in terms of moral duty: "The writer's task is to restore the memory of his murdered people."[36]

Moreover, the *Red Wheel* cycle and the epic of the camps are by no means the only writings in which Solzhenitsyn has tried to present the truth about the past. In a substantial effort at remembering a theme that in his opinion has not received treatment adequate to its importance, he has authored a two-volume study tracing the troubled history of Russian-Jewish relations through two centuries.[37] Other major projects are explicitly dedicated to bringing back from virtual oblivion unjustly forgotten aspects of the Russian past. These include the publication of a large lexicon of words displaced by the urban-oriented and politicized vocabulary of the Soviet period[38] and a series of essays on noteworthy Russian writers and literary works "the memory of which has been fading among my countrymen."[39]

It is important to emphasize, finally, that the missionary zeal with which Solzhenitsyn strives to recover the truth about Russian history and culture transcends any notion of his personal literary ambition. On the contrary, he has called on fellow Russians who witnessed past events to participate in a collective effort of reconstructing an authentic picture of the historical past. To this end, he has financed the establishment of the Russian Memoir Library, at first based on his Vermont estate, and after 1994 incorporated into

Moscow's Library of Émigré Literature (*Biblioteka-Fond "Russkoe Zarubezh'e"*). The Memoir Library has served as a depository for unpublished reminiscences, documents, letters, and other memorabilia illuminating aspects of Russian twentieth-century history, with these materials collected in response to Solzhenitsyn's appeal to Russian émigrés and, later, to his countrymen.[40] In this undertaking, as in all the other projects mentioned, the writer has been inspired by the conviction that the truth about Russia's past must be restored for the sake of a livable future.[41]

Alternative to the Enlightenment

Needless to say, many writers through the ages have operated with the concept of a moral universe. Dante's *Inferno* is the example par excellence of a literary work that depends on this concept, for the punishments (or consequences) of characters' actions are the extensions of those actions—and, in this case, throughout not only time but eternity. Milton's *Paradise Lost* is another crystal-clear example of the moral universe at work, as Adam's original sin is worked out in his life and in the lives of all those who come after him. Dostoevsky painstakingly shows how actions grow out of the habits of the heart and, as in his character Raskolnikov, how actions bring on inevitable consequences that are not subject to the protagonist's intentions. The concept of the moral universe is inescapable throughout the ancient, medieval, and early-modern epochs of Western civilization. It is on display wherever God and his good creation are accepted as givens. For the concept of the moral universe posits as the fundamental reality of human life that God and man intersect and stand in relationship to each other.

This way of talking about the relationship between man and the world seems to many heirs of the eighteenth-century Enlightenment to be primitive and outmoded—just the kind of thing to cause a critic to wave off Solzhenitsyn's thinking as "medieval rubbish."[42] In the late twentieth century, however, a rebellion against the Enlightenment project surfaced, drawing in a wide range of secular and religious thinkers, Solzhenitsyn among them. This is not to say that Solzhenitsyn and other traditionalists see nothing of merit among the effects of the Enlightenment. In the political sphere, for example, they can laud the Enlightenment for advancing human liberty by promoting the rule of law rather than men, for establishing democratic procedures and representative institutions, for recognizing individuals' rights. But at its deepest level—the metaphysical level—the Enlightenment rejected traditional beliefs about the nature of the universe and human beings. Enlightenment thought abandons the conviction that God is necessary. And if God is dispensable, so is a whole array of concomitant principles governing human life—indeed, the very principles that constitute the moral universe.

The culminating sections of Solzhenitsyn's *Harvard Address* provide the clearest distillation of his contrast between a traditional Christian worldview and the Enlightenment worldview. When he refers to "the mistake" that lies "at the root, at the very foundation of thought in modern times," he means "the prevailing Western view of the world" which came into its own in "the Age of Enlightenment." He summarizes this prevailing view as "rationalistic humanism or humanistic autonomy: the proclaimed and practiced autonomy of man from any higher force above him." This "anthropocentricity" denied "the existence of intrinsic evil in man" and "started modern Western civilization on the dangerous trend of worshiping man and his material needs." Also at this juncture in the history of ideas, "a total emancipation occurred from the moral heritage of Christian centuries with their great reserves of mercy and sacrifice." Even democracy, Solzhenitsyn insists, against much of received opinion, can be justified on Christian—as distinct from Enlightenment—grounds. For "in early democracies, as in American democracy at the time of its birth, all individual human rights were granted on the ground that man is God's creature. That is, freedom was given to the individual conditionally, in the assumption of his constant religious responsibility."[43]

Solzhenitsyn's analysis of the Enlightenment climaxes in a call to action—not to pursue some political program but to revisit the underlying matter of metaphysical foundations. "We cannot avoid reassessing the fundamental definitions of human life and human society. Is it true that man is above everything? Is there no Superior Spirit above him?" The Harvard speech's final two paragraphs focus on the issue of the proper relationship between body and soul. Believing that the world "has reached a major watershed in history," he calls upon humanity to rise "to a new level of life, where our physical nature will not be cursed, as in the Middle Ages, but even more importantly, our spiritual being will not be trampled upon, as in the Modern Era."[44] Most commentators on the Harvard address passed over its crucial culminating passage in silence, no doubt finding it either insignificant or baffling.

Of Literary Art

The view of the world that governs the content of Solzhenitsyn's writing also shapes his sense of calling in his role as literary artist. The *Nobel Lecture* is his central statement about art and literature, and a separate essay on it appears elsewhere in this book. The lecture makes clear from the start that Solzhenitsyn frames his literary theory in religious terms.

These terms govern his description of two contrasting kinds of artist in the lecture's opening section. One kind, drawing upon the Enlightenment concept of the autonomous self, "imagines himself the creator of an autonomous spiritual world" that is not necessarily related to the world around him. This attempt is doomed to failure. For "just as, in general, the man who declares himself the center of existence, is unable to create a balanced spiritual system,"[45] so neither can the artist successfully create his reality. Human actions in a novel must conform to the same moral laws that govern ordinary human life.

The other kind of artist understands this principle and views himself as "a humble apprentice under God's heaven." The artist of this second kind, Solzhenitsyn's kind, will not allow literature to be strictly self-referential but will seek to relate literature to life and connect the word to the world. For he has "no doubts about [the] foundations" of the world in which he works. According to the key sentence that follows, it is "given to the artist to sense more keenly than others the harmony of the world, the beauty and ugliness of man's role in it—and to vividly communicate this to mankind." The theological underpinnings of this crucial point should not pass unnoticed. The "harmony of the world" refers to the good order as it was created; the "beauty" and the "ugliness" refer to the effects wrought by human beings, who share in both creation and the fall into sin and thus act sometimes for the better and sometimes for the worse. The artist, whose creative powers derive from the original Creator, is obliged "to vividly communicate this to mankind"—all of this whole mottled reality, for this is the truth about the human condition. And communication is possible precisely because of the "timeless human nature" shared by writers and readers.[46] Thus does art pay its homage to the moral universe.

In his only other essay devoted entirely to literature per se, the 1993 speech to the National Arts Club later titled "Playing upon the Strings of Emptiness," Solzhenitsyn renews his criticism of writers whose work is circumscribed by subjectivity. Such "pseudo-'avant-garde'" writers characteristically exhibit "a rejection of and contempt for all foregoing tradition" and "mandatory hostility toward whatever is universally accepted." He borrows the modish term *postmodernism* to refer to these writers, whose "deep-seated hostility toward any spirituality" leads them to assert that "art need not be good or pure." Their passion for the "new, newer, and newer still, conceals an unyielding and long-sustained attempt to undermine, ridicule, and uproot all moral precepts. There is no God, there is no truth, the universe is chaotic, all is relative. . . . How clamorous it all is, but also—how helpless."[47] In broad terms, Solzhenitsyn collapses the differences between modernist and postmodernist art that postmodernists emphasize, seeing them both as opposing the religious insights on which he builds his literary theory.

Solzhenitsyn has long held that literary art is at its core a spiritual enterprise. In the mid-1960s, while trying to get *Cancer Ward* published at home, he spoke in a spiritual vocabulary to members of the Soviet Writers' Union (the supreme politicizers of literature). The writer's task, he explained to them, is not "to defend or criticize one or another mode of distributing the social product" (that is, in economic terms) nor "to defend or criticize one or another form of government organization" (that is, in political terms). Rather, the writer's task "is to select more universal and eternal questions, the secrets of the human heart and conscience, the confrontation between life and death, the triumph over spiritual sorrow, the laws in the history of mankind that were born in he depths of time immemorial and that will cease to exist only when the sun ceases to shine."[48]

Solzhenitsyn as Historian

For Solzhenitsyn, the craft of the historian is no less important than the art of the literary author. Indeed, he devoted an extraordinarily large portion of his prime years to conducting historical research. His oeuvre itself shows his imagination to be fundamentally historical in orientation. *The Gulag Archipelago* is "an experiment in literary investigation" into the nonfictional history of the Soviet prison-camp system. *The Red Wheel* embeds fictional characters within an inquiry into the historical causes of the Russian Revolution. More broadly, all of his fiction is situated within real history. And *Two Hundred Years Together,* leaving literature behind, is straightforward history writing.

Solzhenitsyn's historical imagination is unquestionably linked to his Christian worldview. This connection is fitting, in the sense that Christianity posits God's personal involvement in human history through creation and through the abiding presence of divine providence. Its central involvement with the time-space continuum lies in the Incarnation of Christ, when the God of the universe took on human form and shared the human lot by living and dying as "one of us." This is Christianity's distinctive way of intertwining the transcendent and the immanent and of implicating the immaterial with the material, heaven with earth. The intersection of the celestial and the terrestrial validates the purposefulness of human activity in this life and imbues that activity with significance for the life to come. This framework silently but ineluctably affects how a writer who is a Christian handles human events, whether working in the literary or in the historical mode (or in some combination of the two).

Solzhenitsyn is well aware that his Christian philosophy of history puts him in conflict with various other philosophies of history. His opposition to Marxism is legendary. Marxism is quasi-religious in character and, like Christianity, has a telos in view (the equality of the classless society) and a means to that end (economics-driven class struggle). But in sharp contrast to Christian teaching, its philosophy of history is rigidly deterministic. In his *Letter to the Soviet Leaders,* Solzhenitsyn tells the high and mighty of the USSR what he is sure they already know in their hearts, namely, that "this grim jest of the twentieth century" called Marxism is an utterly "discredited and bankrupt doctrine."[49]

The Red Wheel is the primary source for Solzhenitsyn's historiography. Tucked in among its profuse events and characters are comments relevant to issues in the philosophy of history. Perhaps surprisingly, in these comments Solzhenitsyn pays more attention to Tolstoy than to Marx.

The opening chapters of *August 1914* intimate the theistic foundations of Solzhenitsyn's historical imagination. On the first page of the work, the "world of small man-made things" is set against the backdrop of the "huge and elemental" realm of nature that God has made. By the second chapter, Leo Tolstoy appears in person when Sanya Lazhenitsyn, a character based on the author's father and presented in the book as a self-declared Tolstoyan, seeks him out. During their conversation Tolstoy intones "that people are evil not by nature but out of ignorance" (a standard Enlightenment idea). Sanya objects: " . . . it's not at all like that, Lev Nikolaevich, it just isn't so!"[50] All the rest of *The Red Wheel* is committed to showing that on this central issue of human nature the disciple speaks more wisely than the master. Indeed, the whole vast work can be understood as, in large part, a running argument against Tolstoy's philosophy of history.

Tolstoy, as we know, heartily embraced Jesus' ethical teachings but denied the supernatural elements of Christianity. All branches of Christianity, despite their differences on doctrinal details, together with—in Solzhenitsyn's understanding—all major religions of the world, place the locus of evil within every human being. Tolstoy, by contrast, follows Rousseau in viewing human nature as essentially innocent and in assigning to social institutions the agency for the evil that is undeniably present in human affairs. For Tolstoy, history is moved by large, impersonal forces, in the face of which individual human beings are passive recipients, lacking the ability to affect events significantly. In other words, Tolstoy promulgates both fatalism and historical determinism.

Solzhenitsyn's views on history are a study in contrast to his grand predecessor. *The Red Wheel* forcefully makes the case that the Bolshevik Revolution was in no way inevitable. Characters act out of free will, and their choices affect the course of their lives and—whether in small ways or large—the course of history. Solzhenitsyn rebuts Tolstoy pointedly and repeatedly. The narrator of *August 1914*, while wondering aloud whether it is possible to pinpoint the decisive battle in a war, muses, "We might look for consolation to Tolstoy's belief that armies are not led by generals, ships are not steered by captains, states and parties are not run by presidents and politicians—but the twentieth century has shown us only too often that they are." Solzhenitsyn engages in a *reductio ad absurdum* when depicting a Russian general who practices in *August 1914* what Tolstoy preached in *War and Peace:*

> [H]e knew that one must never take any abrupt and decisive steps of one's own; that nothing but muddle could ever come of a battle begun before it wants to begin; that warfare always goes its own way, always goes as it must go, irrespective of the plans of mere men; that events follow their inevitable course, and that the best general is the

one who refuses to interfere with them. His whole long
military career had convinced the general that Tolstoy's
views on this subject were correct: nothing was worse
than charging in with one's own decisions—people who
do that always come to grief.[51]

Examples abound of Solzhenitsyn's view that personal agency is
paramount. Indeed, *November 1916* can be summarized as devot-
ing a thousand pages to the proposition that individuals could and
should have acted to avert the looming calamity of revolution but
did not do so. In an act that is symbolic of the general tendency to
shirk responsibility, the fictional Colonel Georgi Vorotyntsev, the
epic's major protagonist who has a track record of taking responsible initiatives for the sake of his beloved Russia, takes time out
at this crucial juncture to dally in an adulterous relationship and
thereby forfeits the opportunity to make a positive contribution to
history. The withdrawal from action of this fictional figure stands
for the lack of constructive effort by the real historical personages
and opens the way for Lenin to work his destructive will—his destructive *free* will. Solzhenitsyn draws a straight line from the actions taken by Lenin to the consequent success of the Bolshevik
Revolution.

A central passage of exposition of Solzhenitsyn's philosophy of
history is expressed by an old intellectual in *August 1914* named
Varsonofiev, who presents it to Sanya Lazhenitsyn and another
student. Believing in the primacy of the individual, Varsonofiev
subordinates the drive for "ordering and perfecting society" to
the need "to perfect the order in our souls," which he calls "our
whole vocation."[52] Solzhenitsyn makes the same point in his own
voice in his address at Liechtenstein: "There can be only one true
Progress: the sum total of the spiritual progresses of individuals;
the degree of self-perfection in the course of their lives."[53] As the
students press for Varsonofiev's view of what constitutes the ideal
social order, he dismissively replies that "we cannot by our own
deliberate efforts devise this best of social systems." From this
anti-ideological position, Varsonofiev moves on to a specifically

anti-Enlightenment stance in denying that history is "governed by reason," insisting instead that history "has its own organic fabric which may be beyond our understanding." He then offers two images to illuminate his philosophy of history. The first suggests why an ideological approach must fail. "History grows like a living tree. Reason is to history what an ax is to a tree. It will not make it grow." If this first image emphasizes the negative, the second image, which follows without a break in the text, emphasizes the positive. "Or, if you prefer, history is a river. . . . The bonds between generations, institutions, traditions, customs, are what keep the stream flowing uninterruptedly." When the students ask, "Where should we look for the laws that govern the stream?" Varsonofiev, sighing, answers, "The laws for constructing the best social order must be inherent in the structure of the world as a whole. In the design behind the universe and in man's destiny." Lazhenitsyn presses further: "What about justice? . . . Surely justice is an adequate principle for the construction of a good society." To this question Varsonofiev answers heartily, "Yes indeed! . . . but not the justice we devise for ourselves, to create a comfortable earthly paradise. Another kind of justice which existed before us, without us, and for its own sake."[54] Throughout, the old sage mediates the concept of the moral universe to the next generation.

Love of Country

One of the most common accusations leveled at Solzhenitsyn over the years has been the assertion that he is "a Russian nationalist," in fact an "extreme" one. The term is notoriously imprecise, but as it is used by hostile critics, it implies some combination of xenophobia, hostility to democracy, and an aggressive stance toward the outside world. Yet each of these qualities is entirely inimical to positions Solzhenitsyn has publicly espoused, and the writer has responded to the charges on a number of occasions.[55]

An episode dating from 1982 illustrates the problem and at the same time points beyond the political misunderstanding to the deeper issues involved. In May of that year President Reagan hosted a lunch in the White House for a group of former Soviet dissidents. Solzhenitsyn received an invitation but refused to attend, despite his genuine admiration for Reagan. According to a *Washington Post* report published a month before the scheduled event, the president had originally intended to invite Solzhenitsyn for a private meeting, but certain officials in his administration had advised against it because the writer "has become a symbol of an extreme Russian nationalist position."[56] Solzhenitsyn was in effect being shunted aside on the strength of a false accusation, and he responded with a letter to the president that he released for publication. The central point is set forth in the following three sentences: "I am not at all a 'nationalist.' I am a patriot. This means I love my country and therefore well understand other people's love for theirs."[57]

The moral issues involved in this position are addressed in many of Solzhenitsyn's works. To begin with, for Solzhenitsyn, patriotism must never lead to immoral actions. On the contrary, it requires "frank assessment of [one's country's] vices and sins, and penitence for them."[58] Love of country, along with all other temporal affiliations and affections, is governed by moral principles and is to be judged by them. In a decisive passage from *"The Russian Question" at the End of the Twentieth Century,* Solzhenitsyn writes:

> There is some truth in the reproaches leveled at Russian ruling and intellectual elites for their belief in Russian exclusivism and messianism. Even Dostoyevsky, despite his incomparable acumen, failed to resist this subjugating influence: the dream of Constantinople, "the East will bring salvation to the West," and even disdain for Europe (an opinion which for a long time now has been impossible to read without shame).[59]

Solzhenitsyn rules out Russian exceptionalism in his *Nobel Lecture* as well. "Nations are the wealth of humanity, its generalized personalities. The least among them harbors within itself a special aspect of God's design."[60] Russia's story in the twentieth century carries paradigmatic lessons for other nations, he believes, but only because all nations are on a par and can learn from the experience of one another.

Solzhenitsyn's works of fiction provide additional evidence, if more is needed, that the author's attitude toward his beloved Russia is not idolatrous. In *Cancer Ward* the protagonist Oleg Kostoglotov tells the nurse Zoya a story from his prison-camp days, in which a gang of Russian hoodlums repeatedly robbed food from the other prisoners, a group of Japanese plus himself and another Russian prisoner. One night, the Japanese turned the tables and beat up the goons. The two Russian politicals "joined forces with the Japs." Zoya, shocked, asks, "Against the Russians?" Oleg answers, "I don't count grafters as Russians."[61] Needless to say, a xenophobe would not write a vignette elevating morally driven human solidarity over the blood ties of nationality.

In *The First Circle* Gleb Nerzhin is tempted to take his moral bearings from the vaunted image, plentifully present in nineteenth-century Russian literature, of "a haloed, silvery-haired People, embodying all wisdom, moral purity, and spiritual grandeur." But he ultimately rejects pegging his worldview to a strictly national source. Prison-camp life has taught him that "the People had no homespun superiority to him." In the most anti-nationalistic terms imaginable, Nerzhin concludes that "the people is not everyone who speaks our language" and that it is "not by birth" that one is "elected into the people." Rather, the true criterion resides in the sphere of moral universals, with qualities common to all humanity taking precedence over any national characteristics: "One must try to temper, to cut, to polish one's soul so as to become a *human being*. And thereby become a tiny particle of one's own people."[62]

The experience of Ignatich, the narrator of "Matryona's Home," is closely similar to the lesson learned by Nerzhin. Attracted by the picturesque qualities of a Russian village and at first impressed by the dignified appearance of its patriarch, Ignatich soon discovers that, except for Matryona, the villagers are greedy, mean-spirited folk with few redeeming moral qualities, and that the Russian décor that had so enchanted him at the beginning is but a thin veneer of no ethical significance.[63]

The Informing Spirit

Much of this chapter has been devoted to showing how thoroughly Solzhenitsyn's overarching vision is infused with moral categories. But it must be emphasized that moral meaning is not self-generating, and a writer's moral vision is not freestanding. Morality is built upon a foundation of some set of beliefs about ultimate realities; it is, in that sense, a dependent term, requiring a prior understanding of the nature of the universe and of human nature. And that is where religion comes into play. The nexus between religion and morality in Solzhenitsyn's works is precisely what Alexander Schmemann explicates in a seminal essay published in 1970. Schmemann argues for the foundational function of Christian concepts in Solzhenitsyn's works. He contends that Solzhenitsyn deserves to be called a "Christian writer" because he takes his bearings from "Biblical and Christian revelation, and only from it."[64] Schmemann's explanation deserves to be quoted in full:

> When I speak of a "Christian writer" and of Solzhenitsyn in particular, I have in mind a deep and all-embracing, although possibly unconscious[,] perception of the world, man, and life, which, historically, was born and grew from Biblical and Christian revelation, and only from it. Human culture as a whole may have had other sources, but only Christianity, only the revelation of the Old and New Testaments contains that perception of the world which, incorporated into human culture, revealed in it the potential, and indeed the reality[,] of a Christian culture. I shall call this perception, for lack of a better term, the *triune intuition of creation, fall, and redemption.* I am convinced that it is precisely this intuition that lies at the bottom of Solzhenitsyn's art, and that renders his art Christian.

Schmemann then expatiates upon these cardinal Christian doctrines as they apply to Solzhenitsyn's writings. As for creation, Solzhenitsyn may write "almost entirely about ugliness, suffering, and evil," but he always assumes "the original goodness of the world and life." As for the fall, evil for Solzhenitsyn is "not found in impersonal 'systems' or 'structures.'" Rather, evil "always remains on a *moral*, and therefore *personal* plane; it is always related to the conscience which is in every man. It is not a failing, an absence of something, a blindness or a lack of responsibility; it is man's betrayal of his humanity; it is his *fall*." Since "only that which is raised on high can fall," the Christian concept of the fall casts a retrospective light on the glory of creation, and that contrast explains how readers should approach the accumulation of horrors in Solzhenitsyn's texts. Those horrors are neither his first nor his last word. And as for redemption, Solzhenitsyn displays not "humanistic optimism" but "an indestructible faith in the possibility of *regeneration* for man, a refusal to 'write off' anyone or anything forever."[65]

Solzhenitsyn called Schmemann's essay "very valuable to me," because it "formulated important traits of Christianity which I could not have formulated myself."[66] Although both men are Russian Orthodox, in his writing Solzhenitsyn refers to specifically Orthodox concepts only rarely, and Schmemann fittingly emphasizes Solzhenitsyn's reliance on generic Christian concepts held in common by Christians of all denominations.

Schmemann's article is based entirely on a consideration of Solzhenitsyn's literary works, since none of the theoretical essays that were examined above had yet made their appearance, and it is therefore appropriate to conclude this chapter with specific examples of Christian symbolism in Solzhenitsyn's writings.

One theme that pervades the entire corpus of Solzhenitsyn's works is the defeat that is transformed into victory, in this sense echoing the central event of Christian history. Schmemann has himself noted the example of Innokenty Volodin, who experiences moral regeneration in the brutally hopeless environment of a Soviet prison.[67]

There are numerous examples of such a pattern of moral rebirth in *The Gulag Archipelago,* the most important one, obviously, being the story of how adversity—prison and critical illness—brought about Solzhenitsyn's own reawakening to moral reality and faith in God.

But the writer also introduces a different paradigm, one in which regeneration occurs not under the press of external forces but rather due to a "kick-start" from an aroused conscience. Three examples can be cited.

The protagonist in *Prussian Nights,* a military officer who participates ever more actively in the rampaging excesses of the Red Army in the closing phases of the war, allows himself to demand sexual favors from a German woman in a newly occupied town. But the act, once consummated, triggers a violent protest of his heretofore slumbering conscience, and the guilt and revulsion at himself that he expresses indicates with incontestable certainty that his subsequent life will be transformed.[68]

In similar fashion, moral transgression moves an aroused conscience to tear loose the ideological blinkers that had distorted the essentially decent nature of Zotov in "Incident at Krechetovka Station." Zotov's propaganda-inspired decision to turn over to the secret police a man who is clearly innocent disturbs his conscience to the point that he is unable to forget this episode for the rest of his life. What Solzhenitsyn is suggesting is not only that conscience is an immutable repository of human values, but that it can, and does, propel morally deficient or ideologically blinded individuals toward ethical regeneration. Schmemann's words apply: "Nothing is closed, condemned or damned."[69]

Part V of *The Gulag Archipelago* presents an especially vivid example of the power of an "activist" conscience to affect behavior. In a chapter titled "The White Kitten," Georgi Tenno, a "committed escaper" who has managed to break out of a Central Asian prison camp, tells the story of an escape attempt that surmounts all physical barriers but is stopped by his instinctive sense of good and evil.

Tenno, who together with a companion had been on the run for more than two weeks, unexpectedly encounters a provincial couple who are moving their entire belongings down the river to their new domicile. He instantly realizes that his dream of freedom would be assured if he were to appropriate this couple's papers. But he understands just as clearly that the only practical way this end could be achieved would be through murder. He hesitates.

> And suddenly—suddenly something very light touched my legs. I looked down: something small and white. I bent over; it was a white kitten. It had jumped out of the boat, and with its tail stiff as a stalk in the air, it purred and rubbed itself against my legs.

> I didn't know what I was thinking. I felt as though the touch of this kitten had sapped my will power. Stretched taut for twenty days, ever since I had slipped under the [barbed] wire, it suddenly seemed to snap. I felt that . . . I could never take the lives nor even the money [of these accidentally encountered people].[70]

Tenno's conscience cuts short his murderous impulse, doing so instinctively and acting directly on his emotions and will, without passing through the process of conscious reflection. And although Tenno comments bitterly on this episode, it is clear that in Solzhenitsyn's opinion the moral calculus points in Tenno's favor.

The concept of moral profit derived from a loss on a different plane can in certain instances also coincide with the idea of "self-limitation" promoted by Solzhenitsyn. These cases are, however, distinguished by an active exercise of will, as when Nerzhin denies himself a sexual rendezvous with Simochka in *The First* Circle,[71] or when Kostoglotov turns back from Vega's door in *Cancer Ward*.[72]

Solzhenitsyn's literary works have only recently begun to be plumbed for religious and specifically Christian patterns of imagery, and a great deal promises to emerge.[73]

Reception

When *One Day in the Life of Ivan Denisovich* appeared in 1962, "The literary talent of Solzhenitsyn was recognized at once: he became a classic overnight."[1] By 1974 a sharply different sentiment came to prevail. "Solzhenitsyn, I am afraid, is not one of us. That is to say he is not a liberal. I don't know what exactly he is, but whatever it is, it is most peculiar."[2] And some two decades later, one could read that "Solzhenitsyn's stock had sunk precipitously," descending "from revered sage and prophet . . . to irrelevant political dinosaur and target of jokes."[3] The trajectory intimated by these scattered references applies primarily to his treatment at the hands of journalists, the very group of people with the most immediate access to shaping public opinion. In partial contrast, there has been a rather steady stream of scholarly books and articles about Solzhenitsyn exhibiting a range of attitudes toward him that are much less dependent on journalistic fashion. Even among journalists, by no means did all of his early admirers, including numerous liberals, abandon him. Furthermore, his standing has remained much higher in some countries, especially France, than in the United States. And his name now routinely appears in scholarly works on the collapse of Soviet communism, the end of the Cold War, and related topics.

In broad terms, nevertheless, an originally positive consensus among opinion-shapers soon turned into a negative consensus

207

from which Solzhenitsyn's reputation has never fully recovered. This radical pivot is most evident in English-speaking countries, especially in the United States, and the present chapter emphasizes English-language journalistic references, to which the reception in France serves as a provocative counterpoint. Untranslated Russian-language responses are mentioned only briefly. The author's reception in his homeland, the terms of which were dictated by the regime, was predictably monotonous until the Soviet straitjacket fell away.[4] Because Solzhenitsyn attained high visibility as a literary author, charting his public reception is a necessary part of tracing his life. In keeping with his sensational life, the subsidiary story of this reception is exceptional for its sheer intrinsic drama. Furthermore, examining his reception turns attention toward what matters most—Solzhenitsyn's writings—and provides occasion to sort through the critical responses to them and clear away the clutter of misrepresentations.

The chronological account that follows can be prepared for by identifying two significant causes of critical confusion about Solzhenitsyn. The lesser of these has to do with literature; the greater has to do with politics. Solzhenitsyn's approach to literature is, according to the tastes prevailing in the second half of the twentieth century, old-fashioned. Literature obviously is guided by aesthetic considerations, but Solzhenitsyn believes that it also should tell the truth. He heartily rejects any notion that literature should avoid moral themes and ethical judgments. Instead, he unapologetically presents many issues in what might be called an ethically absolutist manner. This stance is at odds with the tendency toward moral relativism that permeates modern thought, and it is incompatible with the postmodernist critics' dismissal of all absolutist convictions in principle. Moreover, most of Solzhenitsyn's fiction deals with actual history, and this fact, too, colors his aesthetic in an unfashionable way. He insists that he is "not simply a belletristic writer," but that "in all my books I place myself in the service of historical truth."[5] That is, he self-consciously separates himself from proponents of art for art's sake. In fact, it may be fairly said that his understanding of the function of literature conforms, in general terms, to that of his great predecessors, Dostoevsky and Tolstoy (not to mention such classic writers as Dante and Milton). Thus, the complaint that Solzhenitsyn's fiction is didactic misses the point; he means for it to include a didactic element. To recoil from his moral emphasis is to take exception to what he knowingly and with a will subscribes to as the proper role of literature. That his literary art was initially accepted with enthusiasm, despite its traditionalism, testifies to the intrinsic power of his art to break through the critics' accustomed defenses.

Political issues caused more critics to question Solzhenitsyn—and eventually to distance themselves from him—than did literary issues. Indeed, complaints about his didacticism came to the fore only when suspicions about his politics began to be voiced. In broad terms, Solzhenitsyn and his critics adhered to different hierarchies of values and therefore constructed worldviews that were in conflict. Solzhenitsyn focuses on morality; he is, above all, a moral writer. The majority of his critics, by contrast, whether Soviet or Western, have shown that, at least in practice, they value politics above all other spheres of human activity and thus view everything through the prism of politics. This conflict between the author's chief interest and the critics' chief preoccupation is the central issue of "the Solzhenitsyn affair," as the controversies of the mid-1970s were sometimes called. When Solzhenitsyn first became known, Western critics recognized him as an ally in the fight against totalitarian oppression and thus assumed that he generally shared their political outlook. But when the newly exiled writer accepted invitations to speak, many critics discerned, to their surprise and discomfort, that, despite some common conclusions, he and they had considerably different starting points. Solzhenitsyn recognized not only this disconnection but also its cause: He explained that politics is not his "framework" or "dimension" and therefore that he "cannot be regarded in political terms."[6] This disclaimer Solzhenitsyn reiterated frequently and consistently, in a variety of contexts.

This is not to say that Solzhenitsyn avoids political topics; indeed, he often comments on politics, because political factors form a crucial part of the story that preoccupies him, that of twentieth-century Russia. Solzhenitsyn's political thought is richly textured and well worth studying. Inquiring into the common good is a recurring concern of his, though at the same time a key ingredient of his politics is an insistence on the limits of politics as a means to improving the human condition. Misrepresentation arises when his politics is considered apart from his overarching moral vision and treated as a self-contained sphere. Solzhenitsyn ever keeps his eye trained on the moral issues that reside within every sphere of human activity, including politics. Moral reflection is the habit of his mind. Or, to borrow Marxist imagery, morality is the base, and politics is part of the superstructure. Thus, politics can hold a high place in his thinking, but it simply cannot hold the highest place. Commentators who value politics above all other spheres of human activity tend to ignore this elementary distinction between "high" and "highest." The lamentable result is properly labeled *politicization,* that is, discussing in ideologically charged terms phenomena that are not fundamentally political. And the error of politicizing is compounded when critics of Solzhenitsyn bring into play categories, such as *liberal* and *conservative,* that refer to a Western spectrum of political positions but do not precisely apply to the Russian writer. Some Solzhenitsyn scholars have grasped the proper relationship between politics and morality in Solzhenitsyn and thus have taken a properly nuanced approach to his politics, most notably Daniel J. Mahoney in his book *Aleksandr Solzhenitsyn: The Ascent from Ideology.*[7] But careful scholarship did not determine the main flow of Solzhenitsyn's reception, and the only book that played a significant (though problematic) role in his reception was Michael Scammell's biography.[8] For the most part, it was journalists who determined Solzhenitsyn's reception, and they—all too often—were simply reading one another.

The widespread misunderstanding of the place occupied by politics in Solzhenitsyn's hierarchy of values has been augmented by the no less common incomprehension of his religious convictions. These views are examined in the "Beliefs" chapter, and here it merely needs to be noted that they could not but become an additional factor affecting the tenor of his reception.

Early Praise

The story of Solzhenitsyn's reception begins with Nikita Khrushchev. Beyond permitting Solzhenitsyn to be published for the first time, the Soviet premier also set in motion a way of approaching the author's work that has, in various guises, continued ever since. When Khrushchev allowed *One Day in the Life of Ivan Denisovich* to appear, he did so for an explicitly political reason: to condemn "the evil inflicted on the Communist party" by Stalin.[9] He subordinated the literary to the political when he said, with *One Day* in mind, "The party gives its backing to artistic creations which are really truthful . . . so long as they help the people in their effort to build a new society."[10] True to form, Soviet publications took their cue from Khrushchev; thus, Konstantin Simonov wrote in *Izvestia*, "The party has called writers its helpers. . . . Alexander Solzhenitsyn, in his story, has shown himself a true helper of the Party in a sacred and vital cause."[11] Only Aleksandr Tvardovsky, in his preface to Solzhenitsyn's work, diverged somewhat from Khrushchev's instrumental approach to *One Day*. As a literary man, Tvardovsky emphasized the book's aesthetic quality and noted especially that its moral power lay in its "truthfulness about the nature of man,"[12] rather than truthfulness according to party dicta; even he, however, tinctured his literary appraisal with politics by stubbornly hoping that the book would help cultivate a kinder and gentler communism—much to Solzhenitsyn's chagrin.

The initial Western response to *One Day in the Life of Ivan Denisovich* was enthusiastic. Franklin D. Reeve hailed it as "one of the most powerful prose works of the twentieth century."[13] Similar encomia appeared in profusion, though reservations among some American academics were not entirely absent. Yet even as the literary and moral dimensions of the work were being taken into account, the heavy emphasis on political significance that marked Soviet reactions showed up, in varying degrees, among most Western reactions as well. Thus, it can be said in hindsight that numerous Western critics were distant, albeit unwitting, practitioners of the Khrushchev School of Literary Criticism. Later, as the motivating political issue shifted from the Soviet critics' question of whether Solzhenitsyn was a true Soviet writer to the Western critics' question of whether he was a Western-style liberal, the Khrushchev-initiated approach of viewing Solzhenitsyn through the prism of politics gathered strength, with only *One Day* remaining to some extent exempt from the ensuing detractions.

When *The First Circle* and *Cancer Ward* were published in the West in 1968, they were welcomed warmly as literary achievements. American scholar Deming Brown declared, "No longer can there be the slightest question about [Solzhenitsyn's] literary stature or doubt of its permanence."[14] *The First Circle* received British accolades of "majestic work of genius" and "arguably the greatest Russian novel of the twentieth century."[15] American journalist Jeri Laber called *The First Circle* "a distinguished work" with a "profound" vision and declared that its author "is not a polemicist" but, rather, "the symbol and embodiment of an undaunted creative spirit." Robert Garis demurred, finding the author "immensely honorable" but his talent for fiction "undistinguished."[16] It is crucial to note that even the rare negative assessment of the day gave priority to literary, rather than political, considerations.

When Solzhenitsyn was expelled from the Soviet Writers Union in 1969, Western writers protested. One open letter declaring solidarity was signed by such luminaries as Arthur Miller, John Updike, John Cheever, Truman Capote, Richard Wilbur, Jean-Paul Sartre, and Kurt Vonnegut. Another was signed by W. H. Auden, Günter Grass, Graham Greene, Mary McCarthy, Muriel Spark, and other established authors.[17] Solzhenitsyn gratefully acknowledged this invaluable Western support. Such was the mood that in the next year, 1970, when the Nobel Prize for Literature was bestowed upon Solzhenitsyn. Western satisfaction was virtually unanimous; even French and Italian Communists concurred. The view of Solzhenitsyn that prevailed as late as 1971 is captured by the opening lines of an Italian biography: "Solzhenitsyn is first a great writer and only second a literary sensation. His greatness is not due to the publicity he has received; on the contrary, there would hardly have been such worldwide interest in his fate if he had been a mediocrity."[18]

First Downturn

Solzhenitsyn's reputation took its first downturn in 1972, after he circulated an open letter to Patriarch Pimen about the compromised condition of the Orthodox Church in the Soviet Union, and after a prayer of his was published in the West. The writer's Christian convictions, virtually unremarked in the criticism until then, suddenly became incontrovertibly clear. Moreover, this coincided with the appearance of the initial version of *August 1914*—in Russian in 1971 and in English in 1972—and even the least religiously oriented of critics could not help noticing in it evidence of the author's Christian affinities, particularly as manifested in his fidelity to the religious heritage of Russia that spanned a thousand years. For those with eyes to see, there had been many earlier signs that Solzhenitsyn was, at a minimum, sympathetic toward religion. Father Alexander Schmemann had already observed in an insightful but generally overlooked essay that, whether or not Solzhenitsyn was formally a Christian, his works displayed, perhaps unconsciously, a worldview "which, historically, was born and grew from Biblical and Christian revelation, and only from it."[19] In any case, the revelations of 1972 unsettled a number of his secular admirers and put them on guard for more unwelcome news to come.

The appearance of *August 1914* "disrupted the unanimity of opinion that had enveloped [Solzhenitsyn's] earlier works."[20] Solzhenitsyn himself has dated "the schism among my readers" to this publishing event.[21] Some reviewers expressed hearty approval of *August 1914*. One rhapsodized that it "meets all expectations and indeed surpasses them." Another, lauding the text's "stylistic complexity" and "verbal inventiveness," declared Solzhenitsyn's position as the foremost living Russian writer to be "unassailable on any imaginable literary grounds."[22] A greater number, however, expressed misgivings about the work's aesthetic quality, often softening their tone by praising the man himself. One reviewer found *August 1914* "seriously flawed"; another found its author "a monotonous writer."[23] The work's religious flavor grated on some reviewers. Gore Vidal asserted, "At the book's core there is nothing beyond the author's crypto-Christianity." Philip Toynbee lamented the work's "moments of tired mystical jingoism."[24] Jeri Laber, whose praise for *The First Circle* had been unqualified, wrote in quite a different register four years later about *August 1914.* Characterization seemed strong then, weak now. Religion received no notice then; now she seemed displeased by "this overtly religious novel" and its "pedantic and highly moralistic tone."[25]

Mary McCarthy took it upon herself to say in plain words what was troubling Western reviewers about *August 1914;* it was the author's politics. "Solzhenitsyn himself, to say it straight out, is rude and unfair in his novel to a whole category of society: the 'liberals' and 'advanced circles' of 1914. . . . He has it in for those people, just as he would have it in for you and me, if he could overhear us talking." The deliciously unguarded assumption behind the "you and me" is that the reviewer and her readers share a sense of belonging to elite, "advanced circles." Those readers will want to know that *August 1914* "is *not* the work of a liberal imagination."[26] As Michael Scammell later noted, McCarthy was pointing out that "Solzhenitsyn's novel seemed almost deliberately designed to offend the sensibilities of Western liberals—in other words, the sort of people most likely to be reviewing it."[27] Consensus among cultural elites is a matter not of conspiracy but of intellectual fashion. Elite opinion of the time was identifiably secular as to religion and liberal as to politics. All cultural phenomena were put through the grid formed by these commitments. When Solzhenitsyn was put through this grid, he was correctly seen to be "other," not "one of us" ("you and me"). It takes only a small further step to categorize him as retrograde. And the step after that tends to slide into mishandling evidence in the rush to fill in details of the new portrait—or caricature.

Exile Begins

Solzhenitsyn was welcomed effusively when he reached the West in 1974, though not by everyone. Twenty-five US senators spanning the political spectrum sponsored a resolution to grant Solzhenitsyn honorary US citizenship, but the Republican administration objected. Secretary of State Henry Kissinger, who was promoting a policy of détente with the Soviet Union at the time, recommended against inviting the newcomer to the White House. President Gerald Ford privately called Solzhenitsyn "a goddam horse's ass." Ford's snub of Solzhenitsyn met with universal disapproval. Hundreds of letters received at the White House censured the snub, and sympathy for Solzhenitsyn inspired a plank in the Republican Party's platform of 1976 titled "Morality in Foreign Policy."[28]

Solzhenitsyn's forced arrival in the West followed hard on the heels of the appearance of volume 1 of the Russian text of *The Gulag Archipelago*. In the Soviet press, the Western publication of *Gulag* set loose a torrent of invective-laced denunciations. Vitriolic broadsides from journalists were supplemented by outraged letters to the editor from milkmaids, lathe operators, and other workers who were recruited to castigate a literary work they had not seen, with letters from faraway locations miraculously reaching Moscow overnight. Vituperative name-calling was the norm. Solzhenitsyn was characterized as a psychotic renegade unhinged by hatred for his homeland, a decadent descendant of embittered class enemies, a contemptible Judas dancing to the tune of Western warmongers, a Nazi at heart, and so on. He received threatening phone calls and hate-filled mail. The choreographed tide of Soviet vilifications of book and author are of minimal interest, but the ferocity of the reaction is direct evidence of the pain and damage *Gulag* had inflicted on the regime.

Within the Soviet Union, dissent from the official line came from the dependably brave Andrei Sakharov and Lydia Chukovskaya.[29] It was easier for the Soviet-style "loyal opposition" to speak out. Their most noteworthy representative was Roy Medvedev, a historian who, in rejecting Stalin, remained faithful to the Marxist-Leninist creed. While highlighting his differences from Solzhenitsyn on politics and religion, Medvedev vouched for the general historical accuracy of *Gulag*.[30]

Western reviewers, by contrast, widely welcomed *The Gulag Archipelago* as "both a literary masterpiece and an unparalleled indictment of the Soviet regime."[31] Harrison Salisbury effused, "Against the powerful state stands a single man. . . . The odds against Solzhenitsyn seem tremendous. Yet I know of no Russian writer who would not trade his soul for Solzhenitsyn's mantle, who does not know that one hundred years from now all the world . . . will bow to his name when most others have been forgotten."[32]

A Negative Consensus Begins

Solzhenitsyn's *Letter to the Soviet Leaders* appeared in print in the same general time frame as the first volume of *Gulag* (after the Russian text and before the English translation), and it received a decidedly chilly welcome from most Western commentators. Whereas *August 1914* had troubled a number of influential critics two years earlier, its unfashionably patriotic ideas could be at least partially ascribed to the fictional context. The *Letter,* in contrast, presented its political message in an explicit form that could not be ignored or rationalized away, and its argument for moderate gradualism was instantly misinterpreted by the advocates of radical democratization as evidence of the writer's "authoritarianism," a charge that was destined to become a major—and endlessly recycled—component in Western criticism of Solzhenitsyn.

The negative reactions to *Letter* acted as a brake on enthusiasm for *Gulag*. In particular, several critics viewed Solzhenitsyn's challenge to established interpretations of history as a point against, not for, him. In Joshua Rubenstein's words, "Solzhenitsyn's uncompromising hatred of the Soviet regime leaves him purblind or indifferent to several historical judgments generally accepted in the West." George Steiner sided with Khrushchev's view that the Soviet experiment went wrong with Stalin and faulted *Gulag* for "utterly reject[ing] this version of history."[33] And the fact that Roy Medvedev had embraced *Gulag* while strenuously objecting to *Letter* gave Western leftists confidence in casting their own split verdict.[34]

Nevertheless—and oddly—in most Western countries the little letter had greater immediate impact on the author's reputation than did the monumental *Gulag*. The letter was, in John Dunlop's estimation, "the real watershed for liberals."[35] For a journalist who thought it worth deciding whether Solzhenitsyn belonged to liberals or conservatives, the letter was decisive: "He is a reactionary. . . . No one who reads this letter attentively can doubt that if Solzhenitsyn had been an American citizen in 1972 he would have voted for Richard Nixon against George McGovern."[36] Five days after Solzhenitsyn's deportation, William Safire, of the *New York Times,* announced himself "the first on my block to feel misgivings about Alexander Solzhenitsyn." With an insider's awareness of how intellectual fashions work, Safire anticipated that the broad consensus in Solzhenitsyn's favor would soon come apart: "Some against-the-grain profilists may report him to be crabbier, more messianic and less beatific than is customarily associated with sainthood, and today's intellectual inspiration may become tomorrow's former hero, the old champ who turns into a bore."[37]

Jeri Laber conveyed with perfect pitch the 1974 shift in conventional opinion toward Solzhenitsyn. "The Real Solzhenitsyn"—her title—is "authentically reactionary" in his politics: "Reactionary, authoritarian, chauvinistic—hardly adjectives that sit comfortably with the typical image of a freedom-fighter and Nobel Prize winner." Although this is a new note in her comments on Solzhenitsyn, Laber says that others sounding this note "have done so with surprise," adding, "Many Western admirers of his fight against despotism had considered Solzhenitsyn an advocate of liberal values and had, until the publication of the *Open Letter,* refused to acknowledge what should have been evident from a careful reading of his fiction and his earlier political pronouncements." Among his political offenses, "Solzhenitsyn blames not Stalin but Marxism itself for the system that destroyed millions of his countrymen." Political disagreement then elides into aesthetic disapproval: His art is "didactic" and "often dull and ponderous." Despite her previous high praise for his fiction, she now notes that "many Western readers appear to find his novels heavy-handed, humorless, and monotonous."[38] Her belittlement of Solzhenitsyn's religion is not new, however; it began in 1972. In a subsequent article titled "The Selling of Solzhenitsyn," Laber memorably phrased her main complaint: "he is not the 'liberal' we would like him to be." Conceding that this point "should not really matter," Laber then belabors it at length in her effort to debunk the "misleadingly 'liberal' image" that Solzhenitsyn was "selling."[39]

Jeri Laber was not a fountainhead but a bellwether of opinion. At this same time (1974) and on the same evidence (*Letter*), many journalists were describing Solzhenitsyn in similar—at times almost identical—terms. Nan Robertson, of the *New York Times*, compiled her own list of adjectives: "messianic, patriotic, utopian and religious in tone; anti-democratic, anti-Western." Anthony Astrachan, of the *Christian Science Monitor*, asserted that Solzhenitsyn "is no liberal," noted the Russian's "contempt for the Western world," and alleged that his "nationalism verges on chauvinism and racism though it never falls into the abyss." Jonathan Yardley (today the editor of *Washington Post Book World*), found Solzhenitsyn "neither a 'liberal' nor a 'democrat'" but rather "a not-very-thinly disguised Czarist" and grumbled that Solzhenitsyn "is adroit at self-promotion, and has skillfully used the western press both to enhance his 'image' and to advance his own purposes."[40]

By 1974, according to Timothy Foote, "the going literary view" was that "Solzhenitsyn is a great man, but not a great writer."[41] The process of discrediting the man himself was further advanced than Foote realized, but he was entirely correct in observing that there was such a thing as "the going view." It is remarkable the extent to which, as if in an echo chamber of opinions, many critics said much the same thing—the same *new* thing—at the same time.

As the second and third volumes of *The Gulag Archipelago* made their way into print, Western reviewers accorded them generalized but restrained approval. Even such a favorable review of volume 2 as Patricia Blake's had to concede that "it has become the fashion to dismiss 'Gulag' as 'nothing new.'"[42] Abraham Brumberg's review of volume 3 detoured from the material at hand to complain about the author's "venomous and often fatuous polemical attacks on Western 'liberals'" and to advance the increasingly common hypothesis that "in some essential respects [Solzhenitsyn] is very much a creature of the system he so passionately loathes."[43]

The French Reception

As part of the record of the Western reception of *The Gulag Archipelago*, an intriguing counterpoint to the prevailing pattern comes from France. In that country the work's impact on both intellectuals and the reading public was sensational. A whole generation of leftist intellectuals who had been blind to the true nature of the Soviet regime read the book and changed their minds. *Gulag* undermined the standing of French Communists and discredited "fellow-travelers," most notably Jean-Paul Sartre, and it fueled a new anti-totalitarian consensus. The splashiest testimonies to Solzhenitsyn's influence came from young intellectuals, such as André Glucksmann and Bernard-Henri Lévy, who had participated in the revolutionary upheavals of May 1968 and later were fleetingly dubbed the "New Philosophers" by the media. Lévy called Solzhenitsyn first the Shakespeare, then the Dante, of our time. He observed that French intellectuals had lived with a "monumental deception" about Soviet realities for a half century, then remarked, "All Solzhenitsyn had to do was *to speak* and we awoke from a dogmatic sleep."[44] Though there were of course some holdouts,[45] Solzhenitsyn's impact on French thinking was immediate, deep, and enduring.

A crucial moment in the story of Solzhenitsyn among the French came when he appeared in April 1975 on Bernard Pivot's sophisticated television talk show, *Apostrophes,* to an eager and exceptionally large audience. The headline episode was the confrontation between Solzhenitsyn and Jean Daniel, the editor of the left-of-center Parisian newsweekly *Nouvel Observateur,* who had castigated Solzhenitsyn for being an apologist for reactionary regimes. Thus, the lines were clearly drawn for a showdown about the nature and effects of Soviet communism, and the TV program galvanized proponents on both sides for a long-lasting debate. In short, Solzhenitsyn succeeded in inserting himself into French intellectual life as an active participant—and to a degree that he never attained in any other Western country. The fact that Paris is an important center of intellectual life among émigré Russians worldwide was a contributing factor. Paris is home to YMCA Press, Solzhenitsyn's Russian-language publisher (led by his scholarly friend, Nikita Struve), as well as to the weekly newspaper *Russkaya Mysl* and to Solzhenitsyn's literary agent, Claude Durand, chief editor of the Fayard publishing house. One of the best books about Solzhenitsyn—informed, measured, respectful—came from Georges Nivat, a highly regarded Swiss Slavist (writing in French).[46] Raymond Aron, a renowned scholar, wrote an article contrasting Sartre and Solzhenitsyn and siding with the latter, whom he called perhaps the greatest writer of our time.[47] Bernard Pivot, whose homework in preparation for hosting Solzhenitsyn put American TV interviewers to shame, kept Solzhenitsyn before the French with another interview in 1983, which corrected many errors still perpetuated elsewhere in the West, including such details as the type of fencing that surrounded the Solzhenitsyn family's Vermont property. And it remains true that Solzhenitsyn's works are translated promptly and fully into French and generally receive more-favorable reviews in France than elsewhere.

Examples of Solzhenitsyn's influence in France could be multiplied. Ex-Trotskyist Claude Lefort, a top-notch political philosopher, wrote a major commentary on *The Gulag Archipelago* and remains a great admirer of Solzhenitsyn, despite keeping to Solzhenitsyn's left in general political orientation and not sharing his religious convictions.[48] Raymond Aron drew substantially on Solzhenitsyn in framing his own arguments against Marxism.[49] Alain Besançon is sometimes inspired by and always in accord with Solzhenitsyn in formulating his insightful interpretation of the Soviet Union as an ideological, or "ideocratic," regime.[50] Two influential Paris-based journals founded soon after Solzhenitsyn became a presence in France, *Commentaire* in 1978 and *Débat* in 1980, reflect and reinforce the Solzhenitsyn-inspired anti-totalitarian consensus. Also, it was not uncommon for moderately leftist French thinkers to express admiration for Solzhenitsyn long after Anglo-American liberals settled into firm opposition.

The French appreciation of Solzhenitsyn established in the 1970s persisted through subsequent decades, though detractors remained in evidence as well. *Le Monde* sounded at times like establishment Western newspapers elsewhere in describing his politics as "reactionary" and "anti-democratic." On similar grounds Lévy's initial enthusiasm waned. Boris Souvarine, an old Communist turned anticommunist who had known Lenin personally and who wrote an authoritative biography of Stalin, challenged Solzhenitsyn's account of the Soviet founder in *Lenin in Zurich*. Fierce exchanges between the two authors ensued.[51] Controversies entailed in "the Solzhenitsyn affair" flared up again years later in 1997, when *The Black Book of Communism,* which emanated from French scholars, was published. The appearance of this volume demonstrates that, in the West's familiar scholarly divide between the so-called "revisionist" Sovietologists and the anti-totalitarians, the latter were stronger in France than elsewhere, due in good part to Solzhenitsyn. French reviews of *The Red Wheel* ranged from respectful to admiring, whereas in the Anglo-American world, where a much smaller percentage of the cycle has been translated, it has already been declared a failure. In 1993, when Solzhenitsyn said his public goodbyes to the West before returning to Russia, one of his speeches was delivered in France, whereas none was delivered in the United States; in this way he chose to show gratitude where he thought it most due. While in France, he participated in another televised roundtable discussion. In December 2000 Solzhenitsyn was inducted into the prestigious French Academy of the Moral and Political Sciences in a ceremony held at the French embassy in Moscow. Whatever accounts for the better reception of Solzhenitsyn in France than in other Western countries, the contrast is real. And, at a minimum, it shows the road not taken in other countries.

The Negative Consensus Hardens

In 1975 and 1976 Solzhenitsyn gave a number of speeches and interviews in the United States and Great Britain. A BBC-TV interview in March 1976, while not matching the sensation of the French interview a year earlier, created quite a stir in Britain, though less of one in the United States when it was replayed there. In general, the public performances of these years kept Solzhenitsyn's name in the news, but their blunt rhetoric and unfashionable content only roiled the waters more. Commentators, increasingly unfriendly, observed with displeasure his inflexible opposition to Marxist ideology, his insistence that détente toward the Soviet Union was a mistake in America's foreign policy, his assessment that the West's political behavior lacked moral clarity and political courage, his castigation of the West for those occasions when he thought it failed to implement its vaunted principles of democracy and freedom of speech. Solzhenitsyn's later observations make it clear that he expected a less negative reception to his public utterances than he received. Those who differed from him on ideas would still, he anticipated, welcome an open exchange of views. But things went wrong in the communication process. Auditors who bristled at his views missed the nuances in his arguments; those who turned defensive ignored his expressions of friendship toward the West and of broad appreciation of Western ways. Too often, his tone struck a number of Westerners as peremptory, uncompromising, and combative, thus heightening the wall of resistance to his content. Tone, probably more than any other factor, introduced enough static to cause Western critics to miss the fundamental moderation of his political views and thus to mischaracterize him as an extremist. The negative consensus had become firmer than ever, and expressions of hostility turned strident. A British newspaper column was titled "Solzhenitwit"; and, in a new low, Simon Winchester sided with those willing "to query the author's mental stability." Winchester's fellow Britisher Bernard Levin represented the other side with an essay titled "Solzhenitsyn Among the Pygmies."[52] As publicly expressed attitudes hardened, detractors outnumbered defenders by a substantial margin.

Yuri Andropov, sitting back in the Kremlin, must have been monitoring KGB reports about the author's reception in the West with some satisfaction. Although Andropov surely overstated the efficacy of KGB efforts to plant anti-Solzhenitsyn stories in the Western press, he could cite, chapter and verse, criticisms that were indeed contributing to "a certain reassessment of [Solzhenitsyn's] personality." And so the instigator of a continuing campaign against the man he had exiled could gleefully chortle over what he viewed as "the abrupt decline of interest" among Western intellectuals toward the previously heralded writer.[53] With widespread and varied misunderstandings lingering in the air, Solzhenitsyn left behind him the role of public speaker and returned to the quiet life of a writer. The time had arrived to give uninterrupted attention to *The Red Wheel*, which, with the initial version of *August 1914* published, was well begun but far from done.

The Harvard Episode

Solzhenitsyn's 1978 commencement address at Harvard University was indubitably a major event in his reception, especially by Americans. This episode did not, however, signal a new departure. Instead, it marked the time when the gathering negative consensus attained full consolidation. It was also the time when the elites' disapproval of Solzhenitsyn permeated the consciousness of the public, who sensed that, for whatever reasons, the author's previous lionization had given way to suspicion. The speech's social setting was rife with potential for miscommunication. Into a festive occasion the speech injected somber content. At an event well covered by members of the press, the speaker accused the press of habitually making hasty and superficial judgments. At the academic nursery of the best and brightest, Solzhenitsyn excoriated the nation's intellectual and ruling elites for their lack of courage. At the citadel of enlightened secular thought, he used explicitly religious terms to diagnose Western society's ills and propose his remedies.

By no means was all of the reaction negative. When columnist Mike Barnicle exclaimed in the *Boston Globe* that Solzhenitsyn "was incapable of writing his way out of a paper bag," ninety-four of the one hundred letters the newspaper received rejected Barnicle's broadside.[54] Two years after the event, there appeared a book titled *Solzhenitsyn at Harvard,* comprising the speech itself, twelve early responses, and six later reflections—the very structure of the book suggesting that the speech contained more of value than had initially been perceived. Twenty years after the speech, a magazine published a symposium on the speech's enduring relevance,[55] and twenty-five years afterward, a small commemorative conference was held on Harvard's campus. The text continues to be required reading in selected university courses. Nevertheless, the dominant note in contemporaneous reviews of the address was, by a wide margin, negative.

The most widely expressed opinion was, in the words of a *Washington Post* editorial, that the speaker displayed a "gross misunderstanding of Western society." The *New York Times* editorial cautioned its readers against heeding the man who "believes himself to be in possession of The Truth and so sees error wherever he looks." Columnist James Reston said that the address, titled in printed form *A World Split Apart,* "sounded like the wanderings of a mind split apart." Mary McGrory was one of several who reacted by leaping to America's defense: "The unspoken expectation was that after three years in our midst, he would have to say we are superior, that our way is not only better, but best. . . . It is hard for us to face the fact that the giant does not love us."[56]

Positive reactions, while in the minority, were not negligible in number or in force. Father Theodore Hesburgh, president of the University of Notre Dame, accepted Solzhenitsyn's "highly unfashionable and unpopular truths" about "the moral mediocrity of the times." Labor leader George Meany observed "how violently Solzhenitsyn provoked the knee-jerk minds of the day, immersed as they were in an unhealthy mixture of post-Viet Nam guilt and a fashionable anti-anti-Communism." Theologian Michael Novak called the address "the most important religious document of our time." And it is indeed astonishing how much more critical attention went to the speech's first half, which catalogs current Western weaknesses, than to its second half, which is, in Novak's words, "a profound investigation into the soul and intellectual roots of the West." In referring to the "positive antipathy to religion common among the enlightened," Novak pointed to the deepest problem at Harvard that day, namely, a clash of worldviews.[57] When one party cannot, even temporarily, enter into the worldview of another, communication is stymied. And the fact that resistance to Solzhenitsyn had been hardening among the elites did not help.

The Nadir of the 1980s

Solzhenitsyn's one foray in 1980 into the scholarly discussion among Western Sovietologists, an essay originally titled "How Misconceptions about Russia Imperil America,"[58] did further damage to his reputation. More than ever, his tone gave offense. Even Harvard's Adam Ulam, in an essentially positive review, expressed "a mixed feeling of admiration and exasperation," because Solzhenitsyn, though "so often right," was also "occasionally, and infuriatingly, wrong-headed," the main distraction being "the occasional intemperance and peremptoriness of his historical judgments."[59] Openly hostile respondents mingled complaints about tone with objections to content. Princeton's Robert Tucker resented Solzhenitsyn's "acrimonious and disdainful tone" and rejected his "basic view of communism" as "unsound." Stanford's Alexander

Dallin accused Solzhenitsyn of "characteristic hyperbole" and cheerfully opined that "the Soviet standard of living has gone up at a rather impressive rate." Silvio Treves, in an admittedly "angry, off-the-cuff reaction," called Solzhenitsyn's article "a disparaging and abusive tirade against the American people" by "a not universally welcome guest."[60]

Solzhenitsyn, in turn, expressed his despair of engaging America's established intellectuals in discussion: "It is becoming increasingly clear that no essay of mine, nor ten such essays, nor ten individuals such as I, are capable of transmitting to the West the experience gained through blood and suffering, or even of disturbing the euphoria and complacency that dominate American political science."[61] Solzhenitsyn did eventually—and defensively—comment on the complaints about his tone: "When I fought the dragon of communist power I fought it at the highest pitch of expression. The people in the West were not accustomed to this tone of voice. In the West, one must have a balanced, calm, soft voice; one ought to make sure to doubt oneself, to suggest that one may, of course, be completely wrong. But I didn't have the time to busy myself with this."[62]

During the 1980s Solzhenitsyn mostly stayed out of the limelight. His 1982 speeches in Japan and Taiwan went almost entirely unnoticed, and his important Templeton Lecture in London in 1983 drew limited attention. Plenty continued to be written about him. In the main, attitudes that had been consolidated in the 1970s were crystallized into cliché in the 1980s. Thus, the myriad copies of *The Gulag Archipelago* lay on household bookshelves unread, initial enthusiasm having been dissipated by the word coming down from on high. And for some opinion leaders it was now—subsequent to the Harvard address—open season on Solzhenitsyn. George Feifer titled his particularly vicious attack "The Dark Side of Solzhenitsyn."[63] Olga Carlisle joined Feifer in writing to settle old scores.[64] Solzhenitsyn's Western reputation reached its nadir in the 1980s.

The most important event during the 1980s for Solzhenitsyn's reception was the appearance in 1984 of Michael Scammell's biography. This assiduously researched tome of a thousand pages remains indispensable as the single most valuable repository of information about the writer's life. It also, however, functions as a megaphone for the received opinion shaped during the 1970s, even including the slur that Solzhenitsyn dishonestly managed his image by adopting a "camouflage as a man of left-wing leanings."[65] Faithfully secular, it is thoroughly wrong about the very bedrock of Solzhenitsyn's worldview, his Christian faith. Scammell later conceded that his "treatment of Solzhenitsyn's religious faith is sketchy and unsatisfactory."[66] Scammell labels Solzhenitsyn a Deist—of all things. Furthermore, and most damningly, Scammell asserts, "Religion for him, it seems, is not an essential part of his being, but a contingent tool and even a weapon. The sentimental picture of him as a pious man of God is false. Solzhenitsyn certainly believes in God, though it is not always clear whether it is a Christian God. . . ." A book that begins with a neutral tone shifts perceptibly toward antagonism as it proceeds, until, by the end, Scammell's Solzhenitsyn appears as "an anachronism" and "a tragic personal failure." Scammell declares him wrong about Lenin, wrong about the numbers of those who died in the gulag. He calls Solzhenitsyn's polemical essays and speeches "silly" and notable for their "crudity and coarseness." Time after time, Scammell sums up Solzhenitsyn's actions as mediocre rather than heroic, his motivations as base rather than noble. And why? The problem was, predictably, politics. It was to Scammell that Solzhenitsyn, during the week that the biographer spent at the author's Vermont home for interviews, made his most direct, unambiguous appeal to avoid viewing him through the prism of politics. Astonishingly, Scammell chose to see "an element of disingenuousness in these protestations."[67] That a biography of the magnitude and promise of Scammell's ended up so fatally flawed is the single saddest episode in the story of Solzhenitsyn's Western reception.

The writer was dismayed by Scammell's book. Largely in response to it, he spent the summers of 1985 and 1986 putting together an autobiographical account (still unpublished) covering his life up to the moment of exile.[68] And in 1989, in an interview with David Aikman of *Time,* he summed up his reaction to the various attacks on him in the 1980s: "It is quite extraordinary the extent to which I have been lied about."[69]

Collapse of the Soviet Union

As the 1980s wound down and the ferment in Soviet-bloc countries began in earnest, the integral relationship between the author and his country made the time ripe to reassess Solzhenitsyn. Various occasions during the 1990s served virtually as invitations to begin this process, and they did indeed result in some revision of Solzhenitsyn's image, as if an ice floe blocking a harbor were about to break up with warming weather. Chief among these events were the appearance of his programmatic essay, *Rebuilding Russia;* the momentous collapse of the Soviet Union; his return to Russia, now in its post-Soviet incarnation; and certain publishing events that drew attention back to him. By and large, however, these episodes proved to be missed opportunities. In Russia as well as in the West, the intelligentsia largely retained their negative attitude toward Solzhenitsyn. Apart from some blips of regard, the main plot line of his reception remained almost flat. The times changed radically, but his reputation in the West remained the same.

In 1990, anticipating the imminent end of the Soviet Union, Solzhenitsyn published the Russian original of *Rebuilding Russia* in two Moscow-based periodicals. One of them, *Komsomolskaya pravda,* received more than a thousand letters of reaction.[70] A number of intellectuals expressed appreciation for this essay, but the negative critics were more specific about contentious issues.[71] The welter of activity swirling around the regime's death throes soon crowded out interest in the pamphlet, along with much else. The country had too much on its mind to seek out a sage. When the essay was published in the West in 1991, responses were fewer than in the dying Soviet Union and, as if a familiar tape had been rewound for replay, largely fell along predictable ideological lines.

The meltdown of the Soviet Union that culminated in 1991 brought Solzhenitsyn to some commentators' minds, for he had long predicted this historical moment and had played a writer's role in its coming. Senator Daniel Patrick Moynihan, reviewing *Rebuilding Russia,* gave him due credit: "Well, the Soviet Union has broken up. No one anticipated it more than Solzhenitsyn." David Remnick said, "In terms of the effect he has had on history, Solzhenitsyn is the dominant writer of this century," explaining later that no other writers of any time had been "able to do so much through courage and literary skill to change the society they came from. And to some extent, you have to credit the literary works of Aleksandr Solzhenitsyn with helping to bring down the last empire on Earth." Even a columnist so negatively disposed as to use the title "Shut Up, Solzhenitsyn" had to admit that *The Gulag Archipelago* was the book that "tolled the death knell for the Stalinist security state, and consequently for the Cold War," though he quickly injected a dose of gratuitous disparagement: "To paraphrase Abraham Lincoln's famous appreciation of Harriet Beecher Stowe: Solzhenitsyn is the little man who ended the big war."[72]

Strangely enough, the world-historical events of 1989–91 did little to overturn established judgments on geopolitical matters. There was a burst of euphoria, but it proved unrealistic to hope that scholars whose predictions were being contradicted by events would rush to the head of the *mea culpa* line and open the floodgates of reevaluation. The implosion of the Soviet Union will undoubtedly occupy the attention of historians for years to come, and the related stage in the story of Solzhenitsyn's reception will then be easier to formulate. But the decade that followed the headline events of 1989–91 did not undo the negative Western consensus. What those events did achieve was to shift the grounds for dismissing Solzhenitsyn. The man who two decades earlier had been deemed wrong-headed about the innate instability of the USSR was now described as irrelevant. Paradoxically, the very fact that he had been right about the past was used as an indication that he belonged to the past. Still, his prescience earned a modicum of grudging respect, and Western critics were less unkind toward him after the upheavals than before.[73]

The Return to Russia

The exile's return to Russia in May 1994 provided an irresistible opportunity to reassess the significance of Solzhenitsyn. What could Western journalists who knew "the going view" of him safely say in advance? It was safe to venture the unfalsifiable thesis that Solzhenitsyn should have come home earlier. This widely reiterated speculation had to do entirely with the assumption that practical politics matters most and that Solzhenitsyn now had the opportunity to turn activist. Thus, Elisabeth Rich wrote representatively, "Solzhenitsyn most assuredly would have wielded political influence had he returned earlier." Rich (and others) did allow that, as a sort of second-place prize, "he can still exert influence in the moral and spiritual arena."[74] The *Washington Post* made so bold as to title an editorial "President Solzhenitsyn?" True, the editorialist deemed this prospect unlikely, given Solzhenitsyn's "fundamentalist views" and his having become a "somewhat sidelined figure in the West." But "he appears to retain a broad measure of moral and intellectual authority at home."[75]

Not all hedging of bets was as oversized—or as falsifiable (and risible)—as imagining a Solzhenitsyn presidency, but nervous bet-hedging was indeed the order of the day. The *Economist* reported a "consensus among the Moscow intelligentsia" that Solzhenitsyn's homecoming "will make little difference" but imagined that "he could touch a chord with a much wider range of Russians long-ing for moral guidance"; and it left itself the loophole that "it has never been wise to write off the man who did more than anyone to alert the world to the scale and horror of the gulag archipelago."[76] At one and the same time, Western reporters clung to the consen-sus view that Solzhenitsyn had been marginalized and yet wrote with refrain-like regularity that Solzhenitsyn is "the most admired living Russian" and "remains a moral authority for millions of

Russians."[77] This abiding conundrum compelled a kind of double vision. The resulting blurry focus characterized the accounts of Western journalists trailing Solzhenitsyn across Russia. They typically began in skepticism, were surprised by the degree of adulation displayed toward him, and wondered if they had underestimated him. Solzhenitsyn, for his part, was gravely disappointed to discover that, though his books had become available, few Russians had actually read him.

Solzhenitsyn's reception by the Russian intellectuals tilted toward the negative. Hedging of bets afflicted Moscow as well as Manhattan: "Solzhenitsyn arrives with the illusion that he will say something new. I don't think he will. But maybe he will."[78] A widely cited article by Grigory Amelin, a young author, signaled the nastiness awaiting the returnee: "Solzhenitsyn is a spiritual statue. Let him stay in mothballs forever." Beyond this mixed metaphor, the detractor mocked Solzhenitsyn's "Hollywood beard" and called him "shamelessly out of date," "a walking skeleton," "a hatrack," and "a eunuch, castrated by his fame." Amelin asked, "Who needs him?" and answered, "No one."[79] Alexander Nevzorov, a television producer, expressed the hostility more tersely: "My God, he has been taken out of formaldehyde."[80] Victor Erofeyev anticipated that the "fussy, provincial old man," who already was "80 percent myth and 20 percent reality," was about to "lose the entire halo of myth."[81] Not all intellectuals carped. An editor sympathized, "It's not Solzhenitsyn's fault that things in Russia have changed. Solzhenitsyn is a hero, and any insulting articles, especially at this time, are indecent." Among the outraged rejoinders to Amelin's rudeness, one expressed irritation at the "Who needs him?" question: "Who needs him? I need him, I, I. We all need him, in conditions of freedom as much as in conditions of lack of freedom." And Vladimir Soloukhin, not to be outdone, exclaimed, "I agree with every word of Solzhenitsyn that he has said and written. And I agree in advance with every word that he will say and write."[82]

Reactions from the public, as reported by journalists, also ran the gamut but tipped toward the favorable side. One correspondent, sizing up the crowd reaction to Solzhenitsyn's words of greeting at Vladivostok, judged, "His audience loved him, with good reason." The broad respect for Solzhenitsyn was captured in a schoolteacher's words: "He wants to help Russia. I'm sure he will speak his mind again. That's good for us. There are too few wise people these days."[83] Doubts about the aging writer's relevance were part of the mosaic of responses. A retired seaman at Vladivostok said, "To be frank and not to hide my soul, the years have passed him by." An office worker concurred that "he's a creature from another era," then specified, "People just aren't interested in all that business about the camps any more."[84] Some expressed personal indebtedness. A Muscovite proclaimed, "When I first read Solzhenitsyn, I was on my knees. He helped me stand on my feet as a citizen." A construction worker chose the very same image: "After reading *The Gulag Archipelago* I could get up off my knees." A young woman waiting for his train at the Moscow station thought, "He won't be able to do much here, but you can believe in him. There's no one else to believe in." An enthusiast in Vladivostok cried out simply, "You are our savior! Our people are all supporting you. We've been waiting for you so long."[85] The most intriguing evidence that some Russians were ready for Solzhenitsyn comes from the most unlikely of sources, Tatyana Tolstaya, a writer who has at other times expressed intemperate contempt for him: "Solzhenitsyn is not entirely alone, of course. He has his own unique support group consisting largely—to his credit—of extremely worthy people. As a rule, these are older, decent, conscientious citizens who are concerned with moral issues and are deeply troubled by the political and cultural crisis that Russia is now living through. At one time or another all of them took to heart Solzhenitsyn's moral imperative 'to live not by lies.' They have tried hard to follow it."[86]

A year after Solzhenitsyn's return, the *Moscow Times* editorialized that "this truly great man has failed to live up to the expectations that he made for himself. . . . By his own measure, his return has been a disappointment."[87] And it is true that his public activities tapered off after a year had passed, and he ended up with more time for writing than he would have been able to find had a clamoring arisen for him to take a central role in discussing public affairs. But it is difficult to tailor immediate actions to address what he believed was the root issue: "Communism has remained in our hearts, in our souls and in our minds."[88] Vladimir Bukovsky anticipated that citizens who were complicit in Soviet evils would "hate those who are not soiled, who did not sup from the Communist Party with everyone else. They never forgive that." So Bukovsky took the long view: "It might be possible for [Solzhenitsyn] to have a kind of spiritual appeal to people. I wish him well and I hope he can—but I doubt it's feasible with this generation, it's not prepared for him. The next generation might."[89] Or, in the derisively intended words of a detractor, "Even if Jesus Christ himself returned to Russia, he could not have a great impact."[90]

Signs of an Uptick

Publishing events in the 1990s generated signs of an uptick, though not an upsurge, in Solzhenitsyn's Western reputation, starting with the appearance in 1995 of *Invisible Allies* by Solzhenitsyn and *The Solzhenitsyn Files* about him. A prepublication notice of *Invisible Allies* said, "The Solzhenitsyn met here is less bombastic than his reputation." Thompson Bradley expressed the hope that this book "will encourage those who do not know him to seek out his writings."[91] Robert Conquest and David Remnick judged that *The Solzhenitsyn Files* alone justified a renewed appreciation of Solzhenitsyn.[92] In a noteworthy reversal, the minority report at this juncture came not from them but from Michael Scammell, whose 1970s-style review of *Invisible Allies* still labeled Solzhenitsyn "an archconservative, a nationalist and an Orthodox Christian fundamentalist." Paradoxically, Scammell's work as editor of *The Solzhenitsyn Files* led him to observe that "Solzhenitsyn is shown to be completely correct in his contempt for the government's abilities" and to call attention to "breathtakingly prophetic political remarks" made by the man being bugged by the KGB. Mere months later, however, Scammell took note of the "very low ebb" of Solzhenitsyn's reputation.[93] He declined to take any credit for this state of affairs.

In 1998 D. M. Thomas's biography of Solzhenitsyn was released. While depending heavily on Scammell for information, Thomas revised various conventional judgments, from unmasking critics' liberal/left bias to clarifying the motive force of Solzhenitsyn's Christian faith. Thomas effected renewed sympathy for Solzhenitsyn among some reviewers. Norman Stone was not among these; he called Solzhenitsyn "a rather comical figure in Moscow—a sort of The End Is Nigh, sandwich-board old man," though conceding the little matter that *The Gulag Archipelago* "must stand as *the* book of the twentieth century if you have to choose one."[94] By contrast, A. N. Wilson judged that Thomas "gives us back our reasons for revering Solzhenitsyn while recognising his feet of clay." Wilson also observed that "Solzhenitsyn's point of view has in some ways triumphed. . . . What began inside his head, in the most terrible prison-isolation, as brave and private perceptions, has now become commonplace."[95]

The most instructive review of Thomas for tracing Solzhenitsyn's reception is George Steiner's. In the 1970s Steiner had found "the heart of Solzhenitsyn's meaning" to be "by liberal and rational standards, archaic and menacing." Reviewing Thomas, Steiner emphasized that "what matters is the extent of our continued indebtedness to 'Ivan Denisovich,' to the mapping of the gulag. At so many moments, what our soiled age has had of conscience lay in this one man's angry keeping." Then, turning his attention to the "decline in stature and reputation" of Solzhenitsyn, he asks, "Is it justified? Is it fair?" And he concludes that "the present moment" is "one both appropriate and premature for reevaluation. It may be too late to get certain problems into the requisite perspective. It may be too early to judge a vast textual output still in progress and a life as yet unquenched."[96] A major critic who formerly had been sure what to think about Solzhenitsyn was now, in a retreat from certitude, cautiously putting on the table the issue of reassessment. As Jeri Laber emblematizes the strong shift of opinion into the dark view of the 1970s, so Steiner emblematizes the weak shift out of it in the 1990s. A bemused critic encapsulated the confusion resulting from double vision: "Nobody can quite figure out what to do about Aleksandr Solzhenitsyn."[97]

Other chapters in the story of Solzhenitsyn's reception lie ahead. In 2001–2 the author published *Two Hundred Years Together,* a heavily footnoted—and, in Russia, best-selling—two-volume study of Russian-Jewish relations that evenhandedly dispenses blame and exoneration to both parties. Predictably but ironically, some critics accused of anti-Semitism the author who seeks to combat anti-Semitism. The allegation that Solzhenitsyn is anti-Semitic is of long standing. Among many able refutations, the most influential came from Norman Podhoretz, a Jewish American. Richard Pipes, a prominent Jewish-American historian who has clashed painfully with Solzhenitsyn, also concluded that in *Two Hundred Years* Solzhenitsyn "absolves himself of the taint of anti-Semitism."[98] Yet this odious charge lingers in the air, impervious to rebuttals.[99] The biggest chapter to come will deal with *The Red Wheel,* Solzhenitsyn's chief undertaking. For now, critics who have written it off before reading all of it can be safely ignored.

In 2006 Solzhenitsyn's novel *The First Circle* appeared in a ten-installment-long serial on Russian television, playing to an unexpectedly large and appreciative audience. Although it is impossible to predict further developments, this episode is a reminder that Solzhenitsyn's reception remains an open-ended story.

A New Obstacle

Meanwhile, a significant new development in the American political culture of the early twenty-first century affected Solzhenitsyn's standing in the West. Its genesis lay not in a reassessment of Solzhenitsyn but in an analysis of post-Soviet Russia in general and, once Vladimir Putin acceded to the presidency, of the new leader in particular. Thus, this development only sideswiped Solzhenitsyn. Yet it became a major new obstacle to taking him seriously. What made it new is that it arose within an unlikely quarter: conservatism, especially among those known as neoconservatives.

Over the years American conservatives had generally paid Solzhenitsyn considerable and favorable attention, as befit their tenacious anticommunism and acceptance of traditional religious and cultural outlooks. (Previously, the chief exception was Reagan adviser Richard Pipes, Solzhenitsyn's most visible conservative critic; he placed the onus for the Soviet tragedy on the historical character of the Russian people, whereas Solzhenitsyn blamed ideology.) The new turn, most clearly defined by writers for *The Weekly Standard* and the *Wall Street Journal,* leveled sharp, unremitting criticism at Putin and the new Russia, arguing that Putin was untrustworthy as a potential ally, harbored authoritarianism in his heart (as in "once KGB, always KGB"), and hankered after restoring the power and the glory enjoyed by the Soviet state during the old Cold War days. As self-conscious exporters of Western-style democracy, these neoconservatives advocated relentless NATO expansion to the East (in violation of agreements at the time of the reunification of Germany), supported anti-Putin political parties and personages who were self-declared democrats regardless of their own shady pasts, and brushed aside any appeals to Russia's history and national character, viewing them as impediments to creating a democratic future for that country. In short, they treated Russia as an enemy.

These analysts, while not aiming to pick a fight with Solzhenitsyn, found little to relate to in his writings about the current Russian scene. Although he, too, lamented that Russia had not yet become democratic, mainly he proclaimed that Russia's first and greatest need was to establish the moral groundwork of a free society, from which an indigenous democracy could take root. After what he called "the fifteen-year-long anarchy under Gorbachev and Yeltsin" that had reduced the populace to the misery and demoralization described in his *Russia in Collapse,* it should not be difficult to understand the patriot's appreciation for a new leader who brought to the "ransacked and bewildered country" a measure of economic recovery and political stability.[100] Furthermore, he approved of Russia reasserting its role in the world and worried about an apparent imperialistic drift in American foreign policy. Stopping well short of championing Putin, he offered a balance sheet with pluses and minuses in roughly comparable portions. But most Westerners on the left and now some on the right could not tolerate those plus marks. Overall, Solzhenitsyn's political and historical judgments were distant from and often at odds with those of the neoconservatives, so they largely ignored him. What gets lost—yet again—is attention to the literature of a primarily literary man.

A particularly memorable expression of the new conservative hostility toward Russia which does not ignore Solzhenitsyn comes from Ariel Cohen, a former Russian analyst at the Heritage Foundation and well-connected in conservative circles. He identifies what he calls "a revived Russian Orthodox world view," according to which, allegedly,

> Russia is closer to China and the Muslim world than to the materialistic post-modern "West," which lacks soul and spirit. This is the thesis of Alexander Solzhenitsyn, Putin, and the current Patriarch. In this spirit, the late Polish Pope, who yearned for reconciliation with his Orthodox brothers, was shunned, but the Ayatollahs, Hamas and even Chinese Godless communists are embraced. Catholicism and Protestantism are declared alien, while Islam is hailed as an "authentic" religion of Russia. . . . [101]

In contrast to Cohen's allegation, Solzhenitsyn was saying in a 1994 interview, "If we look far into the future, one can see a time in the twenty-first century when both Europe and the USA will be in dire need of Russia as an ally." This exact wording comes from the previously cited interview with *Der Spiegel* in 2007, when he was saying the same thing.[102]

In sum, an influential bloc of conservatives was abandoning a writer and thinker who once received attention in their publications and adopting as its default position an old, familiar position of the liberal consensus, namely, that Solzhenitsyn did a great thing in writing *The Gulag Archipelago* but thereafter retreated into a chauvinistic nationalism.[103] One who rereads the exchanges between Solzhenitsyn and the liberal academic establishment that followed the appearance of his essay *The Mortal Danger* will see in the new conservative estrangement a reprise of sorts. Those liberals truly believed that they understood Russia better than he.[104] Now it was the turn of some in the conservative camp to believe the same. Maybe it is time to propose a new test: "Tell me what you think of Russia, and I'll tell you what you think of Solzhenitsyn."

Conclusion

Joseph Epstein's intriguingly titled article, "Why Solzhenitsyn Will Not Go Away,"[105] suggests that future generations will answer "the Solzhenitsyn question" for themselves. They will have to deal with not only the author's immense output but also the false leads and confusions left behind by his contemporaries. The passage of time will bring helpful distance from the controversies of an overheated and cataclysmic century. Meanwhile, paradoxically, the most accurate assessments of Solzhenitsyn to date were in some ways the earliest ones. Readers in the 1960s had fragmentary evidence to work with, but they caught his spirit better than those who in the 1970s measured him on the Procrustean bed of prevailing intellectual orthodoxies. Perhaps the future will see again his immense achievements as a witness to and student of history, as a writer of literature, and as an active player on history's stage. Solzhenitsyn wrote mainly with future readers in mind, and there is good reason to think that they will find him.

Beyond the question of "reception" lies the allied concept of influence. Reception is determined by public responses, while influence resides in the private transaction between reader and writer. Testimonies of Solzhenitsyn's influence abound. Though these testimonies cannot be gathered and counted, the mere mention of one of them stirs the imagination to ponder the prospective magnitude of his impact. Václav Havel, the Czech playwright who moved almost in a flash from prisoner of the Communist regime to president of his ex-Communist country, has freely expressed his indebtedness to Solzhenitsyn. Havel accepts large portions of Solzhenitsyn's analysis of the modern world, and a number of his verbal formulations echo lines from Solzhenitsyn. A key part of Havel's appreciation of Solzhenitsyn has to do directly with the power of words to make a difference: "Yes, I really do inhabit a system in which words are capable of shaking the entire structure of government, where words can prove mightier than ten military divisions, where Solzhenitsyn's words of truth were regarded as something so dangerous that it was necessary to bundle their author into an airplane and transport him. Yes, in the part of the world I inhabit the word Solidarity was capable of shaking an entire power bloc."[106] As Havel understood, the pen is mighty. Solzhenitsyn is, first and foremost, a literary figure. Far beyond his critics' misunderstandings, but also even beyond his courageous life story, his words will abide. Reception matters. Influence matters more.

Notes

Introduction

1. "Solzhenitsyn Was Warned of Treason Charge," *The Times* [London], February 15, 1974, 1.
2. Amis, *Koba the Dread: Laughter and the Twenty Million* (New York: Hyperion, 2002), 5; Solzhenitsyn, *The Gulag Archipelago*, vol. 3 (New York: Harper and Row, 1978), x, 36.
3. Joseph Pearce, *Solzhenitsyn: A Soul in Exile* (Grand Rapids, MI: Baker, 2001), 312.
4. *The Gulag Archipelago*, vol. 2 (New York: Harper and Row, 1975), 617. Throughout, the italics in Solzhenitsyn's texts are his.
5. *Grey Is the Color of Hope* (New York: Knopf, 1988), 40.
6. "Reds Scared," *New Yorker*, October 30, 1995, 111.

Life

1. Aleksandr Solzhenitsyn, "Autobiography," in *Aleksandr Solzhenitsyn: Critical Essays and Documentary Materials,* ed. John B. Dunlop, Richard Haugh, and Alexis Klimoff, 2nd ed. (New York: Collier, 1975), 537.
2. *Hope Abandoned* (New York: Atheneum, 1974), 612.
3. *The Little Grain Managed to Land between Two Millstones* [subsequently *Little Grain*], in *Novyi mir*, 2001, no. 4, 125.

4. David Remnick, "The Exile Returns," *New Yorker*, February 14, 1994, 66.

5. Georges Suffert, "Solzhenitsyn in Zurich: An Interview," *Encounter* 46 (April 1976), 10.

6. Ibid., 11.

7. Designation of the Soviet security service between 1922 and 1934.

8. David Aikman, "Russia's Prophet in Exile," interview with Aleksandr Solzhenitsyn, *Time*, July 24, 1989, 59.

9. Suffert, "Solzhenitsyn in Zurich," 11.

10. Lev Kopelev, *Ease My Sorrows: A Memoir* (New York: Random House, 1983), 93.

11. *Little Grain*, in *Novyi mir*, 2001, no. 4, 98.

12. *The Notebooks of Sologdin* (New York: Harcourt Brace Jovanovich, 1973), 263.

13. Kopelev, *Ease My Sorrows*, 12–20. Kopelev's title is the name of the former church that had become part of the *sharashka*.

14. Panin, *The Notebooks of Sologdin*, 296.

15. Kopelev, *Ease My Sorrows*, 61.

16. Ibid., 15.

17. Solzhenitsyn, *The Gulag Archipelago*, vol. 2 (New York: Harper and Row, 1975), 613.

18. Aikman, "Russia's Prophet in Exile," 59.

19. Leopold Labedz, ed., *Solzhenitsyn: A Documentary Record* (Baltimore: Penguin, 1972), 26.

20. "Speech by N. S. Khrushchev on the Stalin Cult," in *Khrushchev Speaks: Selected Speeches, Articles, and Press Conferences, 1949–1961*, ed. Thomas P. Whitney (Ann Arbor, MI: University of Michigan Press, 1963), 207.

21. *The Oak and the Calf: Sketches of Literary Life in the Soviet Union* (New York: Harper and Row, 1980), 17.

22. Sergei N. Khrushchev, *Nikita Khrushchev and the Creation of a Superpower* (University Park, PA: Pennsylvania State University Press, 2000), 664.

23. In his memoirs Khrushchev expressed himself "proud and pleased" by his decision "not to interfere with the publication of" *One Day*, a book that he found "very heavy" but "written well," because the decision allowed

him to "lance the boil" resulting from "the evil inflicted on the Communist party" by Stalin. He reports that only Mikhail Suslov, the Party's chief ideologist, "squawked in opposition" to his recommendation. See *Khrushchev Remembers: The Glasnost Tapes* (Boston: Little, Brown and Company, 1990), 196–98.

24. The actual place name, Kochetovka, was substituted in more recent editions.

25. At the Twenty-Third Congress in March 1966, the first one after Khrushchev's downfall, speeches decried the former leader as nearly treasonous in permitting subversive ideas to surface and called for tightened ideological controls, with the appearance of *One Day* cited as an example of unacceptable laxity. Carl A. Linden, *Khrushchev and the Soviet Leadership, 1957–1964* (Baltimore: Johns Hopkins University Press, 1966), 222–24.

26. The congress convened in part to commemorate the fiftieth anniversary of the 1917 Revolution. The letter was widely republished in the West. See, e.g., *The Oak and the Calf*, 458–62.

27. *Invisible Allies* (Washington: Counterpoint, 1995), 55, 57.

28. *Les Prix Nobel en 1970* (Stockholm: Norstedt and Sons, 1971), 97. The citation is given in French. Solzhenitsyn was the fourth Russian recipient of this award, following Ivan Bunin (1933), Boris Pasternak (1958), and Mikhail Sholokhov (1965).

29. Walter Cronkite, "The Alexander Solzhenitsyn Interview," in *Congressional Record—Senate*, June 27, 1974, 11724.

30. See Solzhenitsyn's letter to Sakharov, in the appendix to *The Oak and the Calf*, 530–31.

31. An appendix to *Invisible Allies* describes this assassination attempt in the words of a conscience-stricken KBG man. The medical aspects of the episode are detailed in a substantial investigative report in *Sovershenno sekretno*, 1992, no. 4.

32. *Time*, April 3, 1972, 31. The translation we cite is by Ignat Solzhenitsyn, in *The Solzhenitsyn Reader*, 624–25.

33. "On Solzhenitsyn," in *Aleksandr Solzhenitsyn: Critical Essays and Documentary Materials*, 28–44. The initial publication in 1970 was in Russian.

34. *Solzhenitsyn: A Biography* (New York: Norton, 1984), 790.

35. *The Oak and the Calf,* 327.

36. "The Tolstoy Connection," *Saturday Review,* September 16, 1972, 80.

37. *The Oak and the Calf,* 537.

38. Ibid., 409.

39. Ibid., 415.

40. "Solzhenitsyn: An Artist Becomes an Exile," *Time,* February 25, 1974, 34.

41. *The Solzhenitsyn Files: Secret Soviet Documents Reveal One Man's Fight against the Monolith,* ed. Michael Scammell, trans. under supervision of Catherine A. Fitzpatrick (Chicago: edition q, 1995), 431–35, 449.

42. The term is from *Invisible Allies,* 19.

43. *The Solzhenitsyn Files,* 273, 278.

44. "Solzhenitsyn Wants Place to 'Work, Work, Work,'" *Des Moines Register,* February 24, 1974, 9A.

45. *The Oak and the Calf,* 13.

46. Quoted in Joseph Pearce, *Solzhenitsyn: A Soul in Exile* (Grand Rapids, MI: Baker, 2001), 315.

47. "The Unexpected Perils of Freedom," *Time,* March 4, 1974, 31.

48. "Solzhenitsyn Was Warned of Treason Charge," *The Times* [London], February 15, 1974, 1.

49. "Solzhenitsyn: An Artist Becomes an Exile," 34.

50. For Schmemann's account of meeting Solzhenitsyn, see *The Journals of Father Alexander Schmemann, 1973–1983* (Crestwood, NY: St. Vladimir's Seminary Press, 2002), 42–44.

51. *Little Grain,* in *Novyi mir,* 1998, no. 9, 88–89.

52. Recorded in *Little Grain,* passim.

53. *Little Grain,* in *Novyi mir,* 1998, no. 9, 108–11.

54. The book was published only in Russian in a tiny press run: Tomáš Řezáč's *Spiral' izmeny Solzhenitsyna,* Moscow: Progress, 1978. See Appendix B in *Invisible Allies,* where a former KGB operative relates Řezáč's visit to Rostov under the aegis of the Soviet security agencies. See further Yuri Andropov's personal promotion of this book in *The Solzhenitsyn Files,* 448, 451–53.

55. *Little Grain,* in *Novyi mir,* 1998, no. 11, 128.

56. Ibid., 132–34.

57. These four chapters had been included in the 1968 edition familiar from the translations of that time. The full edition of *The First Circle*—published in the first two volumes of the Vermont *Collected Works* in 1978—featured, in addition, a chapter surveying Stalin's career as a revolutionary before 1917, including his stint as a double agent for the tsarist secret police.

58. *Little Grain*, in *Novyi mir*, 2000, no. 2, 105. This judgment was based on clippings from the American provincial press as well as on letters sent to the author.

59. English translation appeared in *Survey* 20, no. 2 (1985).

60. *Little Grain*, in *Novyi mir*, 2000, no. 4, 129.

61. Felicity Barringer, "Kremlin Keeping Solzhenitsyn on Blacklist," *New York Times*, November 30, 1988, 1.

62. "Between Earth and Hell," *New York Review of Books*, March 21, 1974, 4.

63. *The Solzhenitsyn Files*, 9–10.

64. *The Oak and the Calf*, 426.

65. Bernard Levin, "Time to Stand Up for Britain," *The Times* [London], May 23, 1983, 11.

66. *Rebuilding Russia* (New York: Farrar, Straus and Giroux, 1991), 3.

67. Remnick, "The Exile Returns," 77.

68. Ibid., 68.

69. Bernard Pivot, "Solzhenitsyn at Work," *Boston Globe*, February 24, 1984, 2.

70. "No President Solzhenitsyn," *Time*, November 15, 1993, 30.

71. *Little Grain*, in *Novyi mir*, 2003, no. 11, 67.

72. Ibid., 52.

73. Remnick, "The Exile Returns," 83.

74. Ibid., 64–83.

75. Sara Rimer, "Shielding Solzhenitsyn, Respectfully," *New York Times*, March 3, 1994. A7.

76. Paul Klebnikov, "An Interview with Aleksandr Solzhenitsyn," *Forbes*, May 9, 1994, 118–22.

77. Remnick, "The Exile Returns," 70.

78. Vitaly Tretyakov, cited in "One Day in the Stormy Life of Solzhenit-

syn," *The Independent,* May 28, 1994, 1.

79. "Return to Russia," *Grand Rapids Press,* May 27, 1994, A3. Associated Press release.

80. Serge Schmemann, "Solzhenitsyn Is in Russia, Hoping for 'Ray of Light,'" *New York Times,* May 28, 1994, 4.

81. John Kohan, "A Voice in the Wilderness," *Time,* June 20, 1994, 46–47.

82. Jonathan Steele, "Solzhenitsyn Slides into His Place in Russia's Pantheon," *Guardian,* May 31, 1994, 9.

83. Richard Beeston, Untitled report from Vladivostok, *The Times* [London], May 28, 1994, 1.

84. Jonathan Steele, "Homecoming Exile Begins Meander to Moscow," *Guardian,* May 27, 1994, 24.

85. Kohan, "A Voice in the Wilderness," 46.

86. "The Homecoming," Transcript of *Frontline* Show #1314, Public Broadcasting Service, Air Date: April 25, 1995, 6.

87. Andrew Higgins, "Solzhenitsyn Warns of 'Manure from West,'" *Independent,* May 31, 1994, 1.

88. Steele, "Homecoming Exile Begins Meander," 24.

89. Alessandra Stanley, "Now on Moscow TV, Heeere's Aleksandr!" *New York Times,* April 14, 1995, A4.

90. Marcus Warren, "There Can Be No Reconciliation unless the Russian People Repent," *Sunday Telegraph,* May 29, 1994, 2.

91. This information comes from the most unlikely of sources, Tatyana Tolstaya, whose contempt for Solzhenitsyn is undisguised and unmodulated. See her *Pushkin's Children: Writings on Russia and Russians* (Boston: Houghton Mifflin, 2003), 165.

92. "Solzhenitsyn Takes Stage, Picks at Fabric of Russia," *Grand Rapids Press,* October 29, 1994, A8. Associated Press news release.

93. Steven Erlanger, "In Parliament, Solzhenitsyn Castigates Russia's Lawmakers," *New York Times,* October 20, 1994, 4.

94. Richard Wallis, "Solzhenitsyn Creates Russian Literary Award," October 21, 1997. Reuters news release.

95. Gareth Jones, "Solzhenitsyn, Russia's Angry Old Man, at 80," December 9, 1998. Reuters news release.

96. Among the most important are P. E. Spivakovskii, *Fenomen A. I. Sol-*

zhenitsyna: Novyi vzgliad (Moscow: Akademiia Nauk, 1998), A. V. Urmanov, *Tvorchestvo Aleksandra Solzhenitsyna* (Moscow: Flinta/Nauka, 2003), and three collections of articles on specific works by Solzhenitsyn, edited by A. V. Urmanov and published in the Eastern Siberian city of Blagoveshchensk: *"Matrenin dvor" A. I. Solzhenitsyna* (1999), *"Odin den' Ivana Denisovicha" A. I. Solzhenitsyna* (2003), and *"Krasnoe Koleso" A. I. Solzhenitsyna* (2005). All three collections have the same subtitle: *Khudozhestvennyi mir. Poetika. Kul'turnyi kontekst.*

97. N. A. Struve and V. A. Moskvin, eds. *Mezhdu dvumia iubileiami (1998–2003): Pisateli, kritiki, literaturovedy o tvorchestve A. I. Solzhenitsyna* (Moscow: Russkii put', 2005).

98. The planned distribution of Solzhenitsyn's writings within the new *Collected Works* is spelled out in Natalia Solzhenitsyn's preface to vol. 1.

99. *The Oak and the Calf*, 95, 374.

100. Remnick, "The Exile Returns," 83.

Works

Early Works

1. Vol. 3 (New York: Harper and Row, 1978), 99–101. Seeing Lithuanian Catholics make rosary beads from pieces of bread, Solzhenitsyn asked their help in stringing a rosary for his ostensible religious use, with every tenth, fiftieth, and hundredth bead shaped distinctively. He could then recite his verse repeatedly, making sure he was remembering every line.

2. Quoted in Joseph Pearce, *Solzhenitsyn: A Soul in Exile* (Grand Rapids, MI: Baker, 2001), 317.

3. This coda is not included in the separately published edition of "Prussian Nights."

4. Vol. 1 (New York: Harper and Row, 1974), 16–19.

5. "The Mason" appears in an excellent translation in *The Gulag Archipelago,* vol. 3, 74.

6. The full texts of the two poems cited here appear in English translation

in *The Solzhenitsyn Reader*, 20, 22.

Miniatures

1. Quoted in Joseph Pearce, *Solzhenitsyn: A Soul in Exile* (Grand Rapids, MI: Baker, 2001), 315.

The First Circle

1. Dimitri Panin, *Notebooks of Sologdin* (New York: Harcourt, 1976), 263.
2. *Ease My Sorrows: A Memoir* (New York: Random House, 1983), 72–75.

One Day in the Life of Ivan Denisovich

1. *Publitsistika*, II, 424.

Matryona's Home

1. See Nikolai Ledovskikh, *Vozvrashchenie v Matrenin dvor, ili Odin den' Aleksandra Isaevicha* (Riazan': Poverennyi, 2003), 32. Also included are photographs of Matryona, of Solzhenitsyn's quarters in her house, and of Matryona's funeral, all taken by the writer while in residence in Miltsevo (31–35).

Incident at Krechetovka Station

1. The description of the chaotic working conditions on a rail station during wartime has many points in common with scenes depicted in Solzhenitsyn's unfinished novel *Love the Revolution*.

What a Pity

1. Vol. 3 (New York: Harper and Row, 1978), 409–14.

Cancer Ward

1. *Sobranie sochinenii* (Vermont), vol. 4, 503.

2. *Invisible Allies* (Washington, DC: Counterpoint, 1995), 104.

3. *The Oak and the Calf* (New York: Harper and Row, 1980), 95.

4. Ibid., Appendix 4, 478.

5. "*Cancer Ward:* Of Faith and Guilt," in *Aleksandr Solzhenitsyn: Critical Essays and Documentary Materials*, ed. John B. Dunlop, Richard Haugh, and Alexis Klimoff, 2nd ed. (New York: Collier, 1975), 277.

The Gulag Archipelago

1. See, e.g., Norman Stone, "The Years of Living Less Dangerously," *Sunday Times Bookshop* [London], February 15, 1998, 6–7; Michael Specter, "Viewing Solzhenitsyn through a Freudian Lens," *New York Times*, March 13, 1998, B40.

2. Michael Nicholson, "Solzhenitsyn: Effigies and Oddities," in *Solzhenitsyn in Exile: Critical Essays and Documentary Materials*, ed. John B. Dunlop, Richard S. Haugh, and Michael Nicholson (Stanford, CA: Hoover Institution Press, 1985), 109.

3. *The Oak and the Calf* (New York: Harper and Row, 1980), vii, 219.

4. Ibid., 212.

5. Quoted from *The Times* [London], January 19, 1974, in Christopher Moody, *Solzhenitsyn* (New York: Harper and Row, 1975), 27a.

6. *The Oak and the Calf*, 387, 389.

7. "Between Earth and Hell," *New York Review of Books*, March 21, 1974, 4.

8. Martin Malia, "A War on Two Fronts: Solzhenitsyn and the Gulag Archipelago," *Russian Review* 36 (January 1977), 50.

9. The cited text has been edited for fidelity to the original.

10. Personal letter cited in the introduction to the abridged version of *The Gulag Archipelago*, ed. Edward E. Ericson, Jr. (New York: HarperCollins, 2002), xx.

Nobel Lecture

1. "On Solzhenitsyn," in *Aleksandr Solzhenitsyn: Critical Essays and Documentary Materials*, ed. John B. Dunlop, Richard Haugh, and Alexis Klimoff, 2nd ed. (New York: Collier, 1975), 39–43.

2. *The Oak and the Calf* (New York: Harper and Row, 1980), 311–12.
3. Ibid., 333–34.

Lenin in Zurich

1. "An Exchange with Boris Souvarine on Lenin in Zurich," in *Solzhenitsyn in Exile: Critical Essays and Documentary Materials*, ed. John B. Dunlop, Richard Haugh, and Michael Nicholson (Stanford, CA: Hoover Institution Press, 1985), 330.

From under the Rubble

1. Solzhenitsyn, quoted in Michael Scammell, *Solzhenitsyn: A Biography* (New York: Norton, 1984), 897.

Letter to the Soviet Leaders

1. *The Oak and the Calf* (New York: Harper and Row, 1980), 387, 402.
2. The *Letter* was read and discussed at several Politburo meetings. See Michael Scammell, ed., *The Solzhenitsyn Files: Secret Soviet Documents Reveal One Man's Fight against the Monolith* (Chicago: edition q, 1995), 249n.

Harvard Address

1. *A World Split Apart* (New York: Harper and Row, 1978). Solzhenitsyn's preferred title is simply *Harvard Address*, which is used in *The Solzhenitsyn Reader*.

Templeton Lecture

1. From chapter 9, *Little Grain*, in *Novyi mir*, 2000, no. 12, 124–25.
2. In *Aleksandr Solzhenitsyn: Critical Essays and Documentary Materials*, ed. John B. Dunlop, Richard Haugh, and Alexis Klimoff, 2nd ed. (New York: Collier, 1975), 44.

The Little Grain

1. The published French translation simplifies this to *Le Grain tombé entre les meules.*

2. Mrs. Solzhenitsyn personally set all twenty volumes of the writer's Vermont-produced *Collected Works* on an IBM compositor.

Invisible Allies

1. *Harvard Address,* in *The Solzhenitsyn Reader,* 569.
2. *The Gulag Archipelago,* vol. 1 (New York: Harper and Row, 1974), 186.

The Red Wheel

1. *The Oak and the Calf* (New York: Harper and Row, 1980), 219 and vii. In the postscript to the first Russian edition of *August 1914* (1971) Solzhenitsyn speaks of his lifelong dedication to this project in similarly forceful terms: "I have never stopped thinking about it. I understood it as the main task of my life [even] while I was deflected to writing other books by the circumstances of my life. . . ." See Leopold Labedz, ed., *Solzhenitsyn: A Documentary Record,* Enlarged ed. (Bloomington, IN: Indiana University Press, 1973), 260.
2. This is exemplified by the fact that Gleb Nerzhin, the author's alter ego in *The First Circle,* compiles voluminous notes on Russian history.
3. Solzhenitsyn offered this explanation in his 1989 interview with David Aikman. See *Time,* July 24, 1989, 57–58.
4. It is important to emphasize that the first edition of *August 1914* (*Avgust chetyrnadtsatogo* [Paris: YMCA Press, 1971] together with its remarkably inadequate English translation by Michael Glenny, *August 1914* [New York: Farrar, Straus and Giroux, 1972]) is incomplete, and that it has been superseded by the greatly expanded edition of 1983 published in vols. 11 and 12 of the Vermont *Sobranie sochinenii* and superbly translated by H. T. Willetts: Aleksandr Solzhenitsyn, *August 1914: The Red Wheel / Knot I* (New York: Farrar, Straus and Giroux, 1989).
5. The Russian term used here by Solzhenitsyn is not *demokratiia,* the

standard designation of the concept used in modern Russian, but rather "*narodopravstvo*," which represents a part-by-part translation of the Greek roots "demos" and "kratia" into equivalent Russian roots, and in this respect resembles "People Power," the American phrase of similar etymological provenance that arose in the 1960s.

6. In the Aikman interview cited in note 3 above, Solzhenitsyn compared the revolution to a cosmic wheel or a spiral galaxy, the enormous inertia of which, once it starts rotating, is almost impossible to stop.

7. *August 1914* (1989), 271. And Lenin is shown thinking of the historical process—in his eyes, associated entirely with revolution—as a huge red wheel of a locomotive, at once dangerous to those who lose sight of its power and immensely useful to those who can utilize its potential (*August 1914*, 175, 189).

8. Ibid., 324, 777.

9. Unpaginated "Author's Note" following the title page in Aleksandr Solzhenistyn, *November 1916: The Red Wheel / Knot II*, translated by H. T. Willetts (New York: Farrar, Straus and Giroux). See also *August 1914* (1989), 531.

10. Until 1918, Russia used the Julian or Old Style (O.S.) calendar that in the twentieth century was thirteen days behind the calendar used in the West. The conventional date of the February Revolution is February 27 (O.S.), which makes it March 12 by the Western calendar. For the same reason of calendar discrepancy, *November 1916* is titled *October 1916* in the Russian original.

11. Interview for the BBC Russian Service, June 29, 1987. Russian text in *Publitsistika*, vol. 3, 273–84.

12. *Publitsistika*, vol. 1, 457–503.

13. See Alexander Solzhenitsyn, *Three Plays* (New York: Farrar, Straus and Giroux, 1983), 210.

Two Hundred Years Together

1. The first volume of *Two Hundred Years Together* is subtitled "1795–1995," but the second volume no longer has this feature because, as Solzhenitsyn explains in a concluding note to that volume, he realized that the Jew-

ish "exodus" from the USSR that began in the 1970s signals an important turning point in Russian-Jewish relations, one that is almost exactly two hundred years distant from 1772.

2. This was the 1911–13 jury trial of a Jewish workman accused of the ritual murder of a Gentile child. Beiliss was acquitted, but the fact that the government persisted so long in prosecuting the obviously weak case attracted huge international attention.

3. An important recent exception is Yuri Slezkin's *The Jewish Century* (Princeton, NJ: Princeton University Press, 2004).

Short Stories of the 1990s

1. Solzhenitsyn has described this concept in *Novyi mir*, 2003, no. 11, 69.

2. In Solzhenitsyn's early plans for *The Red Wheel*, the Tambov uprising was to have been the subject of the last "knot" of the cycle. This goal proved unattainable, and the epic ends with *April 1917*.

3. An English translation of this story appears under the title "No Matter What" in *The Solzhenitsyn Reader*, 67–84.

4. Solzhenitsyn refers briefly to this episode in *The Gulag Archipelago*. See vol. 1 (New York: Harper and Row, 1974), 260.

5. *Novyi mir*, 1999, no. 2, 122–24.

Literary Collection

1. This concern gave rise to Solzhenitsyn's compilation of 1990 in which he gathered some thirty thousand words and expressions (culled from various sources) that he believed should be used to expand and enrich the shrinking Russian vocabulary. See *Russkii slovar' iazykovogo rasshireniia*, sostavil A. I. Solzhenitsyn (Moscow: Nauka, 1990).

Beliefs

1. "Russia's Prophet in Exile," *Time*, July 24, 1989, 59.

2. *Candle in the Wind* (New York: Bantam, 1974). Solzhenitsyn has called this play "the least successful thing I ever wrote." *The Oak and the Calf* (New York: Harper and Row, 1980), 12. Perhaps the reason for his judg-

ment is that the explicit formulation of his beliefs that it communicates has not been sufficiently integrated into the structure of the text.

3. "To Patriarch Pimen of Russia: Lenten Letter," in *Aleksandr Solzhenitsyn: Critical Essays and Documentary Materials*, ed. John B. Dunlop, Richard Haugh, and Alexis Klimoff, 2nd ed. (New York: Collier, 1975), 551–54.

4. Ignat Solzhenitsyn's translations of his father's two written prayers may be found in *The Solzhenitsyn Reader*, 634. The earlier of the two prayers first appeared in English in *The Catholic Worker* 37 (September 1971), 8.

5. In the Orthodox Church, a reading or song of praise.

6. The citations are from Ignat Solzhenitsyn's translations of these two poems in *The Solzhenitsyn Reader*, 21–22. The text of "Acathistus" first appeared in *The Gulag Archipelago*, vol. 2 (New York: Harper and Row, 1975), 614–15.

7. Vol. 1 (New York: Harper and Row, 1974), 611–12.

8. Vol. 2, 614–15.

9. *Little Grain*, in *Novyi mir*, 2000, no. 12, 124–25.

10. "Templeton Lecture," in *The Solzhenitsyn Reader*, 577–84.

11. Jude 3.

12. Quoted in Michael Scammell, *Solzhenitsyn: A Biography* (New York: Norton, 1984), 981.

13. Vol. 1, 168.

14. *From under the Rubble* (Boston: Little, Brown, 1975), 24–25.

15. "We have ceased to see the Purpose," in *The Solzhenitsyn Reader*, 592, 593.

16. *Little Grain*, in *Novyi mir*, 1998, no. 11, 128.

17. James F. Pontuso, *Solzhenitsyn's Political Thought* (Charlottesville, VA: University Press of Virginia, 1990); 2nd ed. as *Assault on Ideology: Aleksandr Solzhenitsyn's Political Thought* (Lanham, MD: Lexington, 2004). Daniel J. Mahoney, *Aleksandr Solzhenitsyn: The Ascent from Ideology* (Lanham, MD: Rowman and Littlefield, 2001).

18. *Gulag*, vol. 2, 612.

19. "Repentance and Self-Limitation in the Life of Nations," in *The Solzhenitsyn Reader*, 534.

20. Ibid., 529.

21. Vol. 1, 168; vol. 2, 615. This image also appears in *Dorozhen'ka*, Sol-

zhenitsyn's early autobiographical poem. See Aleksandr Solzhenitsyn, *Proterevshi glaza* (Moscow: Nash dom—L'Age d'Homme, 1999), 150.

22. "We have ceased to see the Purpose," in *The Solzhenitsyn Reader*, 596.

23. *Warning to the West* (New York: Farrar, Straus and Giroux, 1976), 57–58.

24. *The Mortal Danger*, 2nd ed. (New York: Harper and Row, 1986), 111.

25. "Letter from Solzhenitsyn to Three Students," in *Solzhenitsyn: A Documentary Record*, ed. Leopold Labedz (Baltimore: Penguin, 1972), 151.

26. *The Solzhenitsyn Reader*, 122.

27. *The First Circle* (New York: Harper and Row, 1968), 96.

28. "Repentance and Self-Limitation," in *The Solzhenitsyn Reader*, 551.

29. Georges Suffert, "Solzhenitsyn in Zurich," Interview with Solzhenitsyn, *Encounter* 46 (April 1976), 13–14.

30. "Repentance and Self-Limitation," in *The Solzhenitsyn Reader*, 529, 532, 534.

31. *Rebuilding Russia* (New York: Farrar, Straus and Giroux, 1991), 51.

32. Marcus Warren, "There Can Be No Reconciliation Unless the Russian People Repent," *Sunday Telegraph*, May 29, 1994, 2.

33. *Nobel Lecture*, in *The Solzhenitsyn Reader*, 526.

34. "An Interview on Literary Themes with Nikita Struve, March 1976," in *Solzhenitsyn in Exile: Critical Essays and Documentary Materials*, ed. John B. Dunlop, Richard Haugh, Michael Nicholson (Stanford, CA: Hoover Institution Press, 1985), 307.

35. *Publitsistika*, 3 vols. (Yaroslavl': "Verkhniaia Volga," 1995–97), vol. 2, 323. The translation of this passage in *Encounter* 46 (April 1976, 12) is defective.

36. Quoted in Michael Scammell, *Solzhenitsyn: A Biography* (New York: Norton, 1984), 981.

37. *Dvesti let vmeste*, 2 vols. (Moscow: Russkii put', 2001–2).

38. *Russkii slovar' iazykovogo rasshireniia*, sostavil A. I. Solzhenitsyn (Moscow: Nauka, 1990) and two later reprints.

39. The quotation is from Solzhenitsyn's preface to the first of the essays, *Novyi mir*, 1997, no. 1, 195. Twenty-two essays have been published between 1997 and 2004.

40. Solzhenitsyn's appeal for submissions was widely published in the émigré press as well as (in excerpt form) in the *New York Times*, November 19,

1977. See *Publitsistika*, vol. 2, 471–73, 610.

41. A significant number of the manuscripts submitted to the Memoir Library have been published, in each case financed by Solzhenitsyn.

42. Raymond Rosenthal, "Solzhenitsyn and the Defeated," *Nation*, February 12, 1973, 213.

43. *Harvard Address*, in *The Solzhenitsyn Reader*, 572–73.

44. Ibid., 575.

45. *Nobel Lecture*, in *The Solzhenitsyn Reader*, 513.

46. Ibid., 513, 522.

47. *New York Times Book Review*, February 3, 1993, 3, 17. The newspaper supplied the snide title "The Relentless Cult of Novelty and How It Wrecked the Century." Solzhenitsyn's subsequently chosen title (used in *The Solzhenitsyn Reader*) is "Playing upon the Strings of Emptiness."

48. "Secretariat Meeting with Solzhenitsyn" (September 22, 1967), in *Solzhenitsyn: A Documentary Record*, 147.

49. *Letter to the Soviet Leaders* (New York: Harper and Row, 1974), 43.

50. *August 1914: The Red Wheel / Knot I* (New York: Farrar, Straus and Giroux, 1989), 3, 17.

51. Ibid., 324, 417.

52. Ibid., 346.

53. "We have ceased to see the Purpose," in *The Solzhenitsyn Reader*, 600.

54. *August 1914* (1989), 346–48.

55. See the chapter titled "On Nationalism" in Edward E. Ericson, Jr., *Solzhenitsyn and the Modern World* (Washington, DC: Regnery Gateway, 1993).

56. *Washington Post*, April 8, 1982, A13.

57. *Washington Post*, May 16, 1982, C2. The letter appears under the ironic title "Solzhenitsyn to Reagan: Spasibo, Nyet."

58. "Repentance and Self-Limitation," in *The Solzhenitsyn Reader*, 539.

59. *"The Russian Question" at the End of the Twentieth Century* (New York: Farrar, Straus and Giroux, 1995), 60.

60. *Nobel Lecture*, in *The Solzhenitsyn Reader*, 520.

61. *Cancer Ward* (New York: Farrar, Straus and Giroux, 1969), 172.

62. *The First Circle*, 449, 452.

63. In light of all that was said above, it is strange to read an accusation, in

a book appearing in 2002, that Solzhenitsyn had made an idol of Russia. The charge is spelled out in the posthumously published *Journals* of Alexander Schmemann, an American theologian of the Russian Orthodox tradition, who is also the author of an admiring article on the Christian implications of Solzhenitsyn's writings which will be discussed presently. The contrast between these two assessments is so great, in fact, that one suspects a degree of personal pique behind Schmemann's negative comments. As a strenuous promoter of specifically American Orthodoxy, Schmemann undoubtedly found Solzhenitsyn's single-minded focus on Russia frustratingly unresponsive to his main concerns. See *The Journals of Father Alexander Schmemann, 1973–1983* (Crestwood, NY: St. Vladimir's Seminary Press, 2002).

64. "On Solzhenitsyn," in *Aleksandr Solzhenitsyn: Critical Essays and Documentary Materials*, 39.

65. Ibid., 39–42.

66. In *Aleksandr Solzhenitsyn: Critical Essays and Documentary Materials*, 44.

67. "On Solzhenitsyn," in *Aleksandr Solzhenitsyn: Critical Essays and Documentary Materials*, 43.

68. See the coda articulating the protagonist's repentance in *Proterevshi glaza*, 150.

69. "On Solzhenitsyn," in *Aleksander Solzhenitsyn: Critical Essays and Documentary Materials*, 43.

70. Vol. 3 (New York: Harper and Row, 1978), 178.

71. *The First Circle* (New York: Harper and Row, 1968), 509–18.

72. *Cancer Ward* (New York: Bantam, 1969), 514–15, 528–29.

73. Thus, Svetlana Sheshunova has demonstrated the crucial symbolic role of the Orthodox liturgical calendar in *The Red Wheel*, and Pavel Spivakovskii has traced the image of deliberate apostasy pervading the same cycle. See Sheshunova's "Pravoslavnyi kalendar' v 'Krasnom Kolese,'" in *Mezhdu dvumia iubileiami*, ed. N. A. Struve and V. A. Moskvin (Moscow: Russkii put',' 2005), 468–77, and P. E. Spivakovskii, "Simvolicheskie obrazy v epopee A. I. Solzhenitsyna 'Krasnoe Koleso,'" *Izvestiia RAN. Seriia literatury i iazyka* 62, no. 1 (January/February 2003).

Reception

1. *Solzhenitsyn: A Documentary Record,* ed. Leopold Labedz (Baltimore: Penguin, 1972, 21.

2. Stanley Reynolds, *Guardian,* February 14, 1974. Cited in Robert Conquest, "Solzhenitsyn in the British Media," in *Solzhenitsyn in Exile: Critical Essays and Documentary Materials,* ed. John B. Dunlop, Richard S. Haugh, and Michael Nicholson (Stanford, CA: Hoover Institution Press, 1985), 5.

3. Michael Scammell, "The Solzhenitsyn Archipelago," *New York Review of Books,* December 3, 1998, 38.

4. The responses in the Soviet press between 1962 and 1973 are chronicled by Michael Nicholson in a detailed bibliography included in *Aleksandr Solzhenitsyn: Critical Essays and Documentary Materials,* ed. John B. Dunlop, Richard Haugh, and Alexis Klimoff, 2nd ed. (New York: Collier, 1975), 579–610. A volume containing both official and samizdat (i.e., privately circulated) Russian responses covering the years 1962 to 1974 has appeared in post-Soviet Russia: *Slovo probivaet sebe dorogu: Sbornik statei i dokumentov ob A. I. Solzhenitsyne* (Moscow: Russkii put', 1998). An account of Solzhenitsyn's Western reception considerably more expansive than the present chapter is available in Edward E. Ericson, Jr., *Solzhenitsyn and the Modern World* (Washington, DC: Regnery Gateway, 1993), 46–125; and Ericson, "Solzhenitsyn's Western Reception since 1991," *Transactions of the Association of Russian-American Scholars in the U.S.A.* 29 (1998), 183–213. See also the several surveys in *Solzhenitsyn in Exile,* including Robert Conquest's "Solzhenitsyn in the British Media," 3–23; John B. Dunlop's "Solzhenitsyn's Reception in the United States," 24–55; Birgit Meyer's "Solzhenitsyn in the West German Press since 1974," 56–79; Pierre Daix's "Solzhenitsyn in France after 1974," 80–84; and Michael Nicholson's collection of offbeat and grotesque responses, East and West, "Solzhenitsyn: Effigies and Oddities," 108–42.

5. "On the Fragments by Boris Souvarine," in *Solzhenitsyn in Exile,* 338.

6. Scammell, *Solzhenitsyn: A Biography* (New York: Norton, 1984), 981. Scammell has also preserved a statement that Solzhenitsyn made when he went to Stockholm to collect his Nobel Prize: "We all know that an artist's work can-

not be contained within the wretched dimension of politics" (900).

7. Lanham, MD: Rowman and Littlefield, 2001. Another worthy treatment of Solzhenitsyn's politics is James F. Pontuso, *Assault on Ideology: Aleksandr Solzhenitsyn's Political Thought,* 2nd ed. (Lanham, MD: Lexington, 2004).

8. Scammell, *Solzhenitsyn,* 1984. An assessment of this book appears later in the present chapter.

9. *Khrushchev Remembers: The Glasnost Tapes* (Boston: Little, Brown, 1990), 198.

10. Cited in Labedz, *Solzhenitsyn: A Documentary Record,* 64.

11. "About the Past, in the Name of the Future," *Izvestiia,* November 18, 1962. Cited in Labedz, 41. In the January 1964 issue of *Novyi mir* (pp. 223–45), Vladimir Lakshin in "Ivan Denisovich, His Friends and Foes" pulled together a range of reactions—such as were permitted within Soviet strictures—to *One Day.*

12. Cited in Labedz, *Solzhenitsyn: A Documentary Record,* 39.

13. "The House of the Living," *Kenyon Review* 25 (Spring 1963), 358.

14. "*Cancer Ward* and *The First Circle,*" *Slavic Review* 28 (June 1969), 304.

15. By Julian Symons in the *Sunday Times* [London] and Ronald Hingley in the *Spectator,* respectively. Cited in Scammell, *Solzhenitsyn,* 643.

16. Laber, "Indictment of Soviet Terror," *New Republic,* October 19, 1968, 32–34; Garis, "Fiction Chronicle," *Hudson Review* 22 (Spring 1969), 148.

17. Labedz, *Solzhenitsyn: A Documentary Record,* 223, 224.

18. Giovanni Grazzini, *Solzhenitsyn* (New York: Dell, 1973), 5.

19. "On Solzhenitsyn," in *Aleksandr Solzhenitsyn: Critical Essays and Documentary Materials,* 39. The Russian original appeared in 1970.

20. Scammell, *Solzhenitsyn,* 790.

21. *The Oak and the Calf* (New York: Harper and Row, 1980), 327.

22. Alfred P. Klausler, "Tragic Chaos," *Christian Century,* November 22, 1972, 1192; Simon Karlinksy, Review of *August 1914, New York Times Book Review,* September 10, 1972, 1, 49.

23. Victor Erlich, "Solzhenitsyn's Quest," in *Aleksandr Solzhenitsyn: Critical Essays and Documentary Materials,* 352; William H. Pritchard, "Long Novels and Short Stories," *Hudson Review* 26 (Spring 1973), 225.

24. Vidal, "The Ashes of Hollywood II: The Top 6 of the Top 10," *New York*

Review of Books, May 31, 1973, 16; Toynbee, Review of *August 1914, Critic* 31 (November–December 1972), 68.

25. "Muted Echo of a Masterpiece," *New Republic,* October 7, 1972, 29–30.

26. "The Tolstoy Connection," *Saturday Review,* September 16, 1972, 80, 88.

27. Scammell, *Solzhenitsyn,* 792.

28. Ron Nessen, *It Sure Looks Different from the Inside* (Chicago: Playboy Press, 1978), 229, 345. See also Dunlop, "Solzhenitsyn's Reception in the United States," in *Solzhenitsyn in Exile,* 35–36.

29. For the range of reactions to *The Gulag Archipelago* from within the Soviet Union, see Michael Nicholson, "*The Gulag Archipelago:* A Survey of Soviet Responses," in *Aleksandr Solzhenitsyn: Critical Essays and Documentary Materials,* 2nd ed., 477–500.

30. For Medvedev's essays on each of the three volumes, respectively, see "On Solzhenitsyn's *The Gulag Archipelago,*" in *Aleksandr Solzhenitsyn: Critical Essays and Documentary Materials,* 460–76; "Solzhenitsyn's *Gulag Archipelago:* Part Two," *Dissent* 23 (Spring 1976), 155–63; "Solzhenitsyn: Truth and Politics," *Dissent* 24 (Spring 1977), 141–53.

31. "Solzhenitsyn's Bill of Indictment," *Time,* January 7, 1974, 49.

32. "Why the Kremlin Fears Solzhenitsyn," *Atlantic* 233 (April 1974), 46.

33. Rubenstein, Review of *The Gulag Archipelago,* vol. 1, *New Republic,* June 22, 1974, 22; Steiner, "The Forests of the Night," *New Yorker,* August 5, 1974, 78.

34. "What Awaits Us in the Future?" in *Political, Social and Religious Thought of Russian "Samizdat,"* ed. Michael Meerson-Aksenov and Boris Shragin (Belmont, MA: Nordland, 1977), 76–94.

35. Dunlop, "Solzhenitsyn's Reception in the United States," in *Solzhenitsyn in Exile,* 42.

36. Harry Schwartz, "Solzhenitsyn without Stereotype," *Saturday Review/ World,* April 20, 1974, 24.

37. "Solzhenitsyn without Tears," *New York Times,* February 18, 1974, 25.

38. *Commentary* 58 (May 1974), 32–35.

39. *Columbia Journalism Review* 13 (May/June 1974), 5, 7.

40. Robertson, "A Russian Nationalist Looks to the Past," *New York Times,* March 3, 1974, 26; Astrachan, "Solzhenitsyn 'Contemptuous' of the U.S.,"

Des Moines Register, March 17, 1974, 1A; Yardley, "Solzhenitsyn—A Dispassionate Look at a Modern 'Saint,'" *Des Moines Register*, June 23, 1974, 6A.

41. "Towering Witness to Salvation," *Time*, July 15, 1974, 90.

42. Review of *The Gulag Archipelago*, vol. 2, *New York Times Book Review*, October 26, 1975, 1.

43. "Soviet Terror," *Commentary* 67 (February 1979), 88.

44. *Barbarism with a Human Face* (New York: Harper and Row, 1979), 154–55.

45. See Daix, "Solzhenitsyn in France after 1974," 80–84.

46. *Soljénitsyne* (Paris: Seuil, 1980).

47. "Alexander Solzhenitsyn and European 'Leftism,'" *Survey* 100–101 (Summer/Autumn 1976), 233–41; also available in *In Defense of Political Reason: Essays by Raymond Aron*, ed. Daniel J. Mahoney (Lanham, MD: Rowman & Littlefield, 1994), 115–24.

48. *Un homme en trop* (Paris: Seuil, 1976).

49. See, e.g., *In Defense of Decadent Europe* (South Bend, IN: Regnery Gateway, 1979).

50. See, e.g., "De la difficulté de définir le régime soviétique," *Contrepoint*, no. 20 (1976), 115–28, and *Court traité de soviétologie*, Preface de Raymond Aron (Paris: Hachette, 1975), translated as *The Soviet Syndrome* (New York: Harcourt, 1978).

51. Statements by both men were published as Aleksandr Solzhenitsyn, "An Exchange with Boris Souvarine on *Lenin in Zurich*," in *Solzhenitsyn in Exile*, 329–38. See also Boris Souvarine, "Solzhenitsyn and Lenin," *Dissent* 24 (Summer 1977), 324–36.

52. Conquest, "Solzhenitsyn in the British Media," 14, 18; Levin, "Solzhenitsyn among the Pygmies," *The Times* [London], July 17, 1975, 14.

53. *The Solzhenitsyn Files: Secret Soviet Documents Reveal One Man's Fight against the Monolith*, ed. Michael Scammell, trans. under supervision of Catherine A. Fitzpatrick (Chicago: edition q, 1995), 431–35, 449.

54. Dunlop, "Solzhenitsyn's Reception in the United States," 44; "Solzhenitsyn: 'Con Man' or 'Worshipper of Man'?" *Boston Globe*, June 19, 1978, 13.

55. *Solzhenitsyn at Harvard: The Address, Twelve Early Responses, and Six Later Reflections*, ed. Ronald Berman (Washington, DC: Ethics and Public

Policy Center, 1980); "America: Triumphant or Troubled? A Timely Look Back at the Most Famous Critique of Our Contemporary Society," *American Enterprise*, July/August 1998, 59–65.

56. "Mr. Solzhenitsyn as Witness," in *Solzhenitsyn at Harvard*, 25; "The Obsession of Solzhenitsyn," in *Solzhenitsyn at Harvard*, 23; Reston, "A Russian at Harvard," in *Solzhenitsyn at Harvard*, 37; McGrory, "Solzhenitsyn Doesn't Love Us," in *Solzhenitsyn at Harvard*, 61.

57. Hesburgh, "Unpopular Truths," *Time*, June 26, 1978, 18; Meany, "No Voice More Eloquent," *Time*, June 26, 1978, 21; Novak, "On God and Man," in *Solzhenitsyn at Harvard*, 131–32, 139.

58. *Foreign Affairs*, 58 (Spring 1980), 797–834. Soon thereafter, the essay was published as a book titled *The Mortal Danger: How Misconceptions about Russia Imperil America* (New York: Harper and Row, 1980); a second edition of the book (1981) is supplemented by responses from six critics and Solzhenitsyn's reply, "The Courage to See."

59. "To the Brink," *National Review*, November 14, 1980, 1402.

60. Tucker, 75; Dallin, 97, 102; Treves, 86–87; in *Mortal Danger*, 2nd ed. These were three letters to the editor of *Foreign Affairs*.

61. "The Courage to See," in *Mortal Danger*, 2nd ed., 130.

62. David Remnick, "The Exile Returns," *New Yorker*, February 14, 1994, 74.

63. "The Dark Side of Solzhenitsyn," *Harper's* 260 (May 1980), 51–58. For Robert Conquest's judgment on the question of Feifer's trustworthiness and veracity, see "Solzhenitsyn in the British Media," in *Solzhenitsyn in Exile*, 10, 13.

64. "Reviving Myths of Holy Russia," *New York Times Magazine*, September 16, 1979, 48, 50, 57, 60, 64–65. See also Carlisle's *Solzhenitsyn and the Secret Circle* (New York: Holt, Rinehart and Winston, 1978).

65. Scammell, *Solzhenitsyn*, 849–50.

66. Letter, *Problems of Communism*, July–August 1986, 101. In this letter Scammell was replying to the review of his biography by John B. Dunlop, "Solzhenitsyn: Unfinished Portrait," *Problems of Communism*, September–October 1985, 82–88.

67. Scammell, *Solzhenitsyn*, 928–29, 932, 934, 943–45, 981–82, 992.

68. *Little Grain*, in *Novyi mir*, 2001, no. 4, 125.

69. "Russia's Prophet in Exile," Interview with Aleksandr Solzhenitsyn,

Time, July 24, 1989, 60.

70. The essay was also published in *Literaturnaya gazeta* and had a total distribution of about 27 million copies.

71. For a fuller account, see Ericson, *Solzhenitsyn and the Modern World,* 268–73.

72. Moynihan, "Two Cheers for Solzhenitsyn," *New York Times Book Review,* November 24, 1991, 9; Remnick, "The Exile Returns," 70; transcript of interview of Remnick by Alex Chadwick, National Public Radio, "Morning Edition," May 27, 1994, 20; Alex Beam, "Shut Up, Solzhenitsyn," *Boston Globe,* February 13, 1993, cited in George Bailey, "Solzhenitsyn," *Bostonia,* Summer 1993, 16.

73. In the Soviet Union, meanwhile, Solzhenitsyn's name was entering the public domain in an ever-increasing fashion. See D. B. Aziattsev, N. G. Levitskaia *et al. Aleksandr Isaevich Solzhenitsyn: Materialy k biobibliografii* (St. Petersburg: Rossiiskaia natsional'naia bibioteka, 2007).

74. Rich, "The Exile's Return," *Washington Post Book World,* May 1, 1994, 15; see also, e.g., Deborah Seward, "Exiled Russian Writer Prepares to Return Home," *Grand Rapids Press,* May 1, 1994, A19; Matthew Campbell, "Solzhenitsyn Draws a Shrug," *Sunday Times* [London], May 22, 1994, 15.

75. *Washington Post,* June 1, 1994, A10.

76. "A Conscience Comes Home," *Economist,* May 28, 1994, 41.

77. Anne McElvoy, "The Second Circle," *The Times Magazine* [London], May 21, 1995, 17; John Kohan, "A Voice in the Wilderness," *Time,* June 20, 1994, 46.

78. Sergei Kunyaev, editor of *Nash sovremennik,* cited in Andrew Higgins, "Will Anyone Recognise Alexander Isayevich?" *Independent,* May 25, 1994, 19.

79. Steven Erlanger, "Solzhenitsyn Is Going Home to a Different Russia," *International Herald Tribune,* May 21–22, 1994, 8; Adi Ignatius, "Solzhenitsyn Returns from Exile: Russia Looks for Icon's Role," *Wall Street Journal,* May 27, 1994, A1; John Lloyd, "Who Needs Solzhenitsyn?" *Weekend Financial Times,* May 28–29, 1994, Section II, 1.

80. Cited in Higgins, "Will Anyone Recognise Alexander Isayevich?" 19. Higgins describes Nevzorov as one of "the new breed of leather-jacketed bully-boy 'patriots.'"

81. Cited in Rich, "The Exile's Return," 15.

82. Cited, respectively, in Ignatius, "Solzhenitsyn Returns from Exile," A1; Lloyd, "Who Needs Solzhenitsyn?" 10; Rich, "The Exile's Return," 15.

83. Jonathan Steele, "Solzhenitsyn Slides into His Place in Russia's Pantheon," *Guardian*, May 31,1994, 9; cited in Seward, A19.

84. Cited, respectively, in Steele, "Returning Son Touches Base on 'Tortured' Russia's Soil," *Guardian*, May 28, 1994, 1; Campbell, "Solzhenitsyn Draws a Shrug," 15.

85. Cited, respectively, in Helen Womack, "Russians Sanguine about Solzhenitsyn's Return," *The Independent*, May 14, 1994, 10; Erlanger, "Solzhenitsyn Is Going Home to a Different Russia," 8; Neela Banerjee, "Solzhenitsyn Returns to Moscow, Ending His 20 Years of Exile," *Wall Street Journal*, July 22, 1994, A8; Campbell, "The Angry Old Man on the BBC Train," *Sunday Times* [London], May 29, 1994, 15.

86. *Pushkin's Children: Writings on Russia and Russians* (Boston: Houghton Mifflin, 2003), 165.

87. "Solzhenitsyn One Year On: No Prophet," *Moscow Times*, June 11, 1995, 9.

88. Cited in Campbell, "Angry Old Man," 15.

89. Cited in Lloyd, "Who Needs Solzhenitsyn?" 1.

90. Cited in David Hearst, "Guru of the Gulags," *Guardian*, May 23, 1994, 2.

91. *Publishers Weekly*, October 9, 1995, 68; Bradley, Review of *Invisible Allies*, *America*, November 16, 1996, 23.

92. Conquest, "Does He Love Lenin?" *Times Literary Supplement* [London], January 26, 1996, 3–4; Remnick, "Reds Scared," *New Yorker*, October 30, 1995, 109–11.

93. "Notes from the Underground," *New York Times Book Review*, January 7, 1996, 14; Introduction, *The Solzhenitsyn Files*, xviii, xxxiii.

94. "The Years of Living Less Dangerously," *Sunday Times Bookshop* [London], February 15, 1998, 6. Among other reviewers who have been similarly dismissive toward Solzhenitsyn are Dominic Lieven, "A Voice in the Wilderness," *Sunday Telegraph*, February 15, 1998, 7; and Michael Specter, "Viewing Solzhenitsyn through a Freudian Lens," *New York Times*, March 13, 1998, B40.

95. "He Dared Tell Them Their History, Now Forgotten," *Literary Review*, February 1998, 4–5.

96. "More Notes from Underground," *New Yorker*, October 13, 1975, 169; "In Exile Wherever He Goes," *New York Times Book Review*, March 1, 1998, 9–10.

97. Specter, "Viewing Solzhenitsyn through a Freudian Lens," B40.

98. Podhoretz, "The Terrible Question of Aleksandr Solzhenitsyn," *Commentary* 79 (February 1985), 17–24; Pipes, "Alone Together: Solzhenitsyn and the Jews, Revisited," *New Republic*, November 25, 2002, 28.

99. See, e.g., Cathy Young's review of *Two Hundred Years Together*: "Traditional Prejudices: The Anti-Semitism of Alexander Solzhenitsyn," Reason 36 (May 2004), 20–21. A reply to Young appears in Daniel J. Mahoney, "Traducing Solzhenitsyn," *First Things*, August–September 2004, 14–17.

100. Interview with *Der Spiegel*, Solzhenitsyn, "I Am Not Afraid of Death," *Spiegel Online*, July 23, 2007. http://www.spiegel.de/international/world/0,1518,496211,00.html.

101. "The New Cool War," May 17, 2006. http://www.benadorassociates.com/article/19497.

102. The 1994 interview is by Paul Klebnikov and appeared in *Forbes* magazine, May 9, 1994. Klebnikov specifies that Solzhenitsyn has in mind the threats from expansionist China and resurgent Islam (118).

103. For a clear summary statement of this position, see Zinovy Zinik, "Blue-collar Solzhenitsyn," *Times Online,* March 7, 2007. http://tls.timesonline.co.uk/article/0,,253412617318,00.html.

104. *The Mortal Danger: How Misconceptions about Russia Imperil America*, 2nd ed. (New York: Harper and Row, 1986).

105. *Commentary* 102 (November 1996), 46–50.

106. "Words on Words," *New York Review of Books*, January 18, 1990, 5. For a discussion of the consanguinity between Solzhenitsyn and Havel, see Ericson, "Solzhenitsyn, Havel, and the Historical Moment," in *Political and Ideological Confrontations in Twentieth-Century Europe: Essays in Honor of Milorad M. Drachkovitch*, ed. Robert Conquest and Dusan J. Djordjevich (New York: St. Martin's Press, 1996), 143–58.

Select Bibliography

The literature on Solzhenitsyn is enormous, and the relatively brief list offered here aims to highlight only publications that are particularly valuable for an understanding of the author and his work, as well as those which have been central to his reception in the West. Our list is further limited to secondary literature, since the publication data on the writings of Solzhenitsyn and on the principal English translations have been systematically included in our essays on specific works.

The first three sections below follow chronological order; the fourth, "Critical Works," is alphabetized. With a handful of exceptions, the bibliography is focused on English-language items.

Bibliographies:

Fiene, Donald M. *Alexander Solzhenitsyn: An International Bibliography of Writings by and about Him, 1962–1973* (Ann Arbor, MI: Ardis Publishers, 1973). The most complete available bibliography for the period indicated.

Solzhenitsyn Studies: A Quarterly Review, 1–2 (1980–81) [no more pub-
lished]. A highly detailed bibliographical survey, compiled by Michael
Nicholson.

D. B. Aziattsev, N. G. Levitskaia, *et al. Aleksandr Isaevich Solzhenitsyn:
Materialy k biobibliografii* (St. Petersburg: Rossiiskaia natsional'naia
biblioteka, 2007). Lists more than eight thousand Russian-language
items.

Collections of Documents:

Labedz, Leopold, ed. *Solzhenitsyn: A Documentary Record*, 2nd ed.
(Bloomington, IN: Indiana University Press, 1973). An important
sourcebook, updated from editions published by Penguin (1970) and
Harper and Row (1971). Many of Solzhenitsyn's statements included
here also appear in the appendix to *The Oak and the Calf* (where they
are presented in Harry Willetts's excellent translations).

Scammell, Michael, ed. *The Solzhenitsyn Files: Secret Soviet Documents Reveal One Man's Fight against the Monolith* (Chicago: edition q, 1995).
Discovered after the fall of the USSR, these documents chronicle the
Soviet government's desperate attempts to cope with its "Solzhenitsyn
problem."

Glotser, Vladimir, and Elena Chukovskaia, eds. *Slovo probivaet sebe dorogu:
Sbornik statei i dokumentov ob A. I. Solzhenitsyne, 1962–1974* (Moscow:
Russkii put', 1998). A collection of Russian-language commentary
on Solzhenitsyn appearing in the Soviet press as well as in unofficial
(samizdat) materials during the period indicated.

Biographies and General Works:

Moody, Christopher. *Solzhenitsyn,* 2nd ed. (New York: Barnes & Noble, 1975). A stimulating general introduction. The second edition takes account of *The Gulag Archipelago.*

Nivat, Georges. *Soljénitsyne* (Paris: Seuil, 1980). Written in French by a Swiss Slavist, this is the best introduction to Solzhenitsyn in any language. An updated Russian translation was published in 1984, but there is no English version.

Scammell, Michael. *Solzhenitsyn: A Biography* (New York: Norton, 1984). A massive tome partially based on interviews with the writer, containing a plethora of useful detail but marked by the critic's frequently skeptical tone and his corresponding lack of sympathy for Solzhenitsyn's religious views.

Remnick, David. "The Exile Returns," *New Yorker,* February 14, 1994, 64–83. A lucid overall evaluation on the eve of the writer's return to Russia.

Thomas, D. M. *Alexander Solzhenitsyn: A Century in His Life* (New York: St. Martin's, 1998). Leans heavily on Scammell's research, but presents independent and generally reliable judgments and literary interpretations.

Pearce, Joseph. *Solzhenitsyn: A Soul in Exile* (Grand Rapids, MI: Baker, 2001). Also greatly indebted to the Scammell biography, but with particular attention to moral and religious issues. Based in part on interviews with Solzhenitsyn after the writer had returned to Russia.

Saraskina, Liudmila. *Aleksandr Solzhenitsyn* (Moscow: Molodaia gvardiia, 2008). A major new biography in the *Zhizn' zamechatel'nykh liudei* (*Lives of Remarkable Individuals*) series, based on archival documents and extensive interviews with Solzhenitsyn.

Critical Works:

Berman, Ronald, ed. *Solzhenitsyn at Harvard: The Address, Twelve Early Responses, and Six Later Reflections* (Washington, DC: Ethics and Public Policy Center, 1980).

Brown, Edward J. "Solzhenitsyn and the Epic of the Camps," in his *Russian Literature since the Revolution* (Cambridge, MA: Harvard University Press, 1982). An excellent overview of all the major works except *The Red Wheel*, with particularly fine comments on *The Oak and the Calf.*

Dunlop, John B., Richard Haugh, and Alexis Klimoff, eds. *Aleksandr Solzhenitsyn: Critical Essays and Documentary Materials*, 2nd ed. (New York: Collier, 1975). A large collection, containing essays on most of Solzhenitsyn's works available by 1974. Includes a consideration of Solzhenitsyn's link to the *samizdat* network and a review of the quality of the English-language translations of his writings.

Dunlop, John B., Richard Haugh, and Michael Nicholson, eds. *Solzhenitsyn in Exile: Critical Essays and Documentary Materials* (Stanford, CA: Hoover Institution Press, 1985). Includes literary analyses, important surveys of Solzhenitsyn's reception in Europe and the U.S., and a striking memoir by Lydia Chukovskaya.

Ericson, Edward E., Jr. *Solzhenitsyn and the Modern World* (Washington, DC: Regnery Gateway, 1993). The most detailed available account of Solzhenitsyn's reception in the West, primarily in the United States. The account is carried forward in the same author's essay "Solzhenitsyn's Western Reception since 1991," *Transactions of the Assn. of Russian-American Scholars in the U.S.A.* 29 (1998), 183–213.

———. *Solzhenitsyn: The Moral Vision* (Grand Rapids, MI: Eerdmans, 1980).

Feuer, Kathryn, ed. *Solzhenitsyn: A Collection of Critical Essays* (Englewood Cliffs, NJ: Prentice-Hall, 1976). A well-edited collection with an excellent introduction.

Kennan, George F. "Between Earth and Hell," *New York Review of Books*, March 21, 1974, 3–7. The most striking Western review of *The Gulag Archipelago.*

Kern, Gary. "Ivan the Worker," *Modern Fiction Studies* 23 (1977), 5–30. Interesting commentary on *One Day in the Life of Ivan Denisovich.*

Klimoff, Alexis, ed. *One Day in the Life of Ivan Denisovich: A Critical Companion* (Evanston, IL: Northwestern University Press, 1997). Contains analytical essays together with detailed materials bearing on the work's sensational appearance.

Mahoney, Daniel J. *Aleksandr Solzhenitsyn: The Ascent from Ideology* (Lanham, MD: Rowman & Littlefield, 2001). A powerful argument against the politicization of Solzhenitsyn.

———. "Solzhenitsyn on Russia's 'Jewish Question,'" *Society* 40 (November/December 2002), 104–9, and "Solzhenitsyn, Russia, and the Jews Revisited," *Society* 41 (July/August 2004), 72–82. Together with Geoffrey Hosking's review in *TLS* (March 1, 2002), this is a calm and reasoned commentary on Solzhenitsyn's *Two Hundred Years Together,* a work that has provoked some heated controversy.

Mathewson, Rufus W., Jr. "Solzhenitsyn," in his *The Positive Hero in Russian Literature,* 2nd ed. (Stanford, CA: Stanford University Press, 1975), 279–340. Incisive analyses of *The First Circle, Cancer Ward,* and *August 1914.*

Nicholson, Michael. "Solzhenitsyn as 'Socialist Realist,'" in H. Chang, *et al.,* eds., *In the Party Spirit: Socialist Realism and Literary Practice in the Soviet Union, East Germany, and China* (Amsterdam: Rodopi, 1996), 55–68. The definitive analysis of a question sometimes raised about Solzhenitsyn's writings.

Pontuso, James F. *Assault on Ideology: Aleksandr Solzhenitsyn's Political Thought,* 2nd ed. (Lanham, MD: Lexington, 2004).

Shturman, Dora. *Gorodu i miru: O publitsistike A.I. Solzhenitsyna* (Paris and New York: Tret'ia volna, 1988). The best, and most detailed, commentary on Solzhenitsyn's many public statements.

Toker, Leona. "*The Gulag Archipelago*" and "The Gulag Fiction of Aleksandr Solzhenitsyn," in her *Return from the Archipelago: Narratives of Gulag Survivors* (Bloomington, IN: Indiana University Press, 2000), pp. 101–21 and 188–209. Excellent analyses, presented in contrast to other writers on the same theme.

Transactions of the Assn. of Russian-American Scholars in the U.S.A. 29 (1998). A volume dedicated in part to Solzhenitsyn, with essays focused on aspects of the *Red Wheel* epic, on a recent short story, and on a survey of recent Western reception.

Index

About the Authors

Edward E. Ericson, Jr., is professor emeritus of English at Calvin College, where he taught for twenty-six years. He is the author of two books on Solzhenitsyn, editor of the one-volume authorized abridgment of Solzhenitsyn's *The Gulag Archipelago*, and coeditor of *The Solzhenitsyn Reader: New and Essential Writings, 1947–2005*, published by ISI Books in 2006.

Alexis Klimoff is Professor of Russian Studies at Vassar College. His publications on Solzhenitsyn include the coeditorship of *Aleksandr Solzheniysyn: Critical Essays and Documentary Materials*, the editorship of *One Day in the Life of Ivan Denisovich: A Critical Companion*, translations of various essays and addresses by Solzhenitsyn, and reviews of translations of his works into English.